IRON

OR

THE WAR AFTER.™

by

S.M. Vidaurri

Published by
ARCHAIA™
Los Angeles, California

For My Grandfather

ORIGINAL DESIGN by
Howling Monkey Studios

SOFTCOVER EDITION DESIGN by
Scott Newman

EDITED by
Rebecca Taylor

Ross Richie..CEO & Founder
Joy Huffman..CFO
Matt Gagnon...Editor-in-Chief
Filip Sablik......................President, Publishing & Marketing
Stephen Christy.................................President, Development
Lance Kreiter......Vice President, Licensing & Merchandising
Phil Barbaro......Vice President, Finance & Human Resources
Arune Singh....................................Vice President, Marketing
Bryce Carlson....Vice President, Editorial & Creative Strategy
Scott Newman............................Manager, Production Design
Kate Henning...Manager, Operations
Spencer Simpson...Manager, Sales
Sierra Hahn..Executive Editor
Jeanine Schaefer..Executive Editor
Dafna Pleban...Senior Editor
Shannon Watters..Senior Editor
Eric Harburn...Senior Editor
Whitney Leopard...Editor
Cameron Chittock..Editor
Chris Rosa...Editor

Matthew Levine..Editor
Sophie Philips-Roberts....................................Assistant Editor
Gavin Gronenthal...Assistant Editor
Michael Moccio...Assistant Editor
Amanda LaFranco.......................................Executive Assistant
Jillian Crab...Design Coordinator
Michelle Ankley..Design Coordinator
Kara Leopard...Production Designer
Marie Krupina...Production Designer
Grace Park..Production Design Assistant
Chelsea Roberts.........................Production Design Assistant
Elizabeth Loughridge....................Accounting Coordinator
Stephanie Hocutt........................Social Media Coordinator
José Meza...Event Coordinator
Holly Aitchison...............................Operations Coordinator
Megan Christopher..............................Operations Assistant
Rodrigo Hernandez......................................Mailroom Assistant
Morgan Perry.........................Direct Market Representative
Cat O'Grady..Marketing Assistant
Breanna Sarpy..Executive Assistant

ARCHAIA.

BOOM! Studios, 5670 Wilshire Boulevard, Suite 400, Los Angeles, CA 90036-5679. Printed in China. First Printing.

ISBN: 978-1-68415-298-8, eISBN: 978-1-64144-151-3

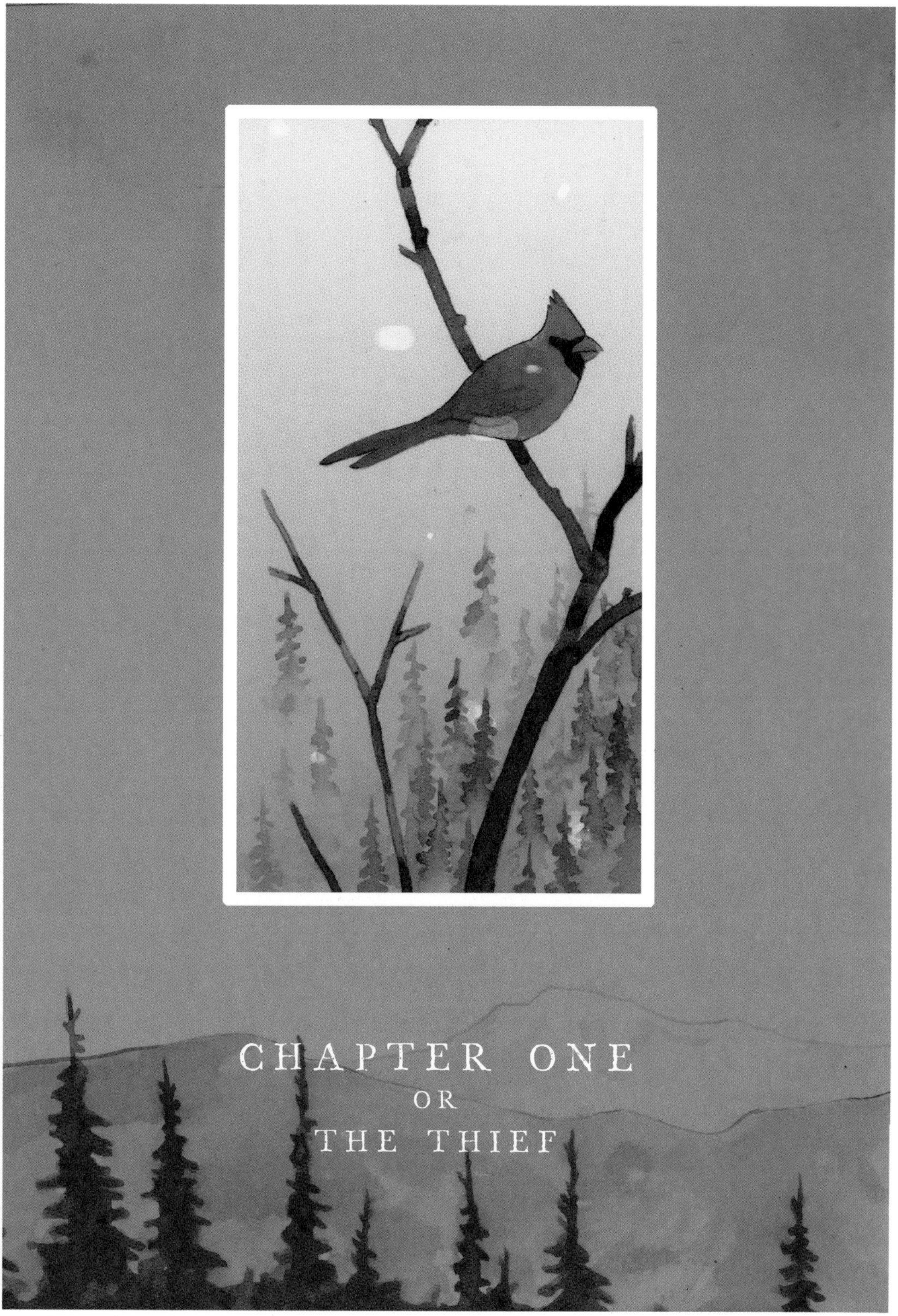

CHAPTER ONE
OR
THE THIEF

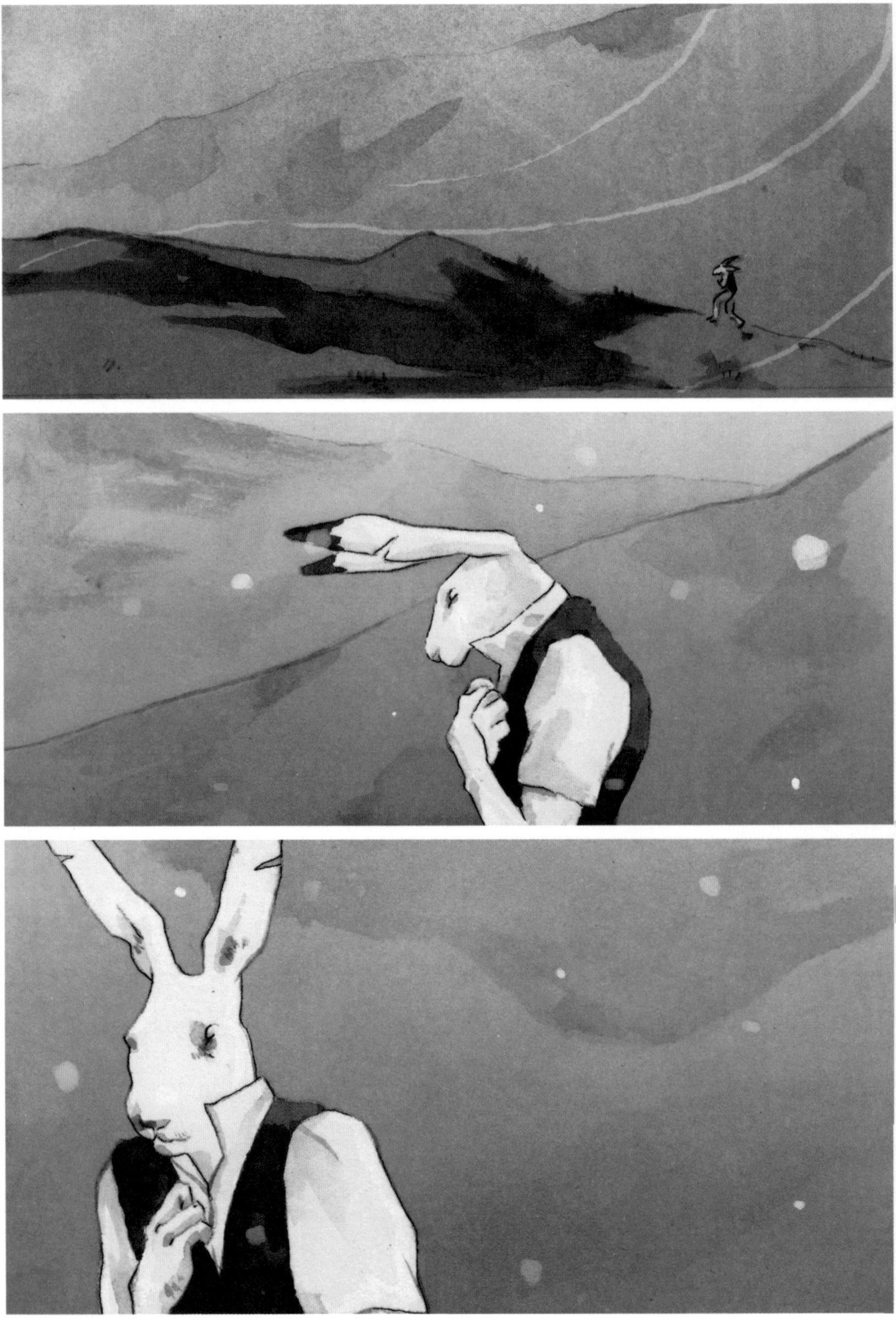

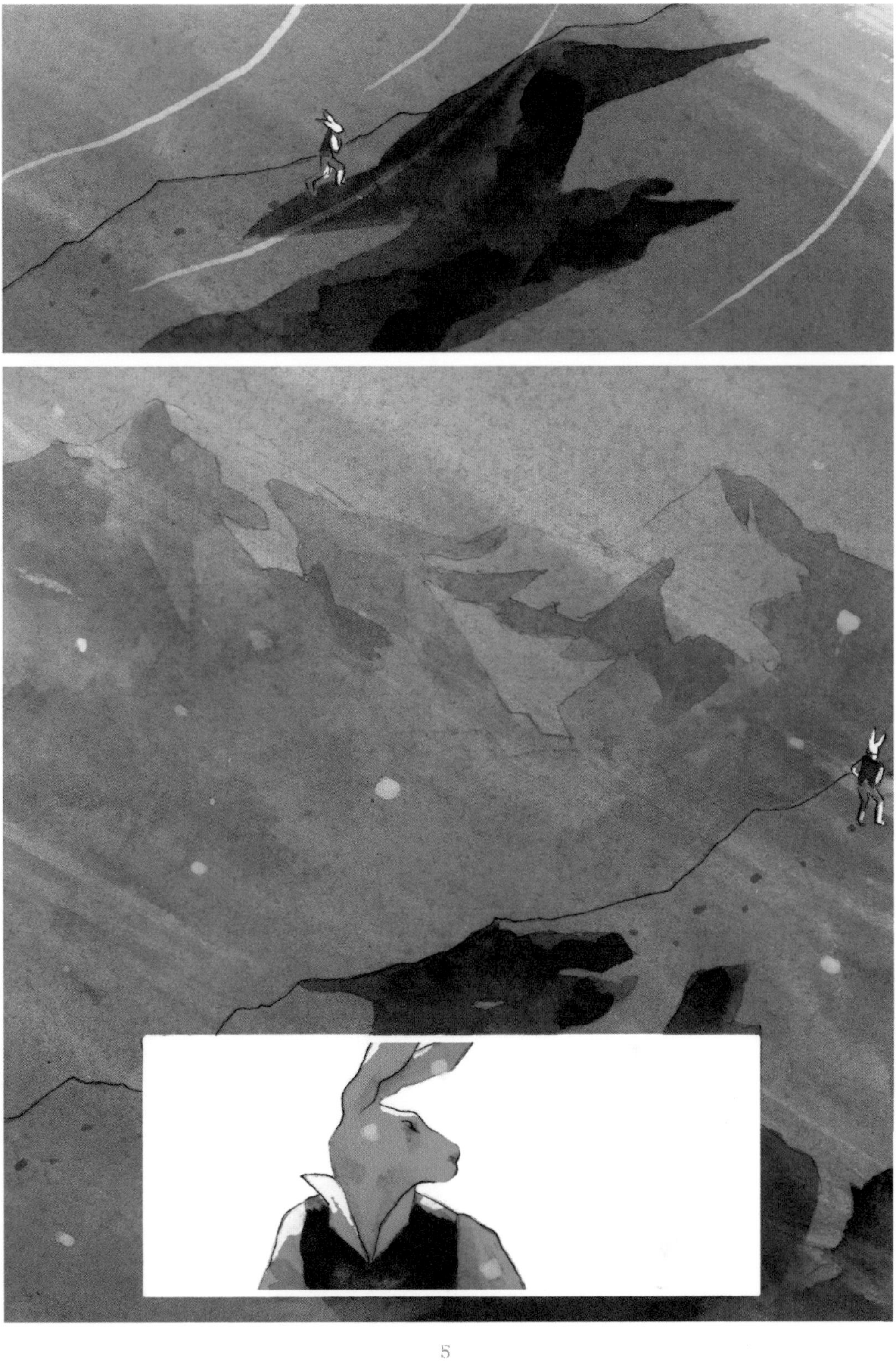

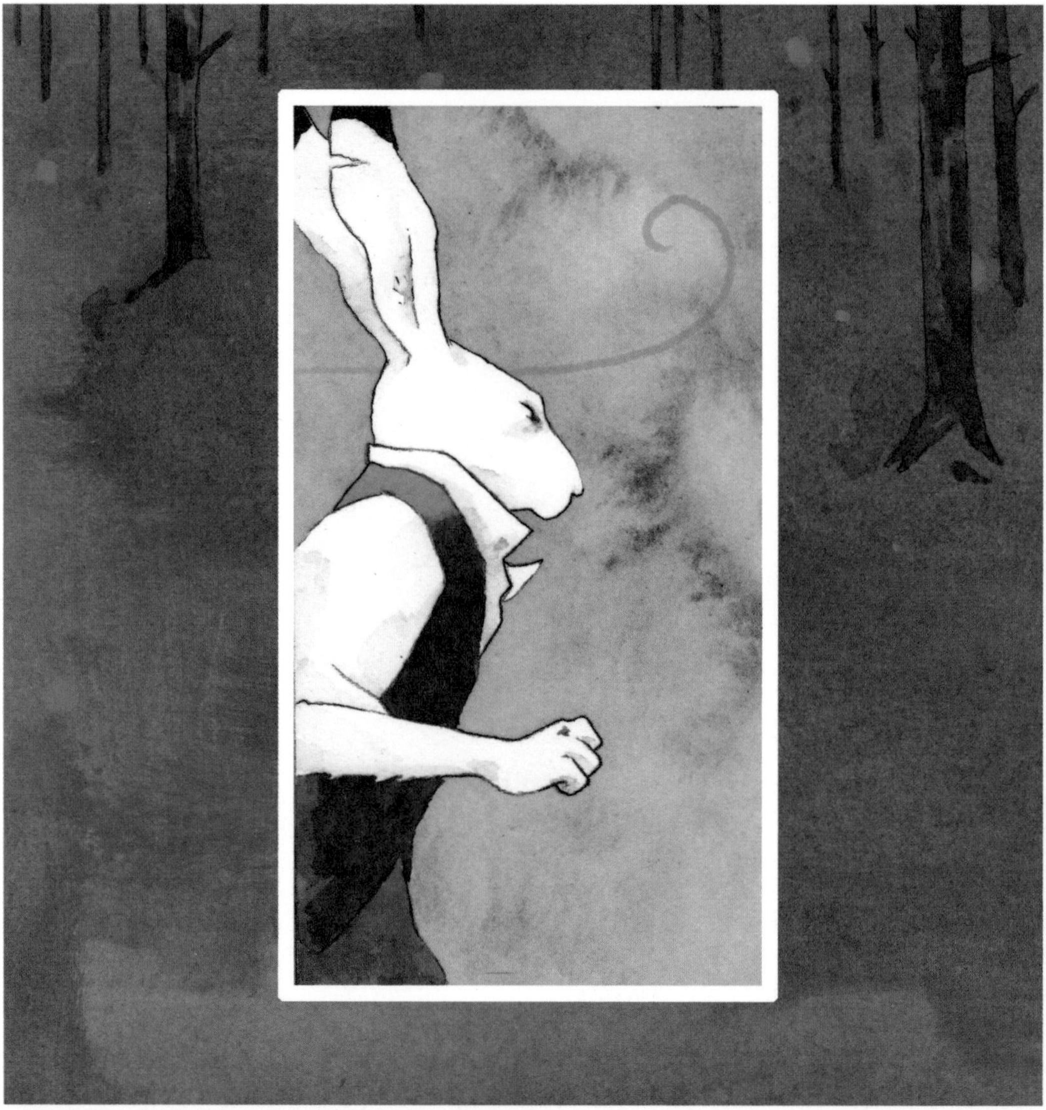

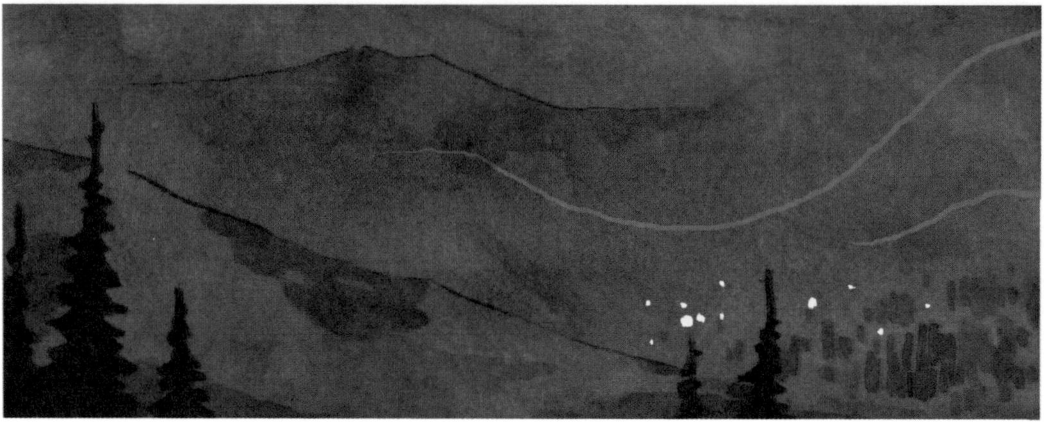

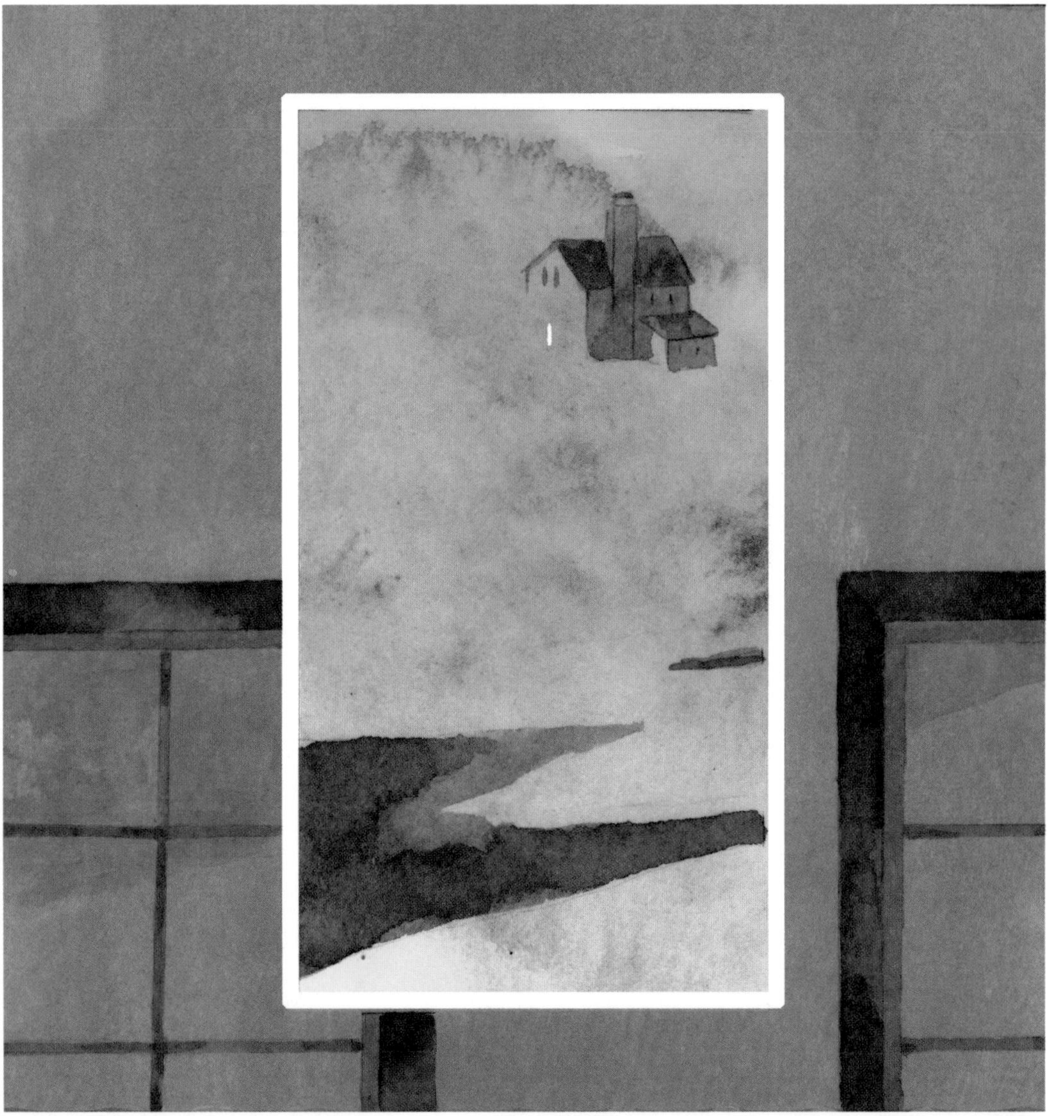

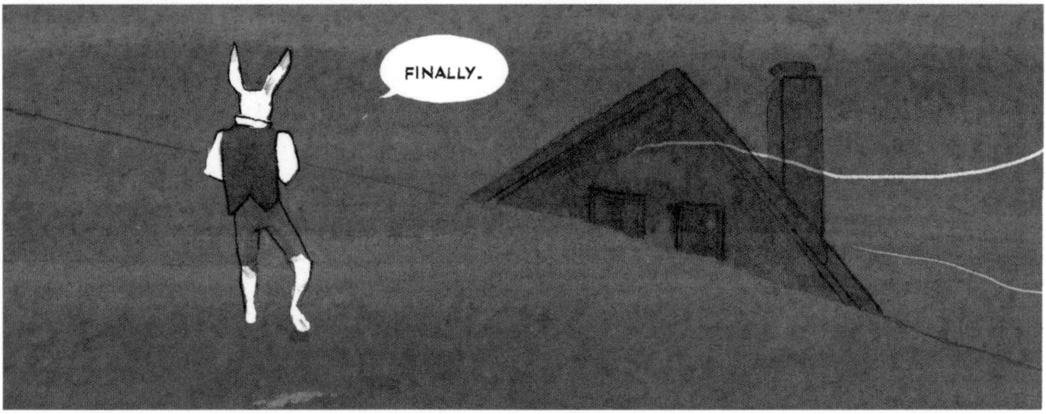
FINALLY.

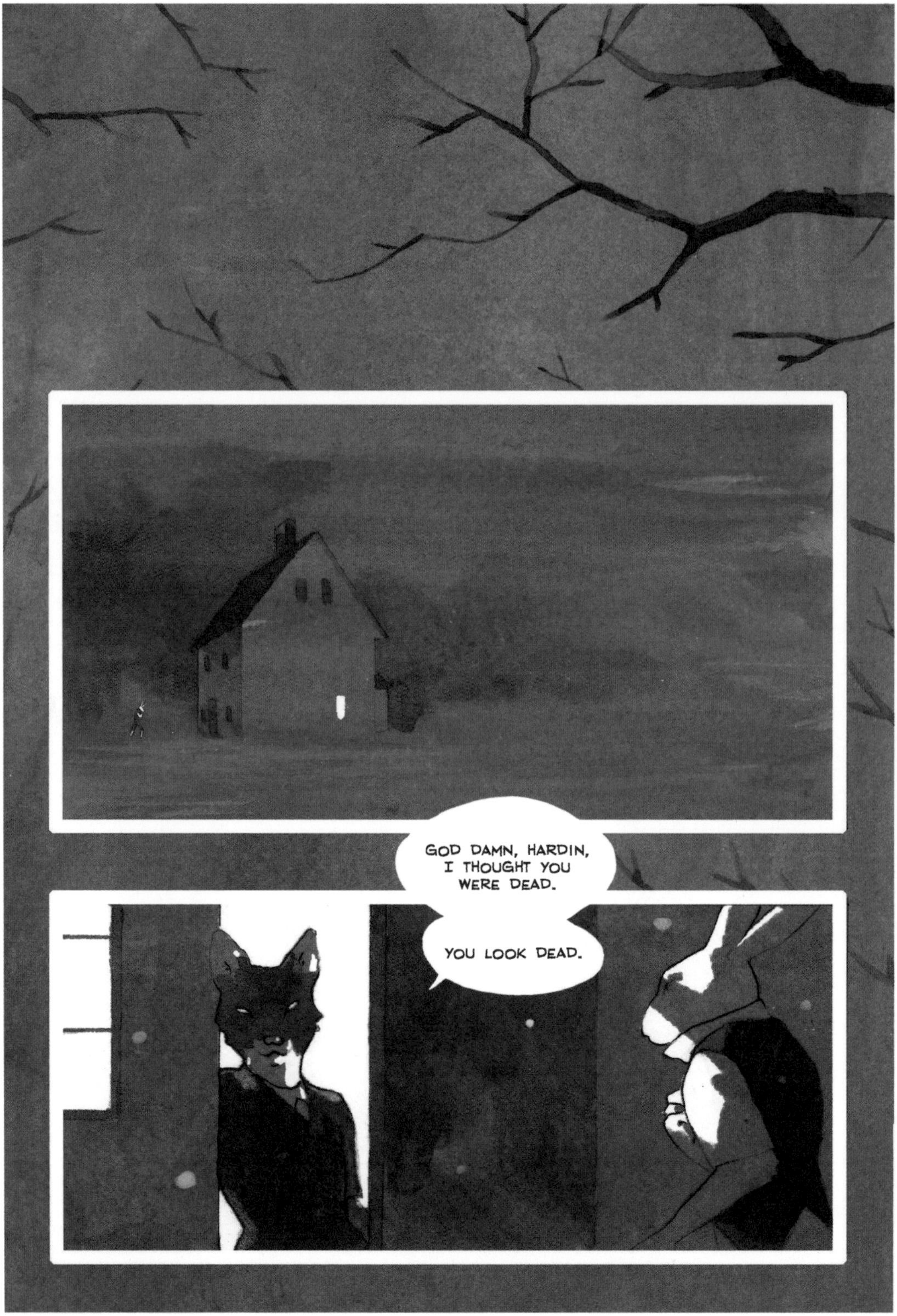
GOD DAMN, HARDIN, I THOUGHT YOU WERE DEAD.
YOU LOOK DEAD.

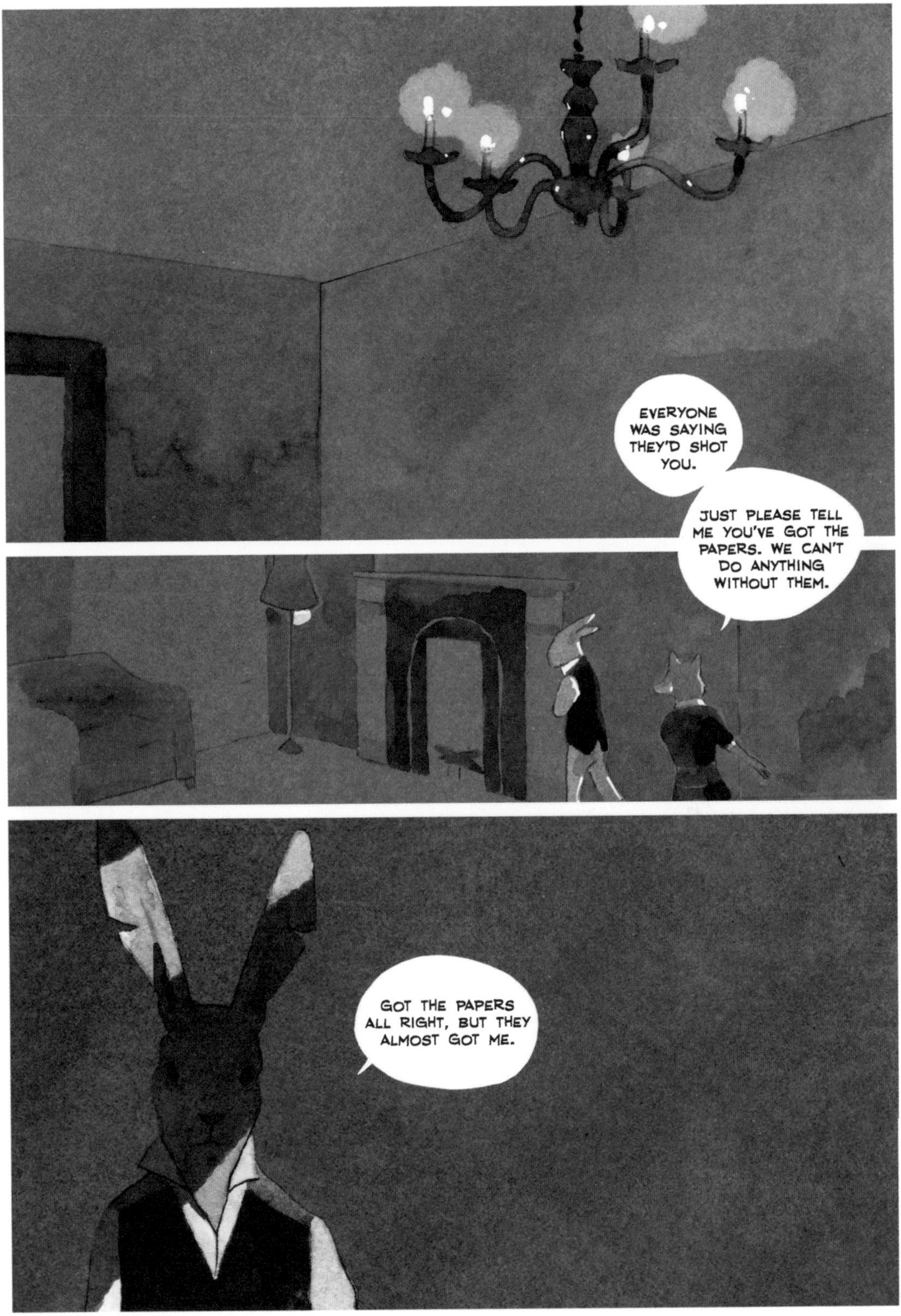
EVERYONE WAS SAYING THEY'D SHOT YOU.
JUST PLEASE TELL ME YOU'VE GOT THE PAPERS. WE CAN'T DO ANYTHING WITHOUT THEM.
GOT THE PAPERS ALL RIGHT, BUT THEY ALMOST GOT ME.

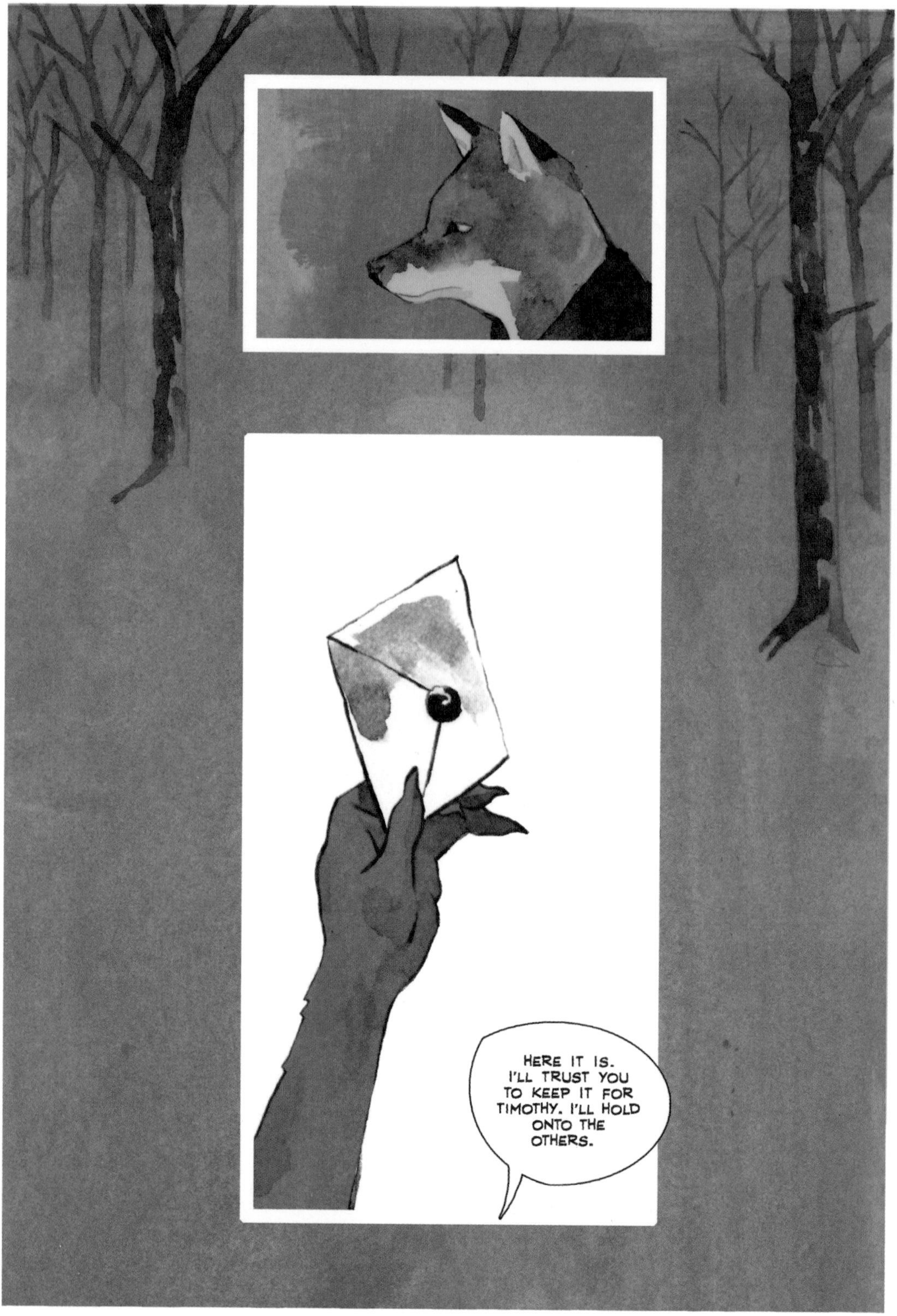
HERE IT IS. I'LL TRUST YOU TO KEEP IT FOR TIMOTHY. I'LL HOLD ONTO THE OTHERS.

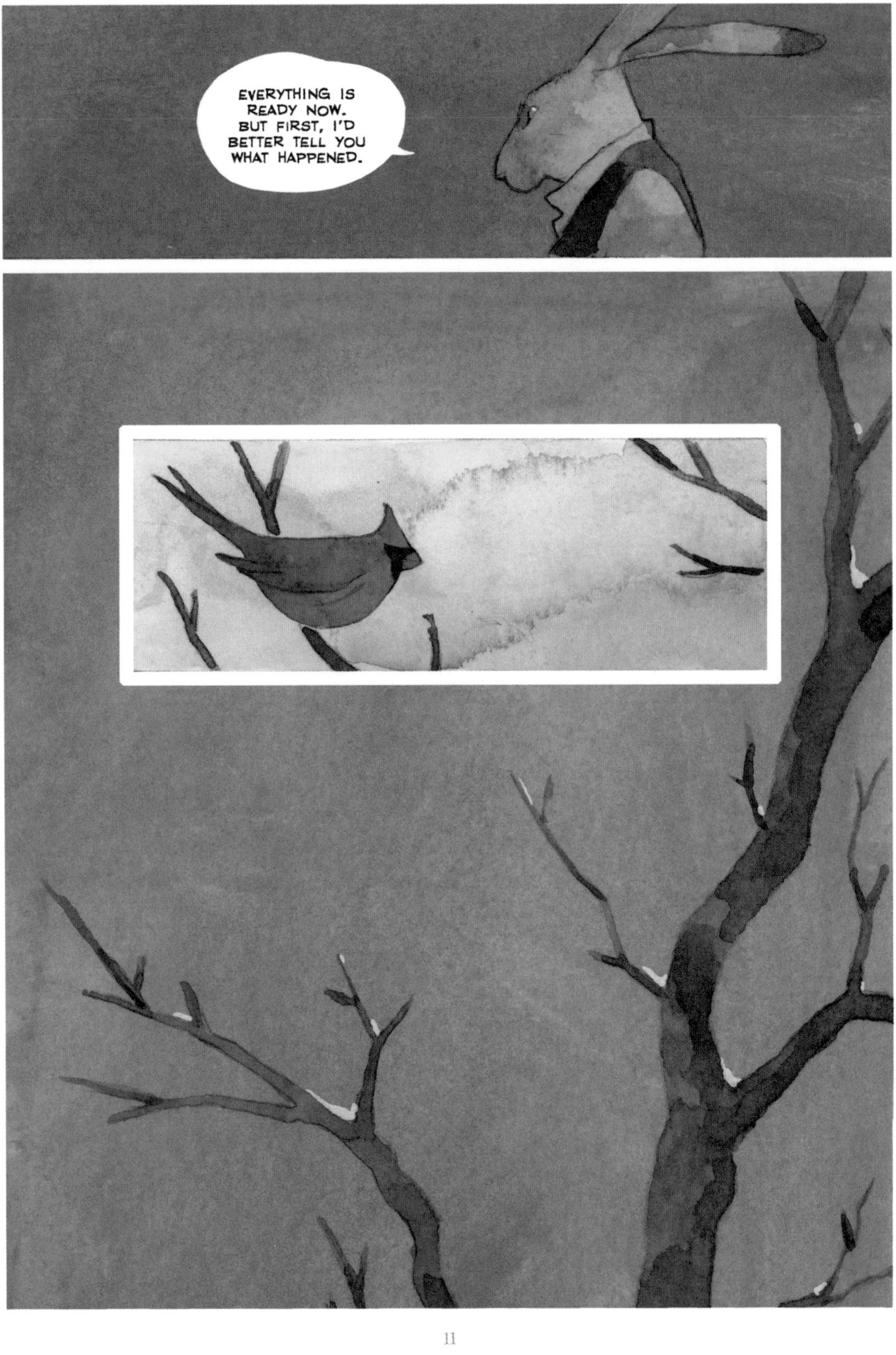
EVERYTHING IS READY NOW. BUT FIRST, I'D BETTER TELL YOU WHAT HAPPENED.

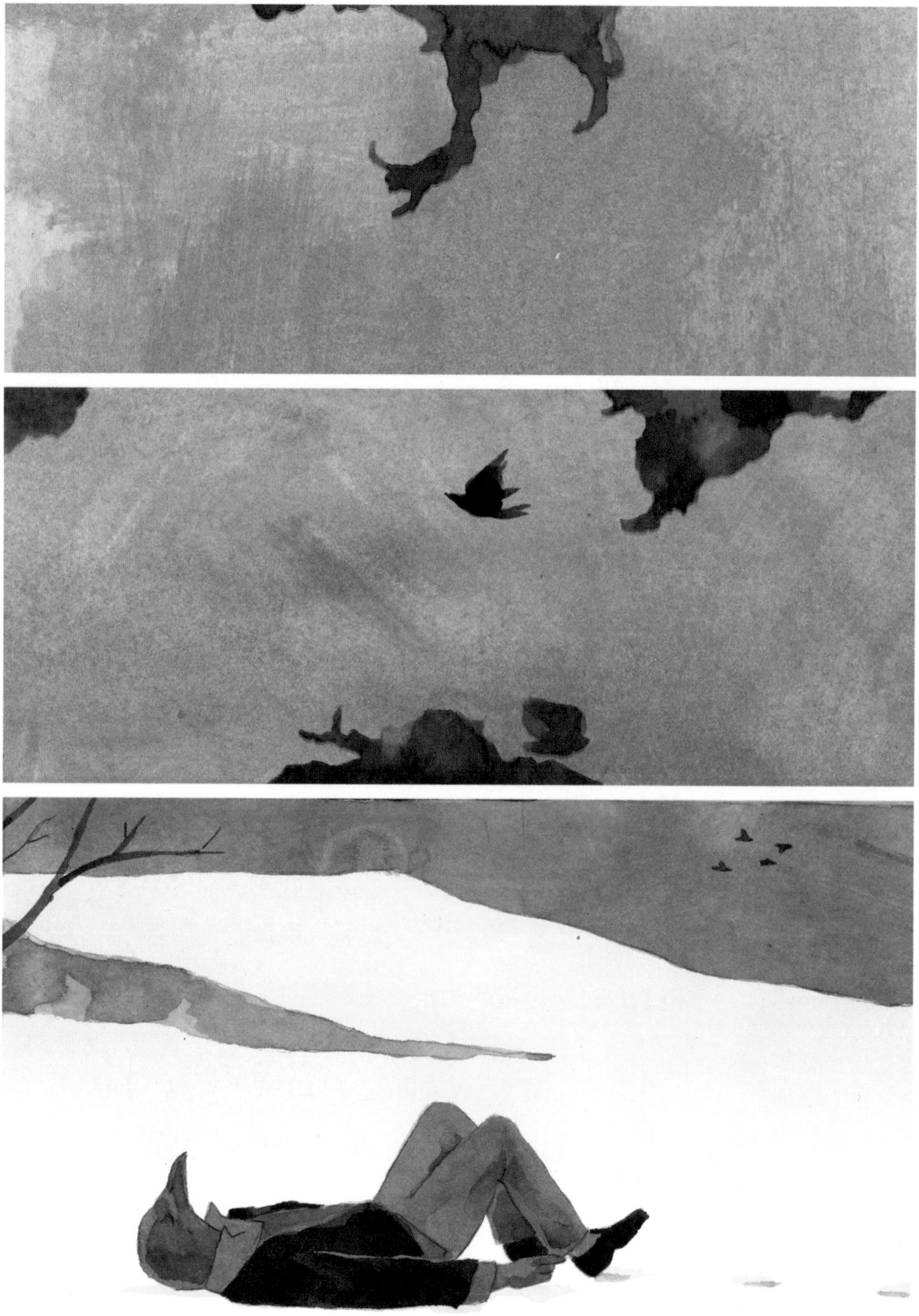

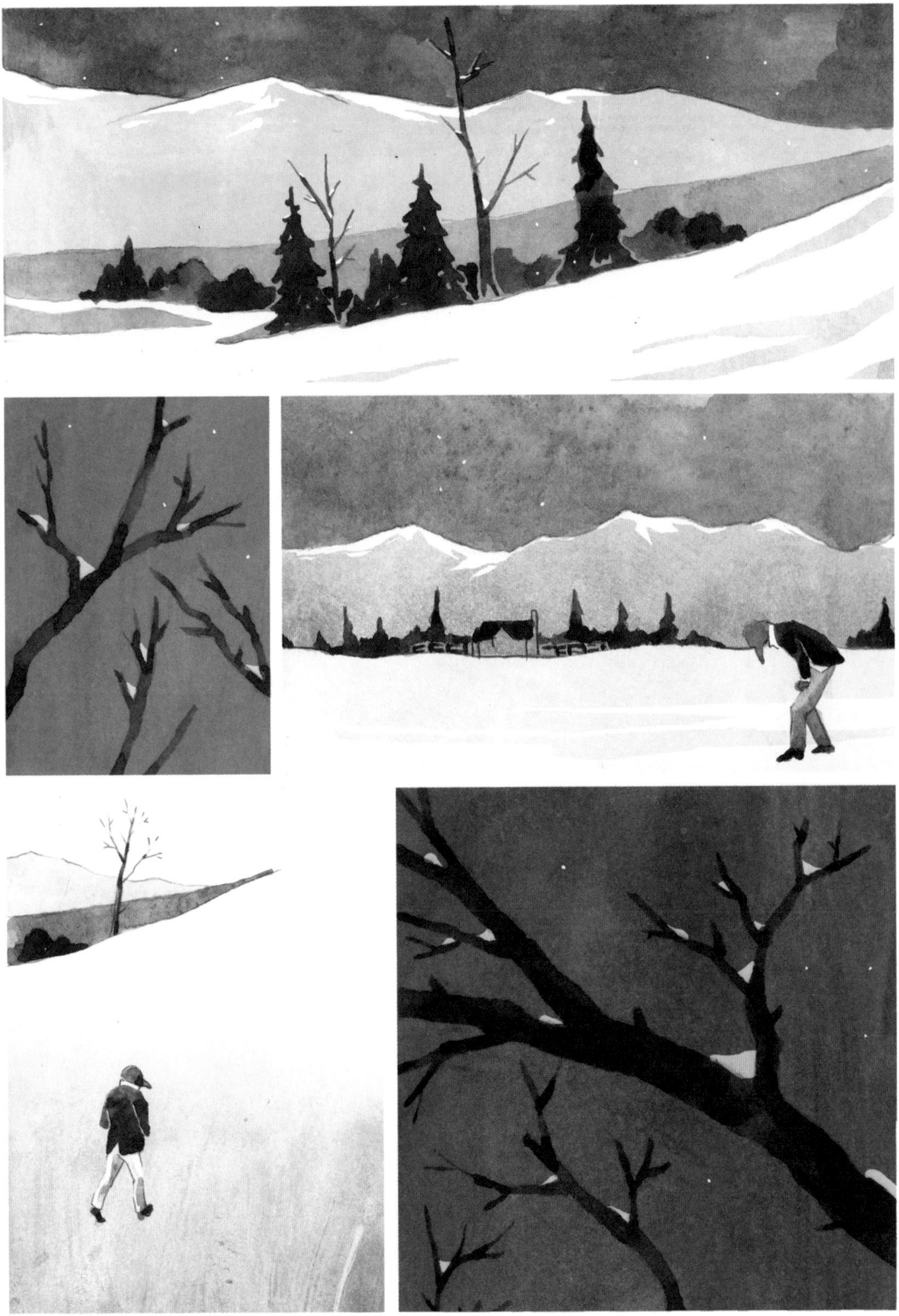

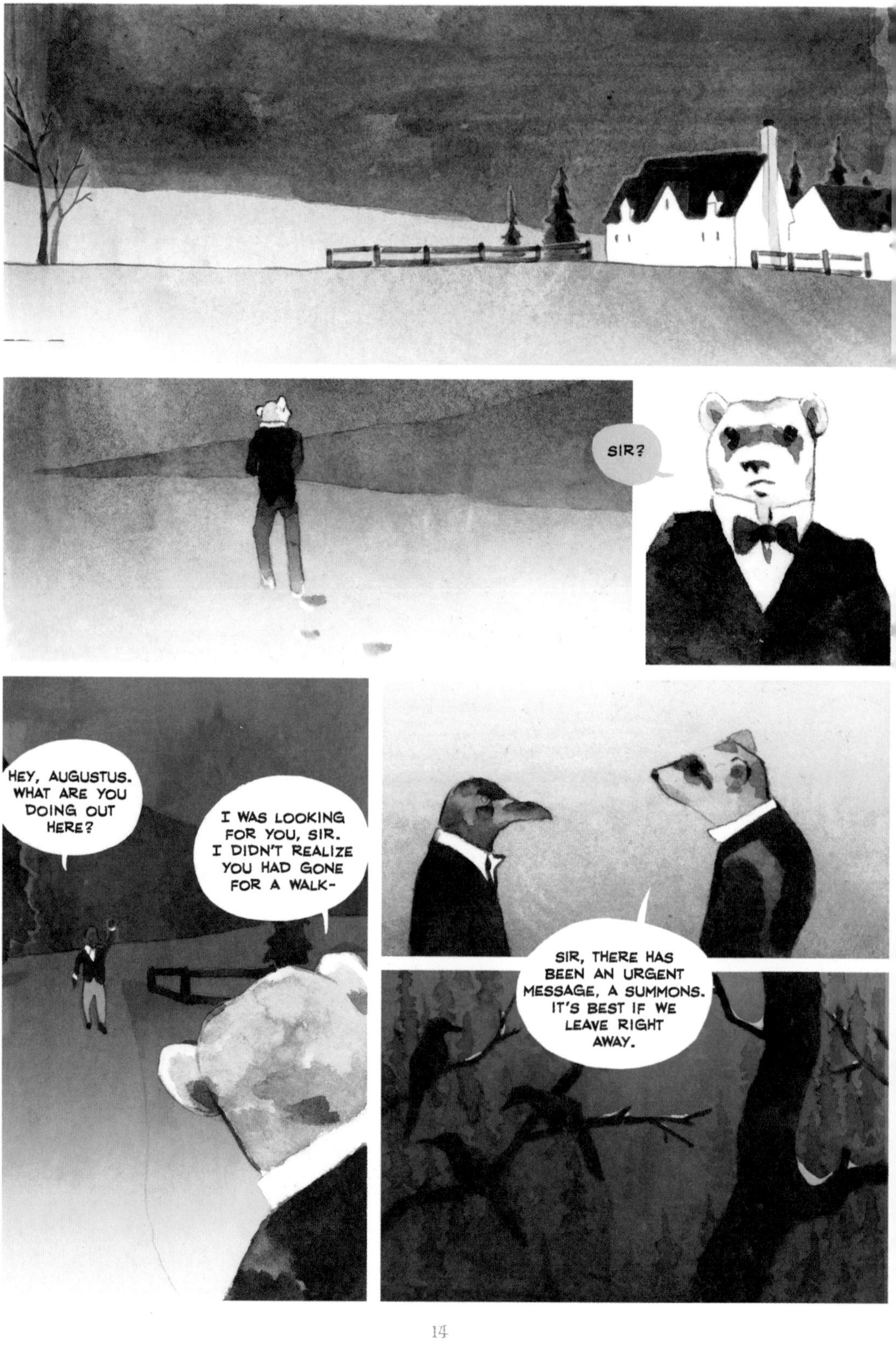
SIR?
HEY, AUGUSTUS. WHAT ARE YOU DOING OUT HERE?
I WAS LOOKING FOR YOU, SIR. I DIDN'T REALIZE YOU HAD GONE FOR A WALK-
SIR, THERE HAS BEEN AN URGENT MESSAGE, A SUMMONS. IT'S BEST IF WE LEAVE RIGHT AWAY.

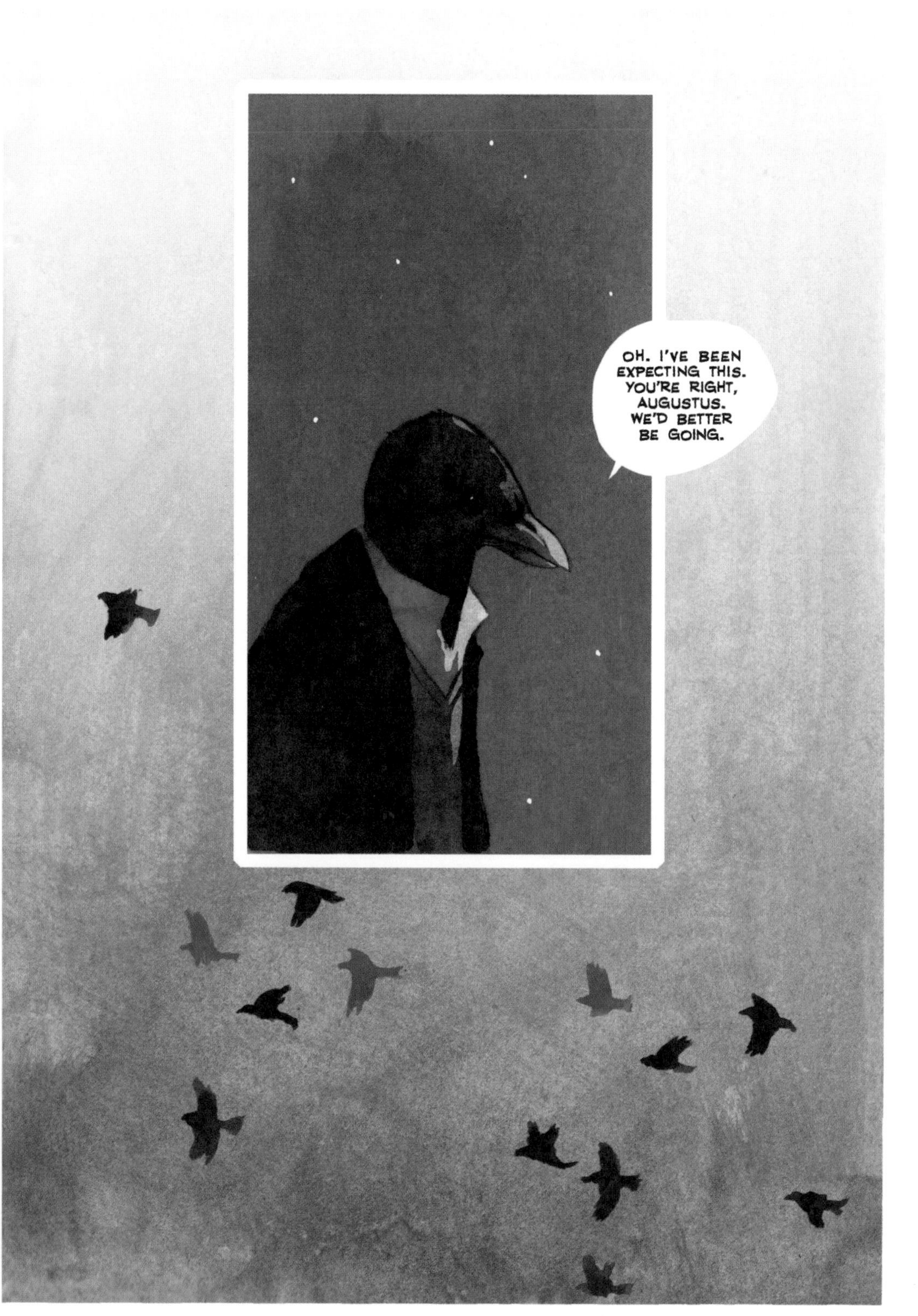
OH. I'VE BEEN EXPECTING THIS. YOU'RE RIGHT, AUGUSTUS. WE'D BETTER BE GOING.

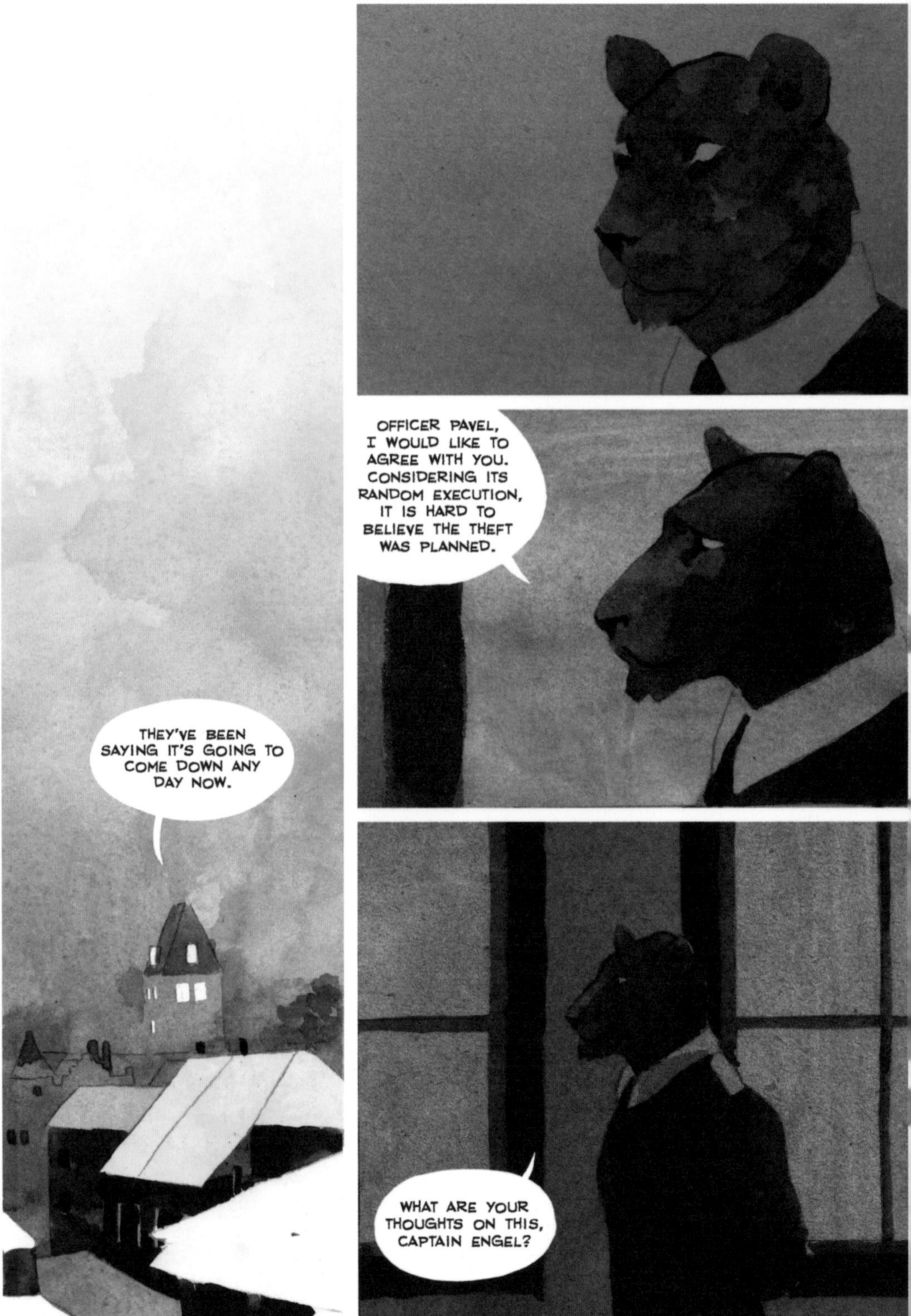
THEY'VE BEEN SAYING IT'S GOING TO COME DOWN ANY DAY NOW.
OFFICER PAVEL, I WOULD LIKE TO AGREE WITH YOU. CONSIDERING ITS RANDOM EXECUTION, IT IS HARD TO BELIEVE THE THEFT WAS PLANNED.
WHAT ARE YOUR THOUGHTS ON THIS, CAPTAIN ENGEL?

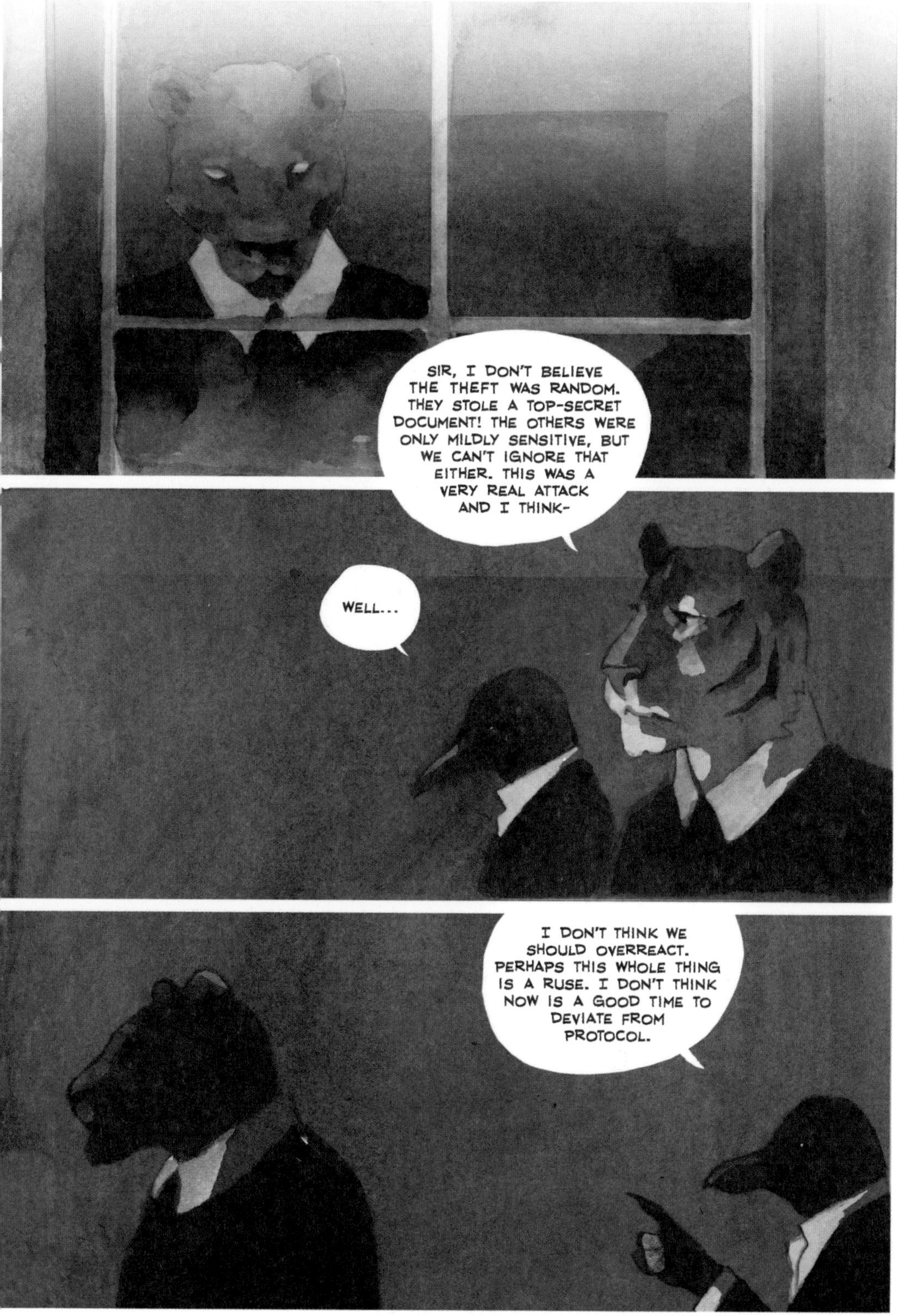
SIR, I DON'T BELIEVE THE THEFT WAS RANDOM. THEY STOLE A TOP-SECRET DOCUMENT! THE OTHERS WERE ONLY MILDLY SENSITIVE, BUT WE CAN'T IGNORE THAT EITHER. THIS WAS A VERY REAL ATTACK AND I THINK-
WELL...
I DON'T THINK WE SHOULD OVERREACT. PERHAPS THIS WHOLE THING IS A RUSE. I DON'T THINK NOW IS A GOOD TIME TO DEVIATE FROM PROTOCOL.

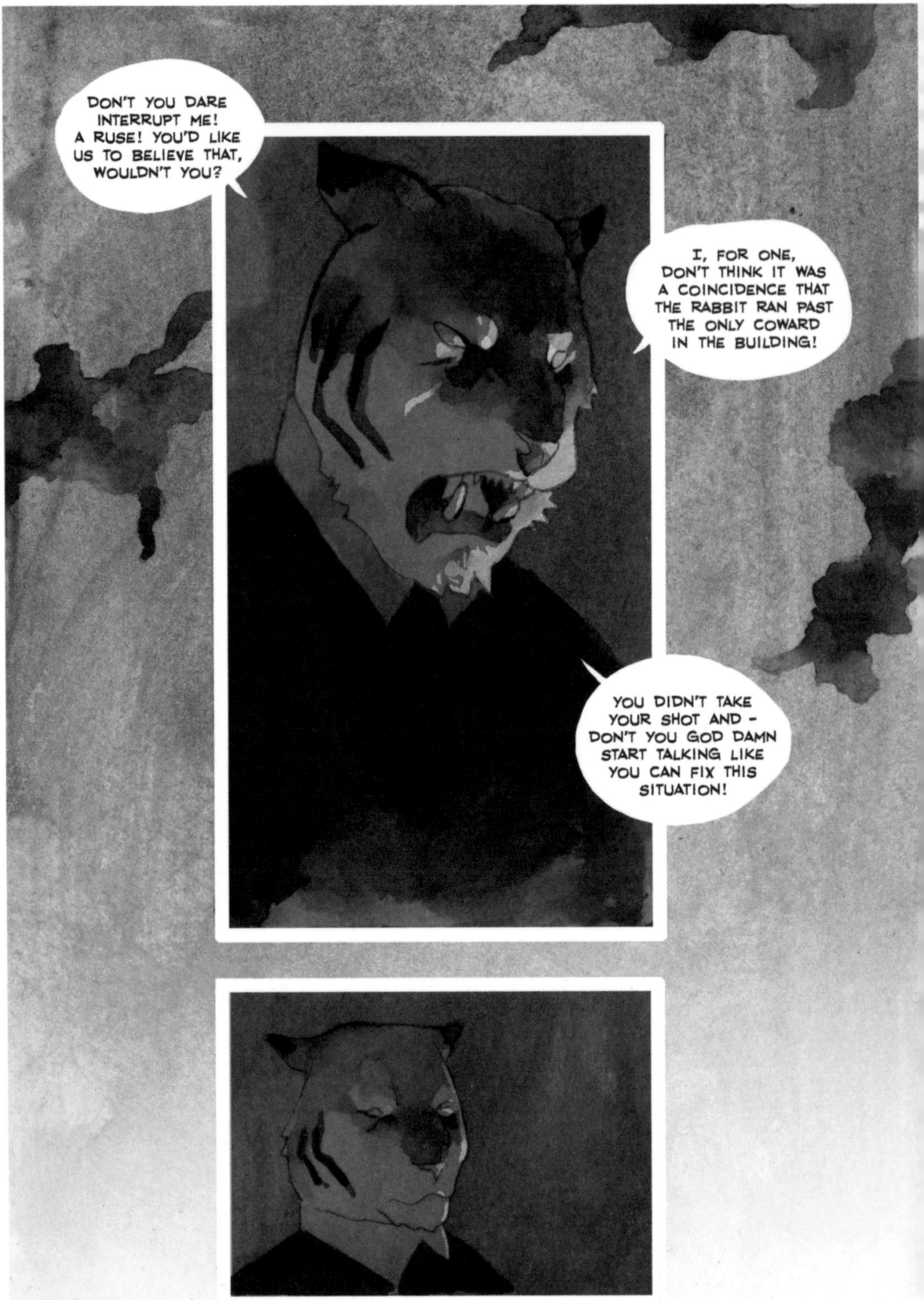
DON'T YOU DARE INTERRUPT ME! A RUSE! YOU'D LIKE US TO BELIEVE THAT, WOULDN'T YOU?
I, FOR ONE, DON'T THINK IT WAS A COINCIDENCE THAT THE RABBIT RAN PAST THE ONLY COWARD IN THE BUILDING!
YOU DIDN'T TAKE YOUR SHOT AND - DON'T YOU GOD DAMN START TALKING LIKE YOU CAN FIX THIS SITUATION!

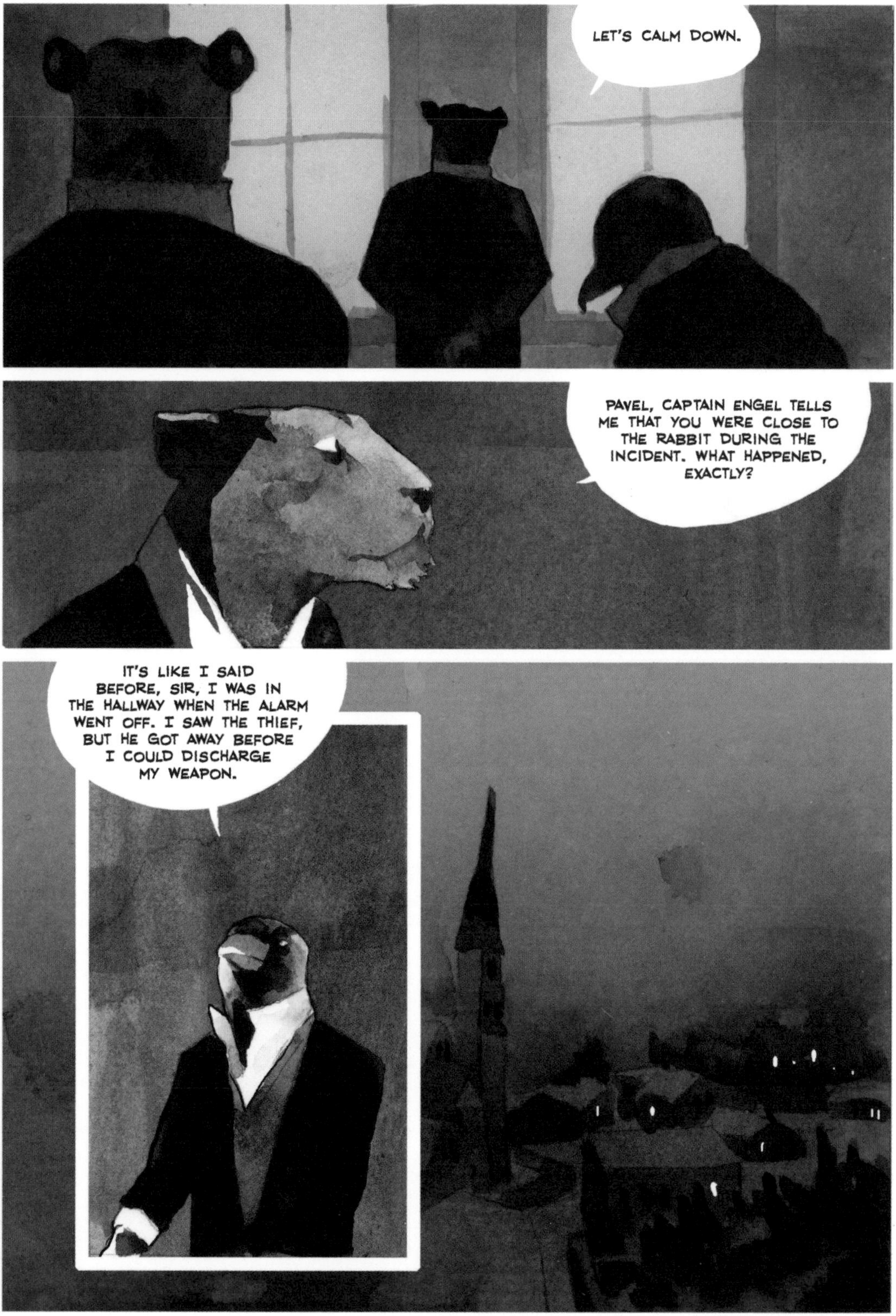
LET'S CALM DOWN.
PAVEL, CAPTAIN ENGEL TELLS ME THAT YOU WERE CLOSE TO THE RABBIT DURING THE INCIDENT. WHAT HAPPENED, EXACTLY?
IT'S LIKE I SAID BEFORE, SIR, I WAS IN THE HALLWAY WHEN THE ALARM WENT OFF. I SAW THE THIEF, BUT HE GOT AWAY BEFORE I COULD DISCHARGE MY WEAPON.

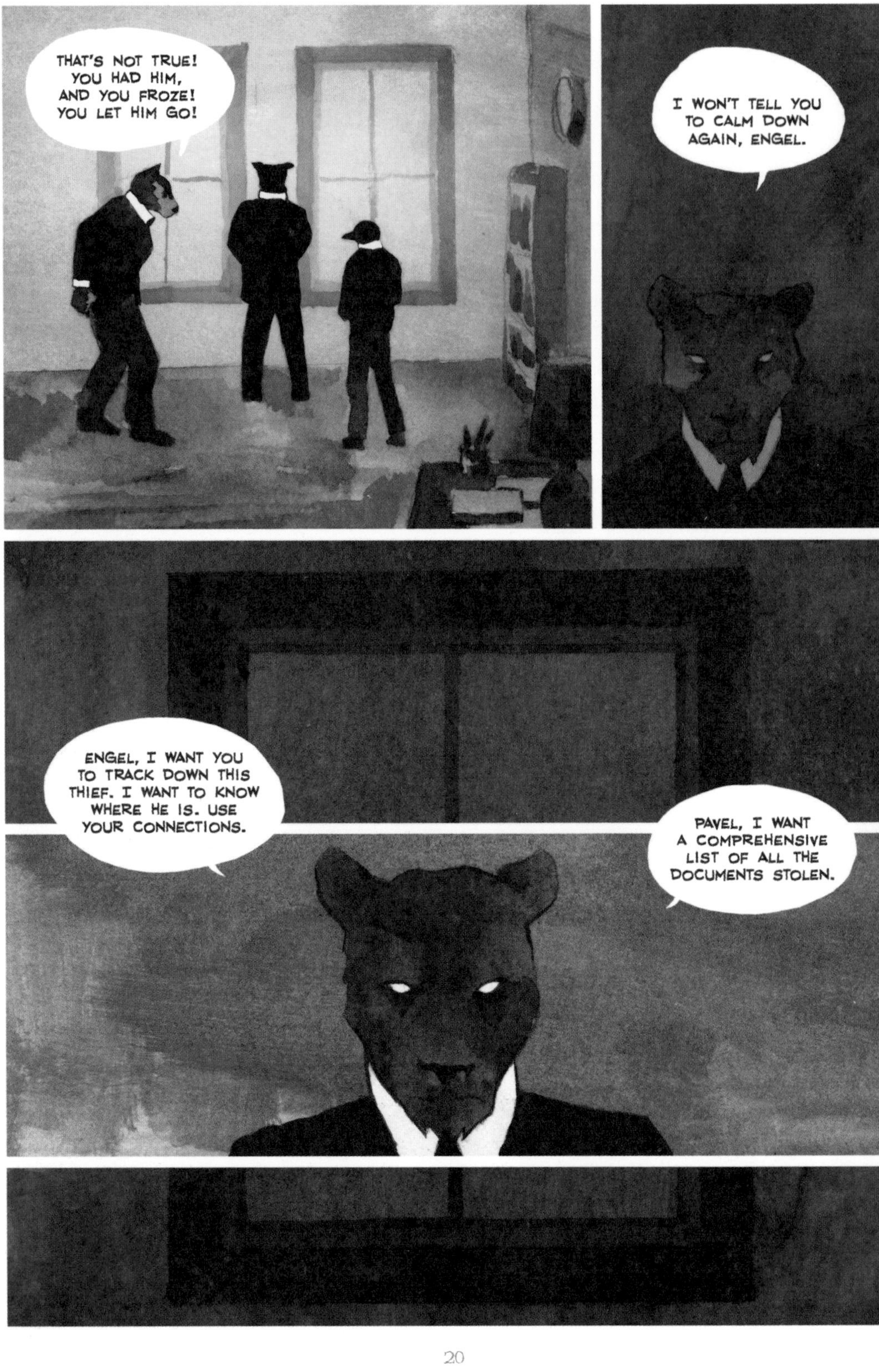
THAT'S NOT TRUE! YOU HAD HIM, AND YOU FROZE! YOU LET HIM GO!
I WON'T TELL YOU TO CALM DOWN AGAIN, ENGEL.
ENGEL, I WANT YOU TO TRACK DOWN THIS THIEF. I WANT TO KNOW WHERE HE IS. USE YOUR CONNECTIONS.
PAVEL, I WANT A COMPREHENSIVE LIST OF ALL THE DOCUMENTS STOLEN.

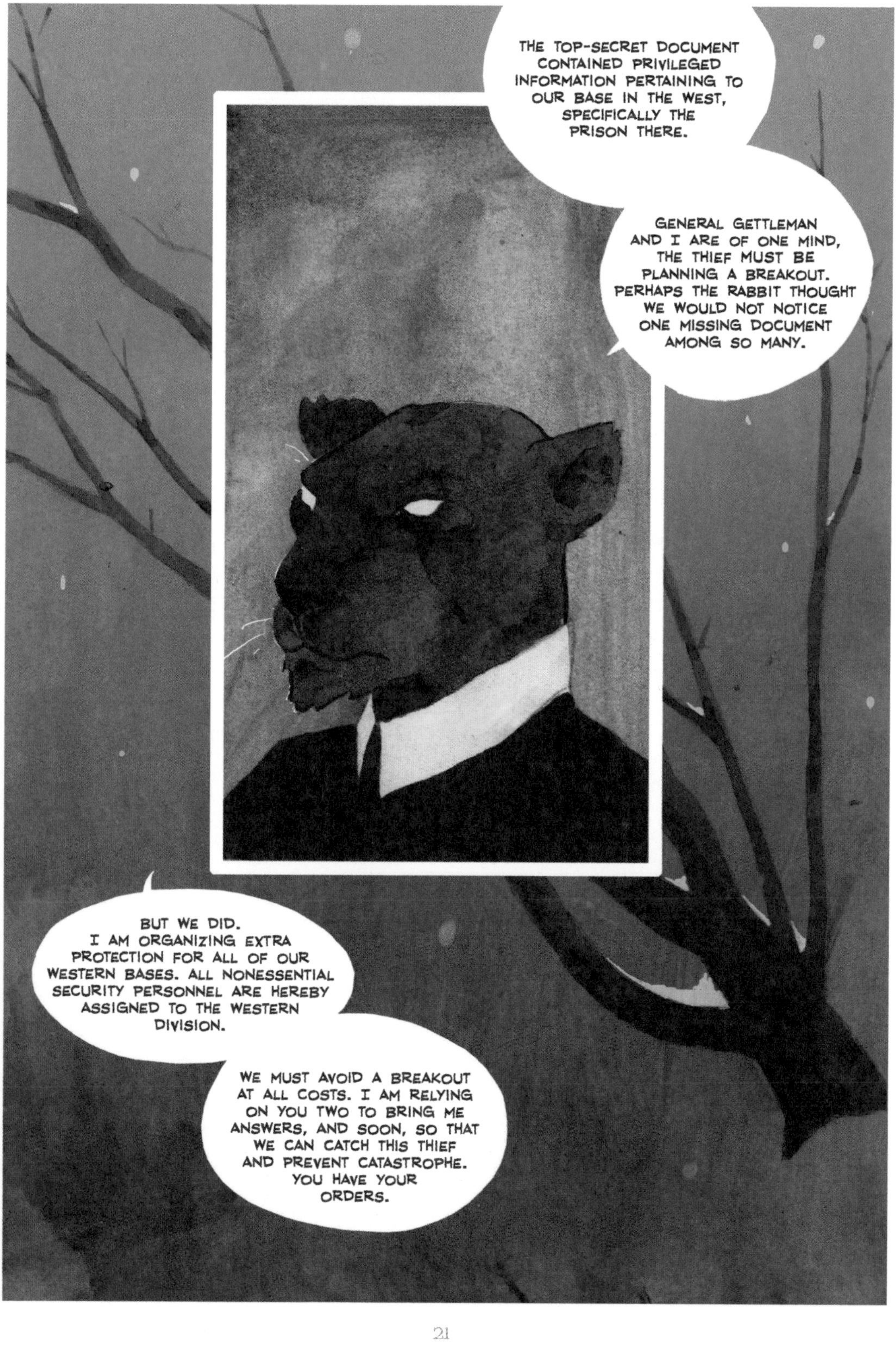
THE TOP-SECRET DOCUMENT CONTAINED PRIVILEGED INFORMATION PERTAINING TO OUR BASE IN THE WEST, SPECIFICALLY THE PRISON THERE.
GENERAL GETTLEMAN AND I ARE OF ONE MIND, THE THIEF MUST BE PLANNING A BREAKOUT. PERHAPS THE RABBIT THOUGHT WE WOULD NOT NOTICE ONE MISSING DOCUMENT AMONG SO MANY.
BUT WE DID. I AM ORGANIZING EXTRA PROTECTION FOR ALL OF OUR WESTERN BASES. ALL NONESSENTIAL SECURITY PERSONNEL ARE HEREBY ASSIGNED TO THE WESTERN DIVISION.
WE MUST AVOID A BREAKOUT AT ALL COSTS. I AM RELYING ON YOU TWO TO BRING ME ANSWERS, AND SOON, SO THAT WE CAN CATCH THIS THIEF AND PREVENT CATASTROPHE. YOU HAVE YOUR ORDERS.

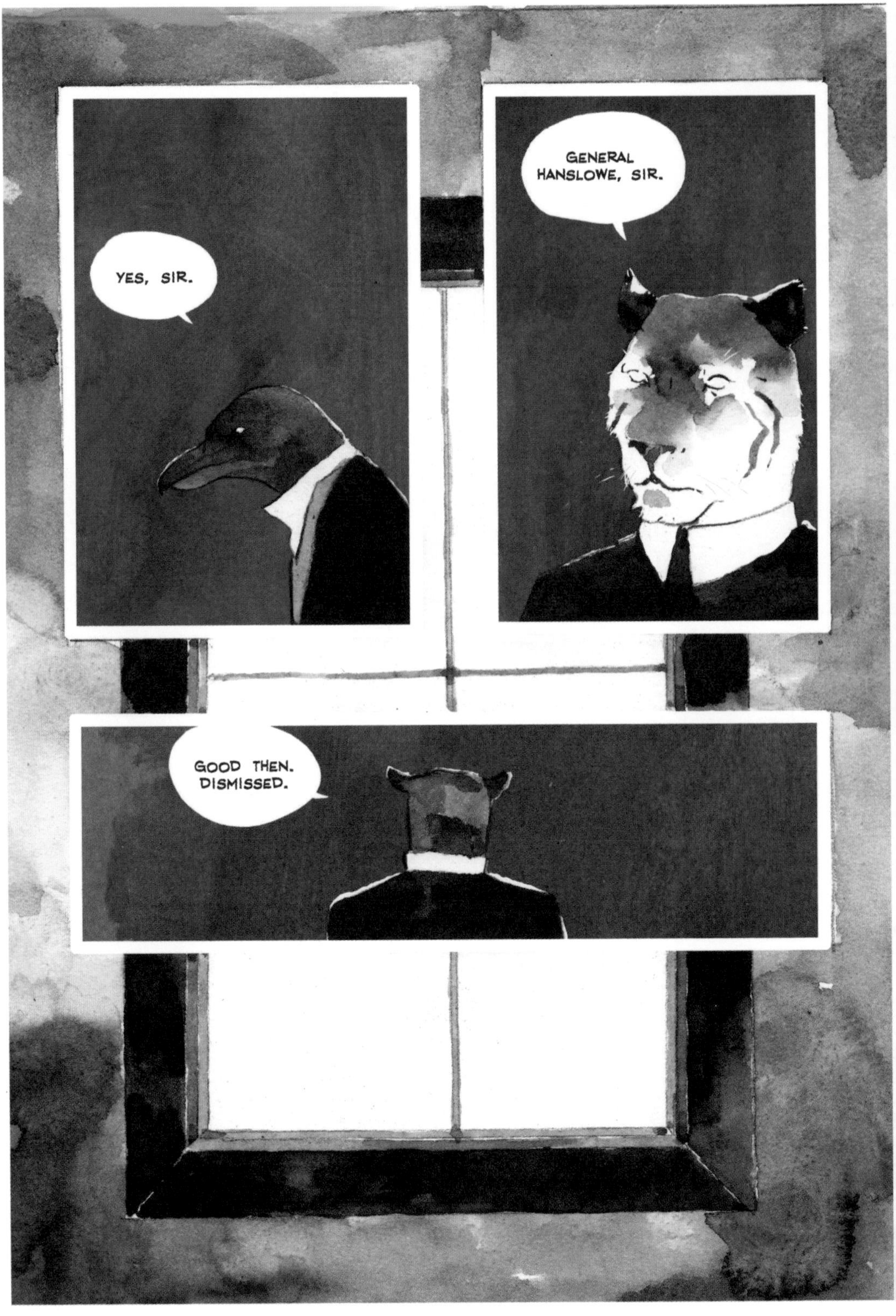
YES, SIR.
GENERAL HANSLOWE, SIR.
GOOD THEN. DISMISSED.

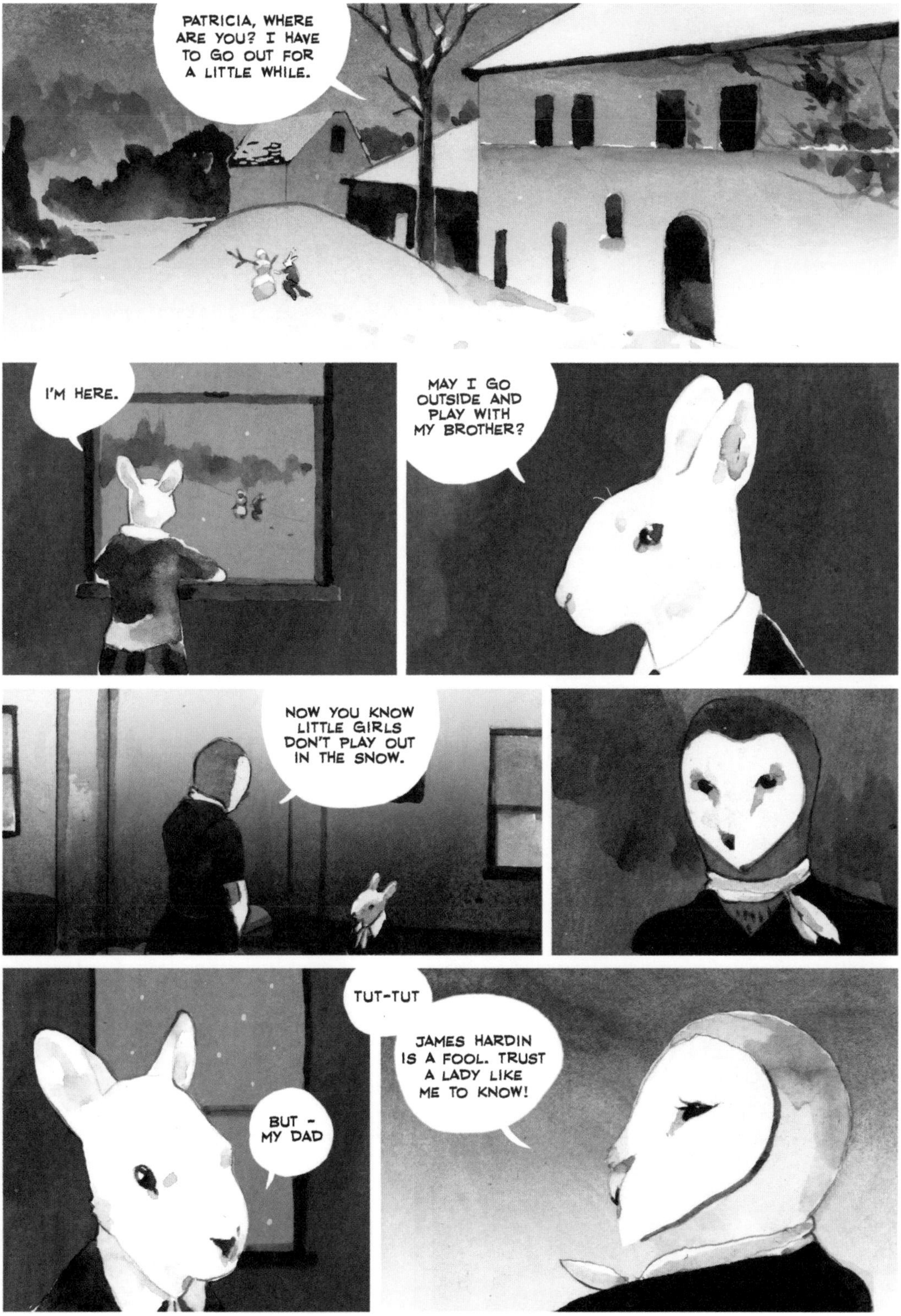
PATRICIA, WHERE ARE YOU? I HAVE TO GO OUT FOR A LITTLE WHILE.
I'M HERE.
MAY I GO OUTSIDE AND PLAY WITH MY BROTHER?
NOW YOU KNOW LITTLE GIRLS DON'T PLAY OUT IN THE SNOW.
BUT - MY DAD
TUT-TUT
JAMES HARDIN IS A FOOL. TRUST A LADY LIKE ME TO KNOW!

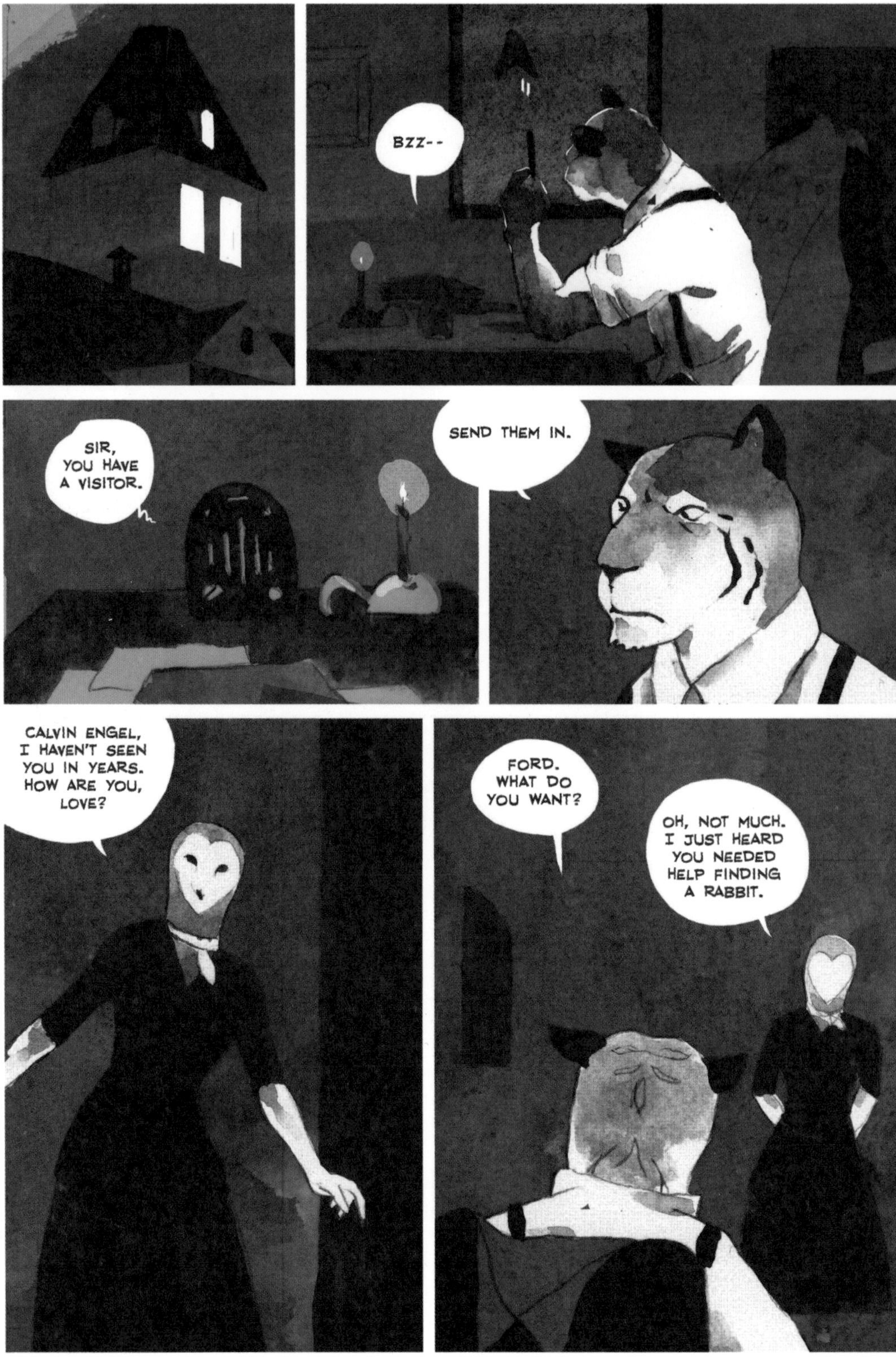
BZZ--
SIR, YOU HAVE A VISITOR.
SEND THEM IN.
CALVIN ENGEL, I HAVEN'T SEEN YOU IN YEARS. HOW ARE YOU, LOVE?
FORD. WHAT DO YOU WANT?
OH, NOT MUCH. I JUST HEARD YOU NEEDED HELP FINDING A RABBIT.

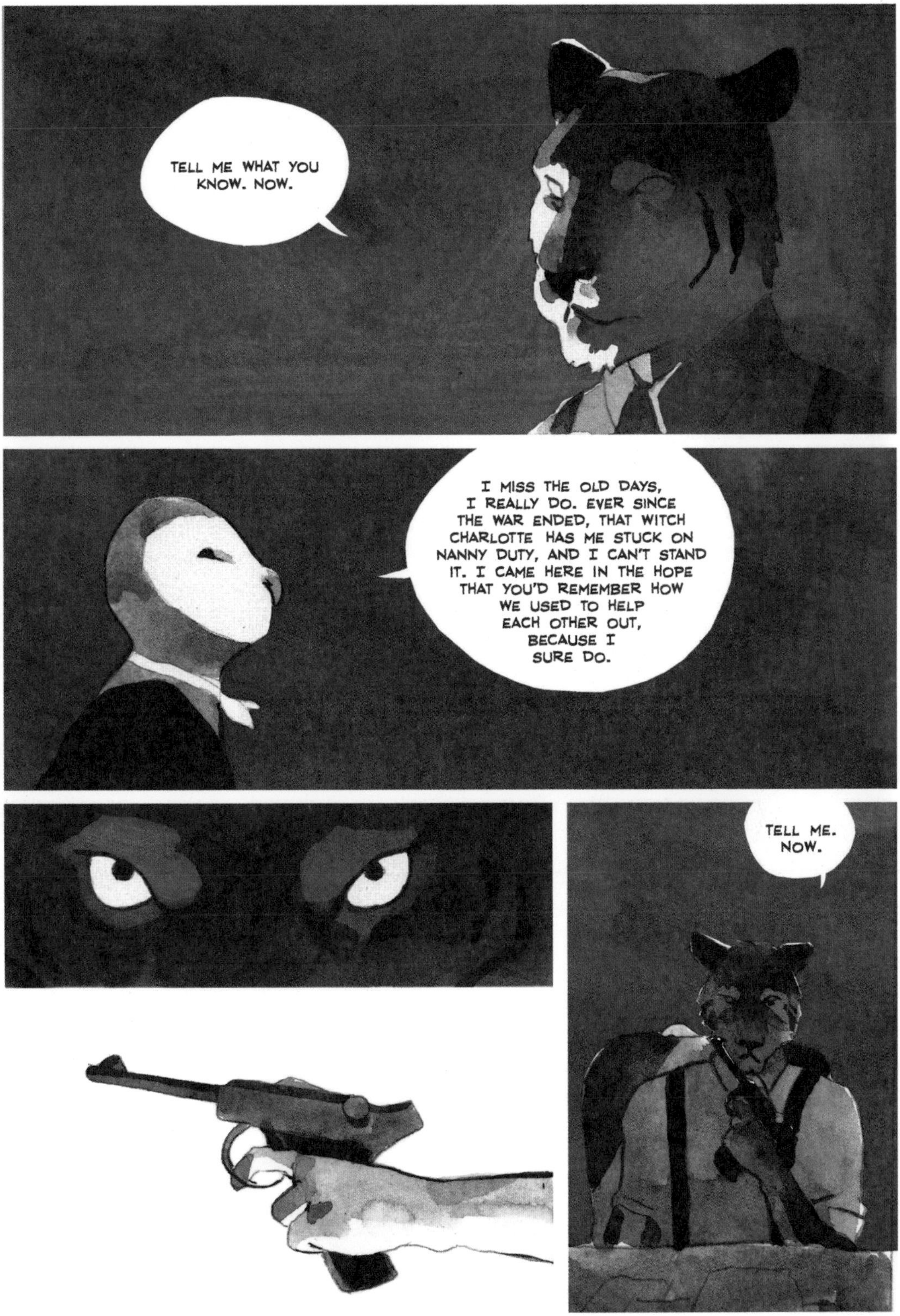
TELL ME WHAT YOU KNOW. NOW.
I MISS THE OLD DAYS, I REALLY DO. EVER SINCE THE WAR ENDED, THAT WITCH CHARLOTTE HAS ME STUCK ON NANNY DUTY, AND I CAN'T STAND IT. I CAME HERE IN THE HOPE THAT YOU'D REMEMBER HOW WE USED TO HELP EACH OTHER OUT, BECAUSE I SURE DO.
TELL ME. NOW.

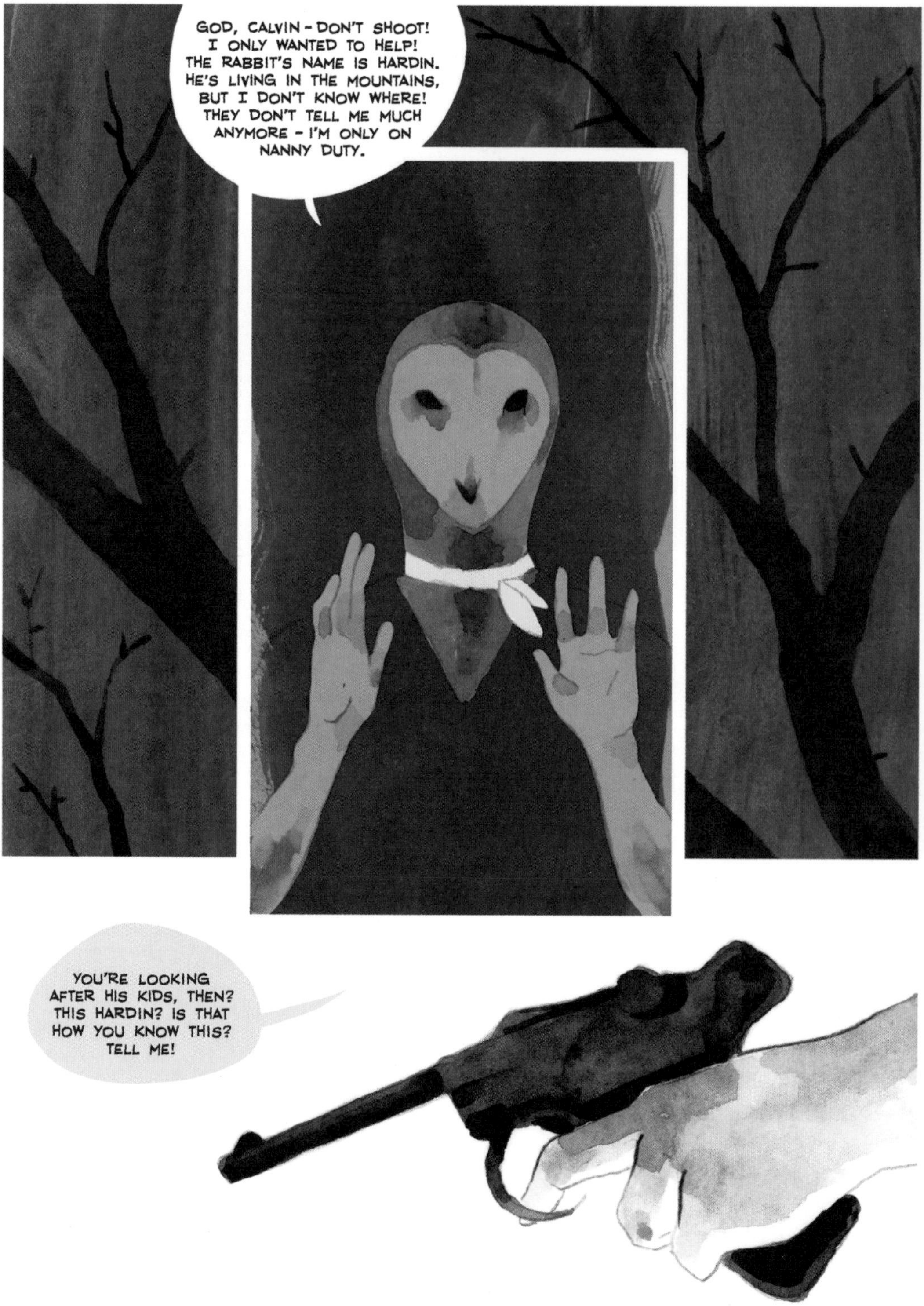
GOD, CALVIN - DON'T SHOOT! I ONLY WANTED TO HELP! THE RABBIT'S NAME IS HARDIN. HE'S LIVING IN THE MOUNTAINS, BUT I DON'T KNOW WHERE! THEY DON'T TELL ME MUCH ANYMORE - I'M ONLY ON NANNY DUTY.
YOU'RE LOOKING AFTER HIS KIDS, THEN? THIS HARDIN? IS THAT HOW YOU KNOW THIS? TELL ME!

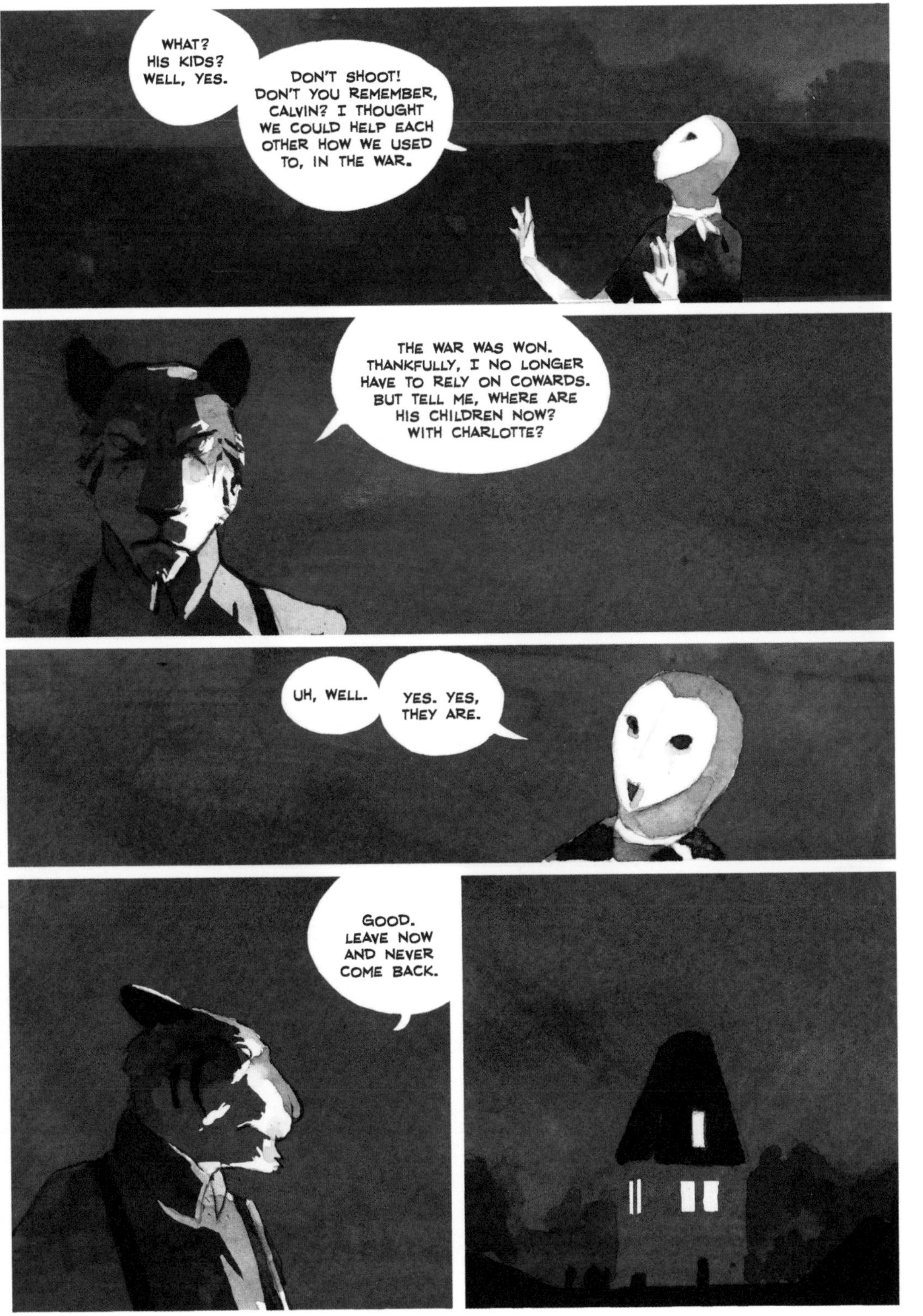
WHAT? HIS KIDS? WELL, YES.
DON'T SHOOT! DON'T YOU REMEMBER, CALVIN? I THOUGHT WE COULD HELP EACH OTHER HOW WE USED TO, IN THE WAR.
THE WAR WAS WON. THANKFULLY, I NO LONGER HAVE TO RELY ON COWARDS. BUT TELL ME, WHERE ARE HIS CHILDREN NOW? WITH CHARLOTTE?
UH, WELL.
YES. YES, THEY ARE.
GOOD. LEAVE NOW AND NEVER COME BACK.

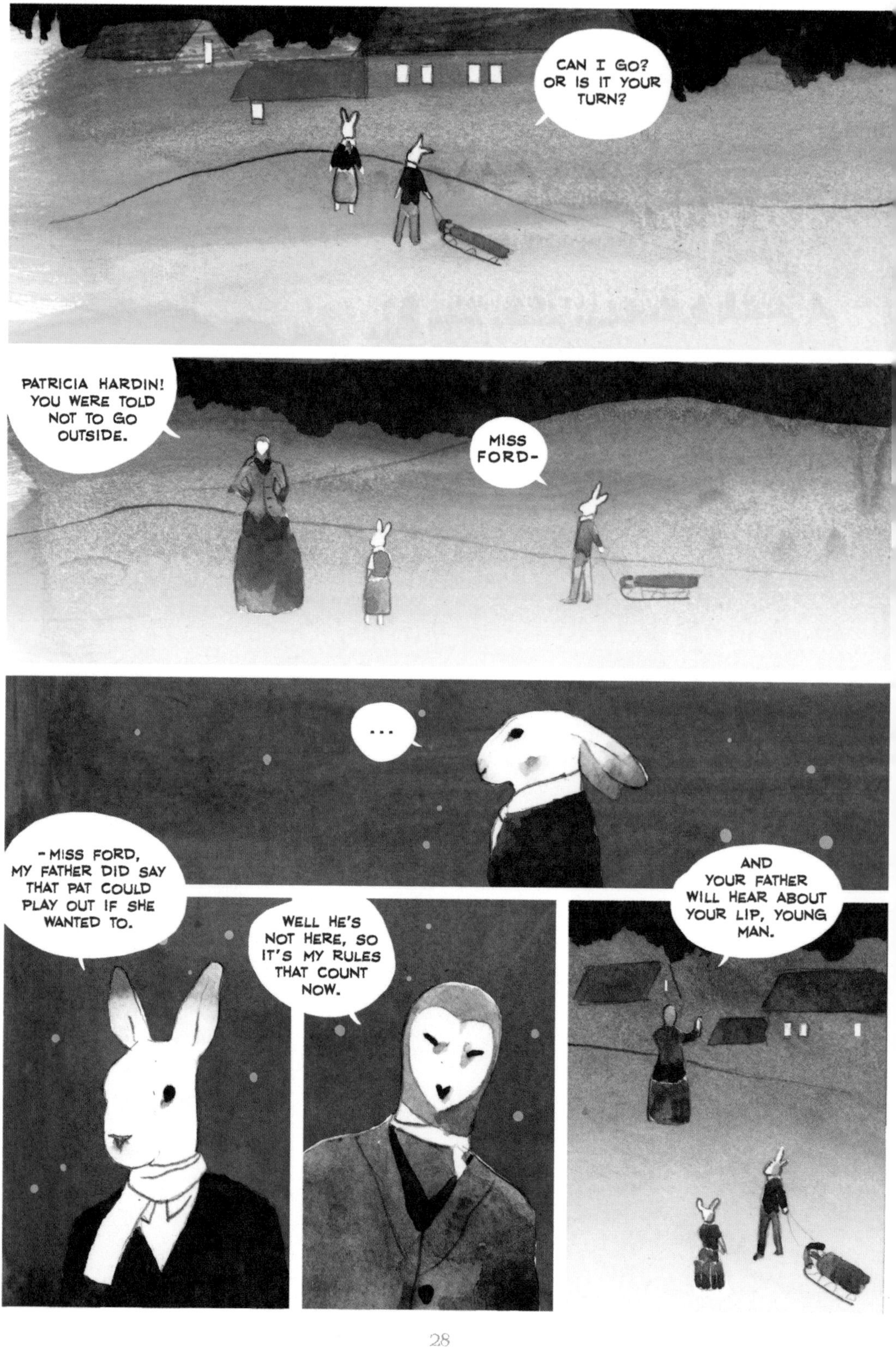
CAN I GO? OR IS IT YOUR TURN?
PATRICIA HARDIN! YOU WERE TOLD NOT TO GO OUTSIDE.
MISS FORD-
...
-MISS FORD, MY FATHER DID SAY THAT PAT COULD PLAY OUT IF SHE WANTED TO.
WELL HE'S NOT HERE, SO IT'S MY RULES THAT COUNT NOW.
AND YOUR FATHER WILL HEAR ABOUT YOUR LIP, YOUNG MAN.

CHARLOTTE WOOLF? YES, I REMEMBER HER. SHE USED TO BE A CONGRESS-WOMAN.

REALLY? WHO WAS YOUR SOURCE ON THIS?

BECAUSE I THINK I SHOULD KNOW.

TOMORROW? WELL, THEN I REALLY WOULD LIKE TO KNOW YOUR SOURCE-

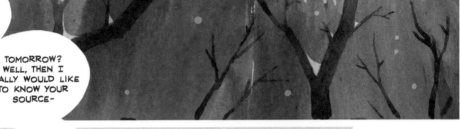

YES, I CAN IDENTIFY THE RABBIT.

DON'T GET ALL UPSET, ENGEL. I DIDN'T SAY I WOULDN'T GO, I JUST SAID-

HM.

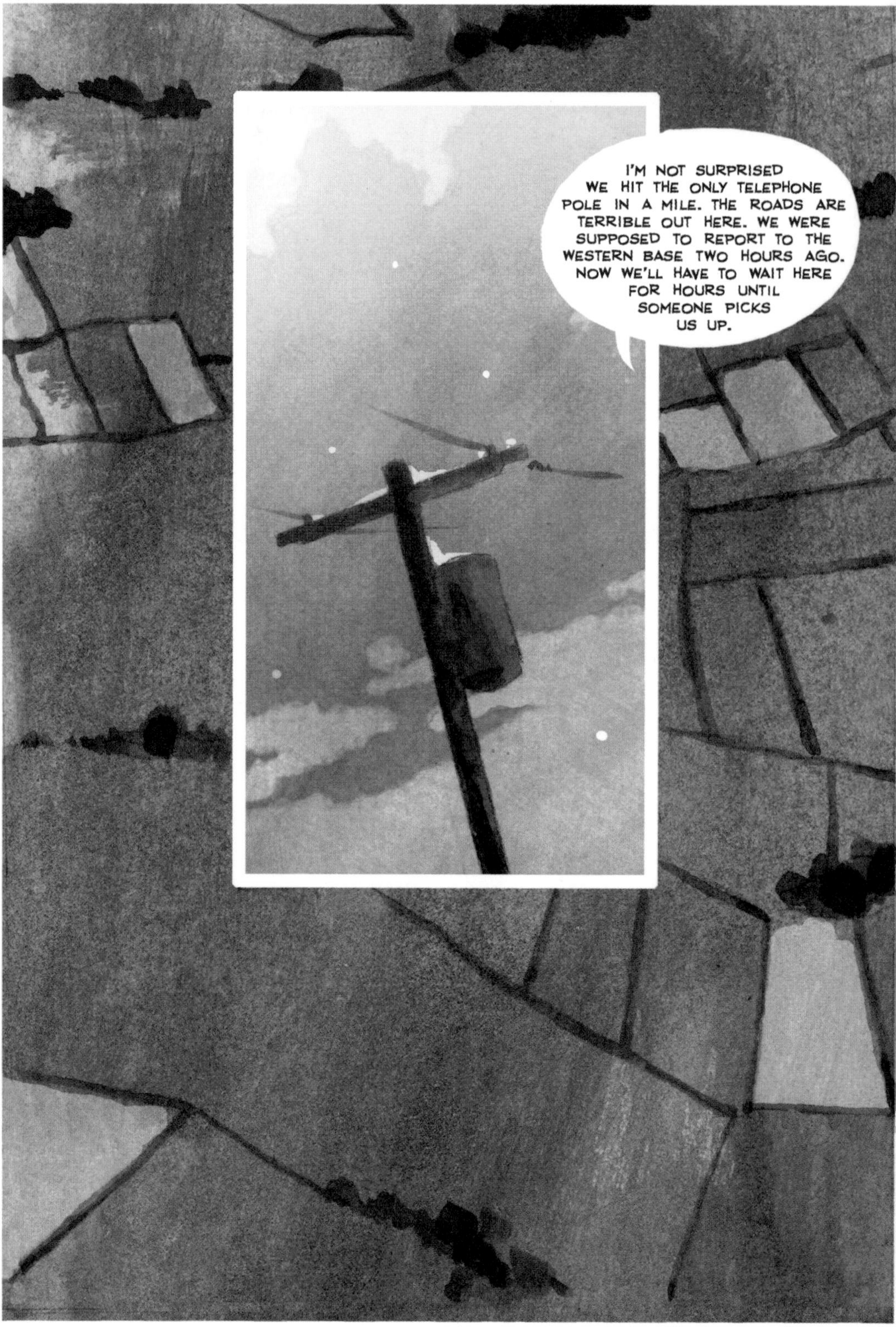
I'M NOT SURPRISED WE HIT THE ONLY TELEPHONE POLE IN A MILE. THE ROADS ARE TERRIBLE OUT HERE. WE WERE SUPPOSED TO REPORT TO THE WESTERN BASE TWO HOURS AGO. NOW WE'LL HAVE TO WAIT HERE FOR HOURS UNTIL SOMEONE PICKS US UP.

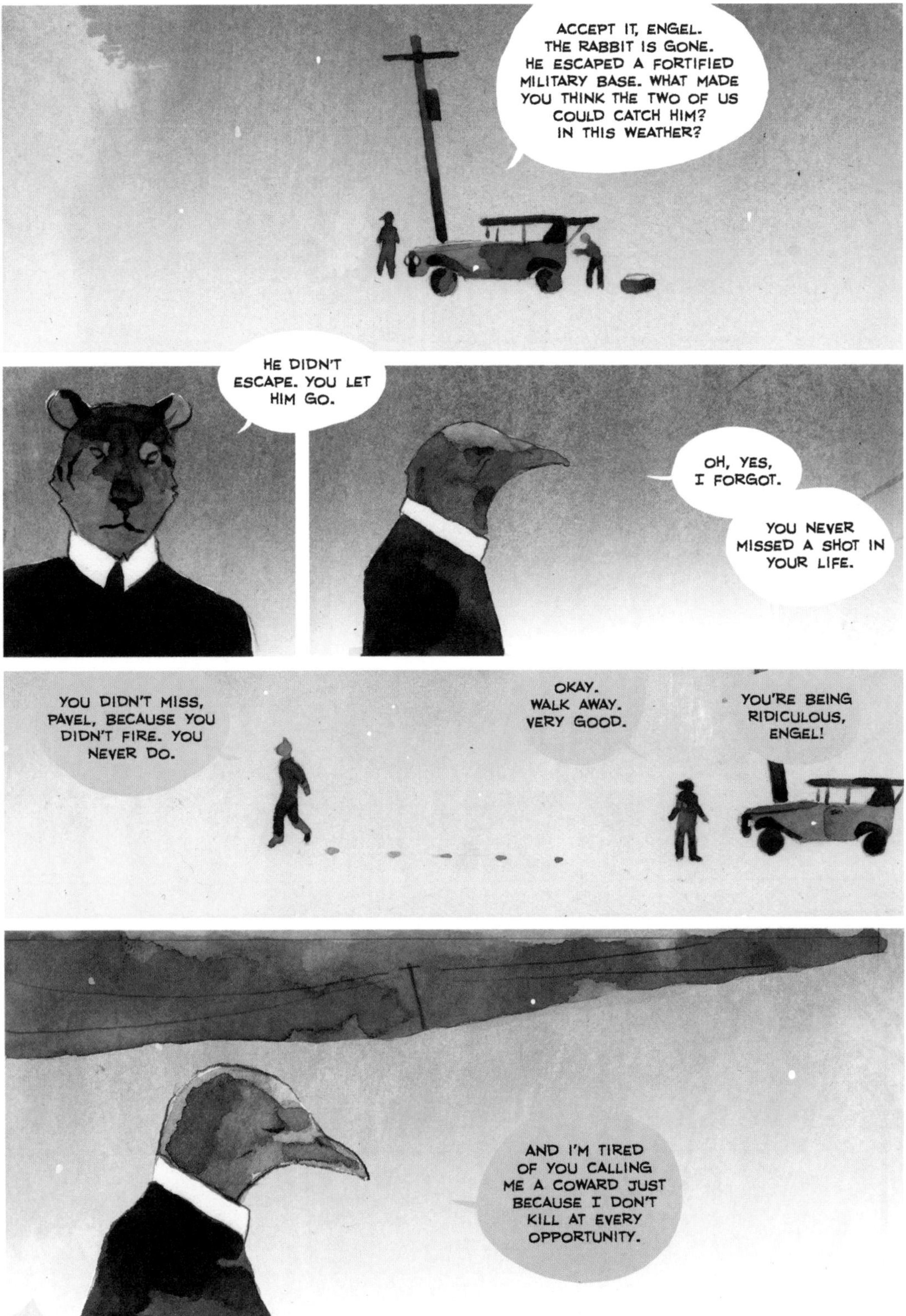
ACCEPT IT, ENGEL. THE RABBIT IS GONE. HE ESCAPED A FORTIFIED MILITARY BASE. WHAT MADE YOU THINK THE TWO OF US COULD CATCH HIM? IN THIS WEATHER?
HE DIDN'T ESCAPE. YOU LET HIM GO.
OH, YES, I FORGOT.
YOU NEVER MISSED A SHOT IN YOUR LIFE.
YOU DIDN'T MISS, PAVEL, BECAUSE YOU DIDN'T FIRE. YOU NEVER DO.
OKAY. WALK AWAY. VERY GOOD.
YOU'RE BEING RIDICULOUS, ENGEL!
AND I'M TIRED OF YOU CALLING ME A COWARD JUST BECAUSE I DON'T KILL AT EVERY OPPORTUNITY.

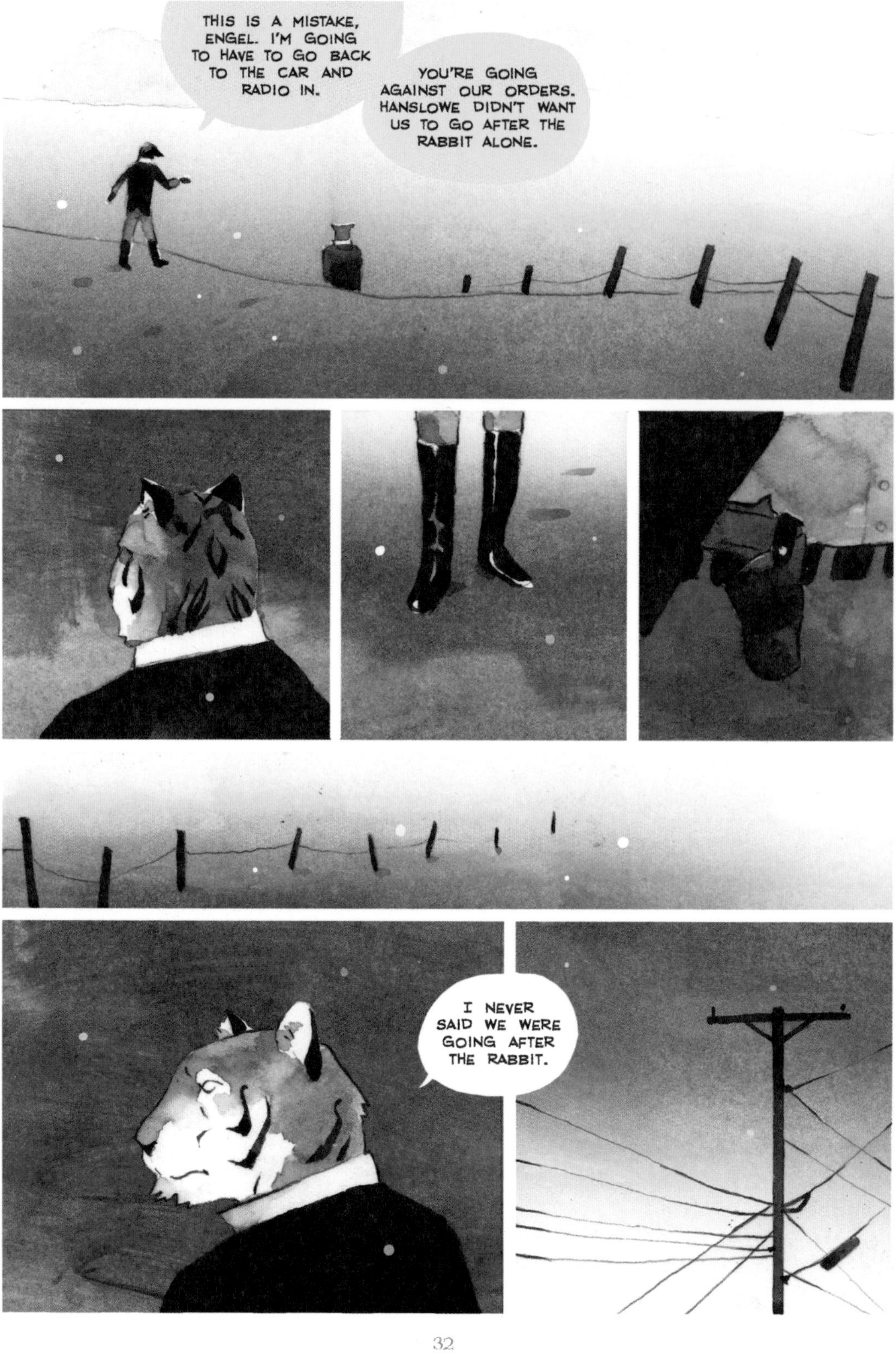
THIS IS A MISTAKE, ENGEL. I'M GOING TO HAVE TO GO BACK TO THE CAR AND RADIO IN.
YOU'RE GOING AGAINST OUR ORDERS. HANSLOWE DIDN'T WANT US TO GO AFTER THE RABBIT ALONE.
I NEVER SAID WE WERE GOING AFTER THE RABBIT.

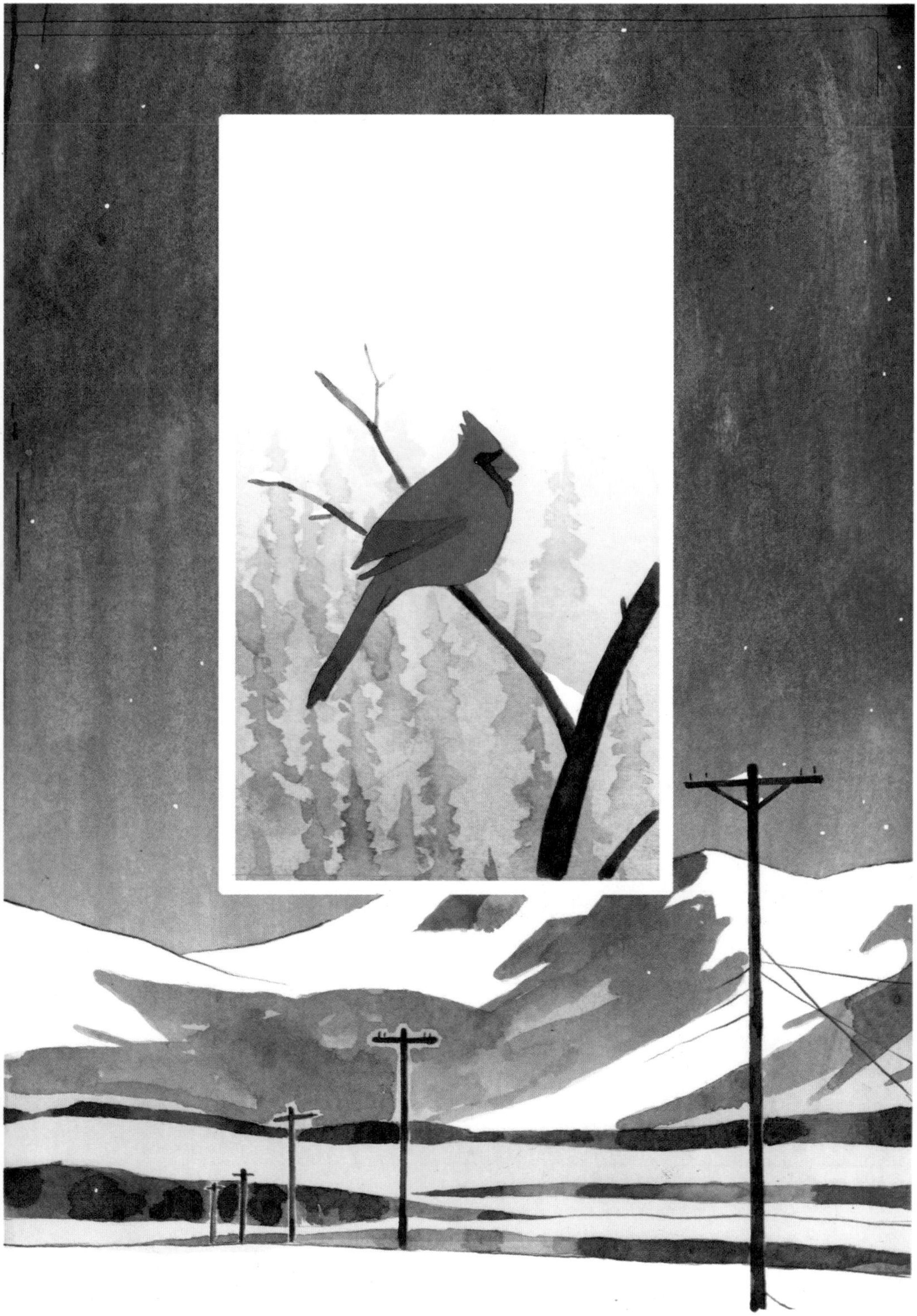

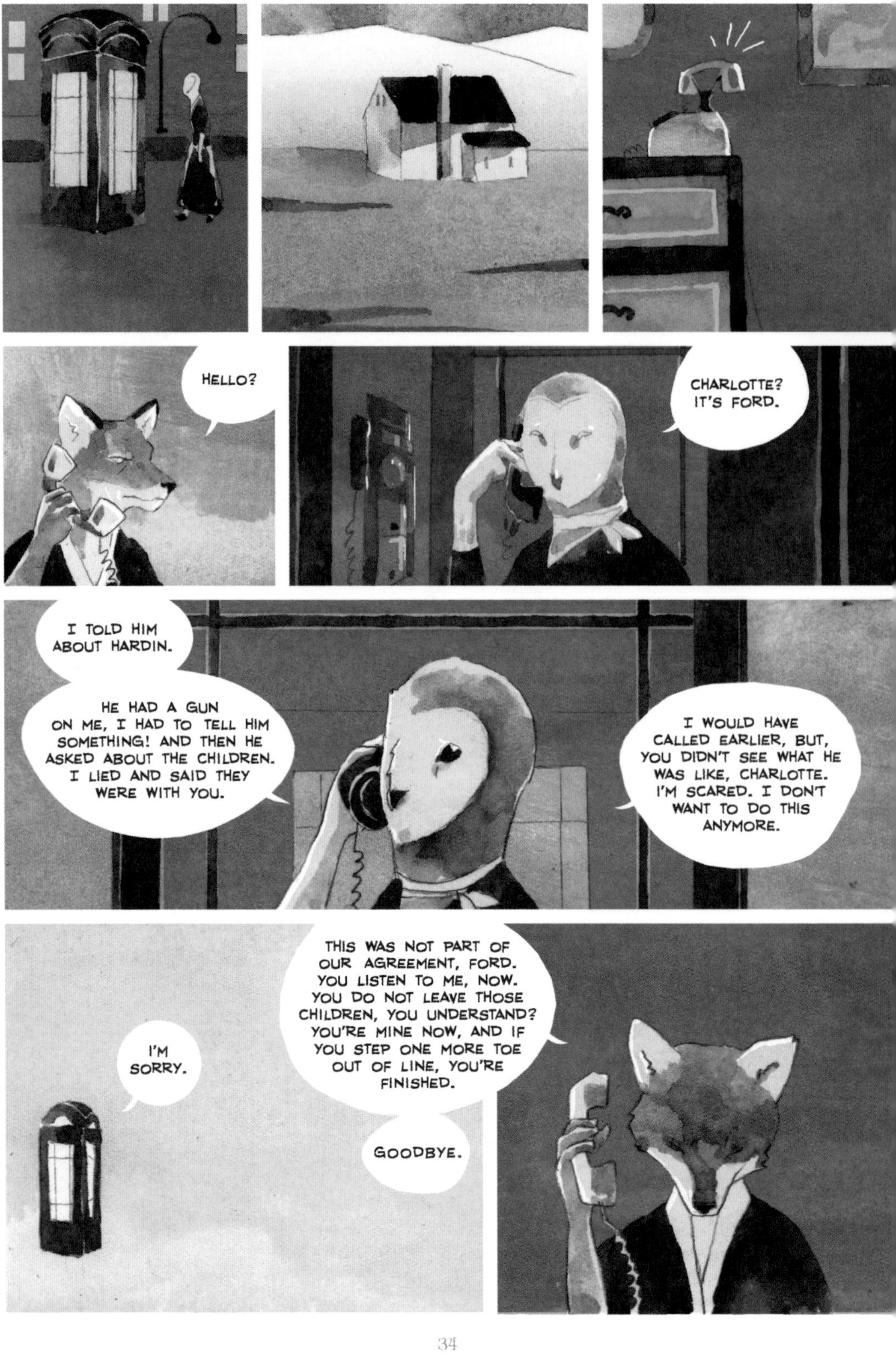
HELLO?
CHARLOTTE? IT'S FORD.
I TOLD HIM ABOUT HARDIN.
HE HAD A GUN ON ME, I HAD TO TELL HIM SOMETHING! AND THEN HE ASKED ABOUT THE CHILDREN. I LIED AND SAID THEY WERE WITH YOU.
I WOULD HAVE CALLED EARLIER, BUT, YOU DIDN'T SEE WHAT HE WAS LIKE, CHARLOTTE. I'M SCARED. I DON'T WANT TO DO THIS ANYMORE.
I'M SORRY.
THIS WAS NOT PART OF OUR AGREEMENT, FORD. YOU LISTEN TO ME, NOW. YOU DO NOT LEAVE THOSE CHILDREN, YOU UNDERSTAND? YOU'RE MINE NOW, AND IF YOU STEP ONE MORE TOE OUT OF LINE, YOU'RE FINISHED.
GOODBYE.

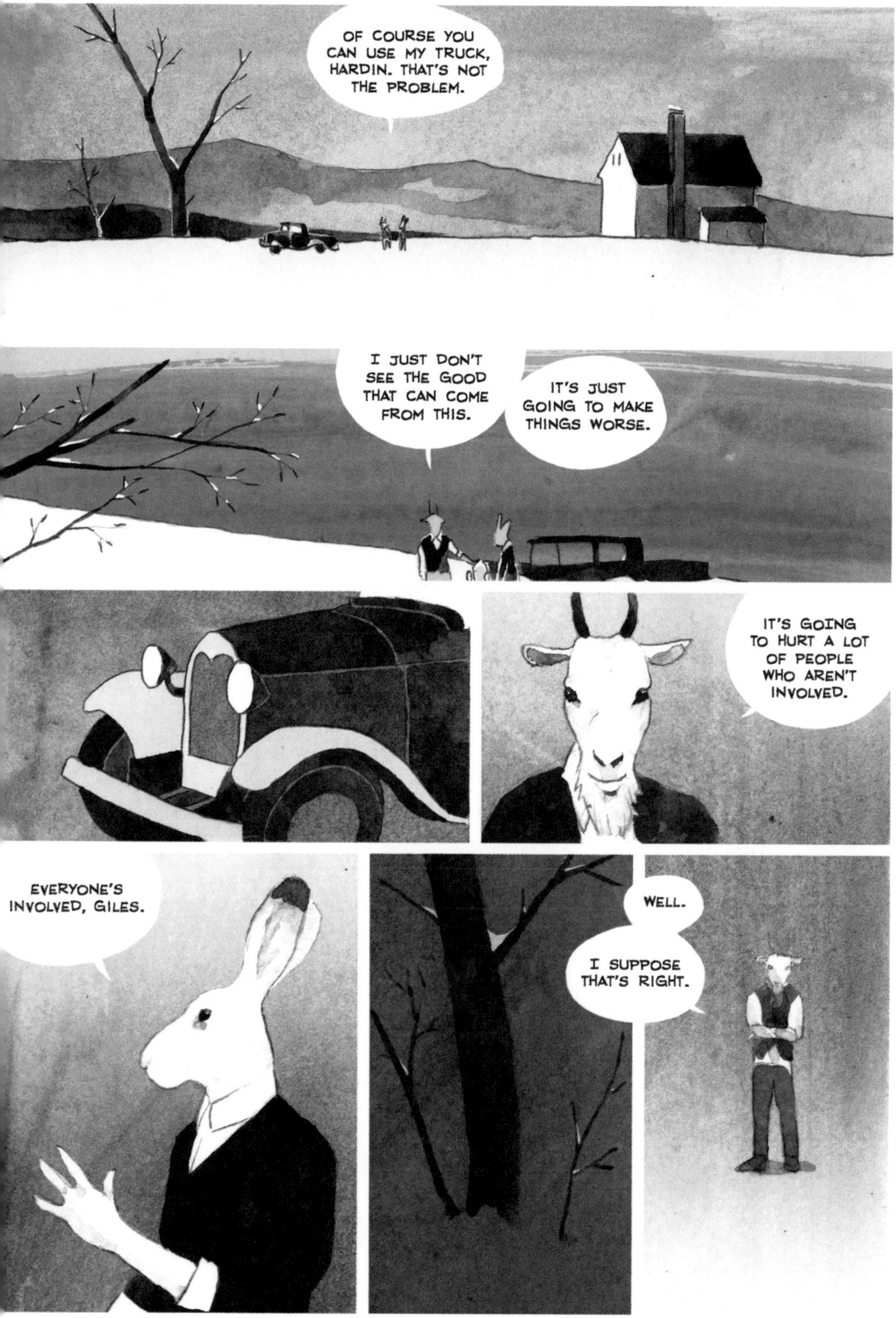
OF COURSE YOU CAN USE MY TRUCK, HARDIN. THAT'S NOT THE PROBLEM.
I JUST DON'T SEE THE GOOD THAT CAN COME FROM THIS.
IT'S JUST GOING TO MAKE THINGS WORSE.
IT'S GOING TO HURT A LOT OF PEOPLE WHO AREN'T INVOLVED.
EVERYONE'S INVOLVED, GILES.
WELL.
I SUPPOSE THAT'S RIGHT.

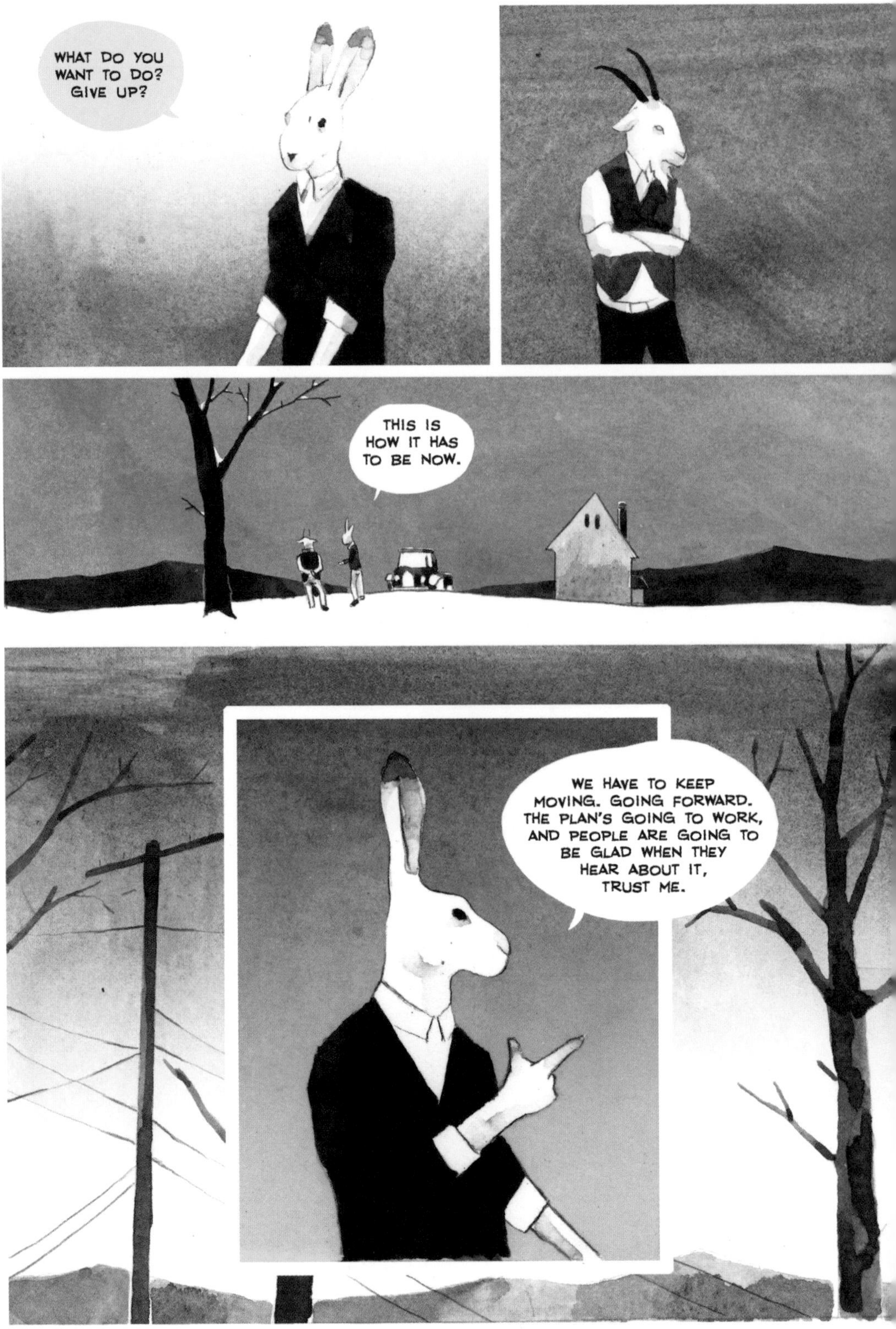
WHAT DO YOU WANT TO DO? GIVE UP?
THIS IS HOW IT HAS TO BE NOW.
WE HAVE TO KEEP MOVING. GOING FORWARD. THE PLAN'S GOING TO WORK, AND PEOPLE ARE GOING TO BE GLAD WHEN THEY HEAR ABOUT IT, TRUST ME.

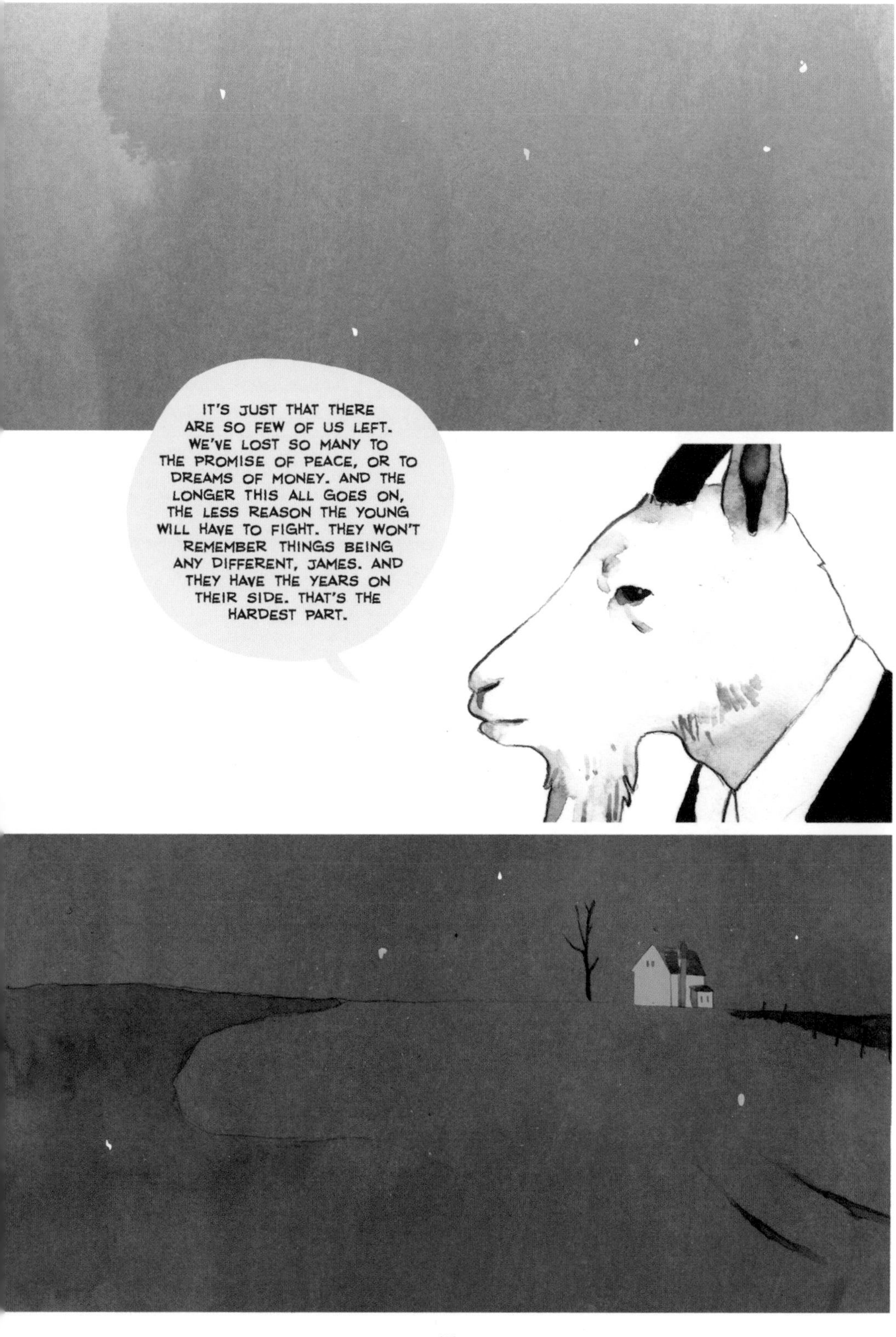
IT'S JUST THAT THERE ARE SO FEW OF US LEFT. WE'VE LOST SO MANY TO THE PROMISE OF PEACE, OR TO DREAMS OF MONEY. AND THE LONGER THIS ALL GOES ON, THE LESS REASON THE YOUNG WILL HAVE TO FIGHT. THEY WON'T REMEMBER THINGS BEING ANY DIFFERENT, JAMES. AND THEY HAVE THE YEARS ON THEIR SIDE. THAT'S THE HARDEST PART.

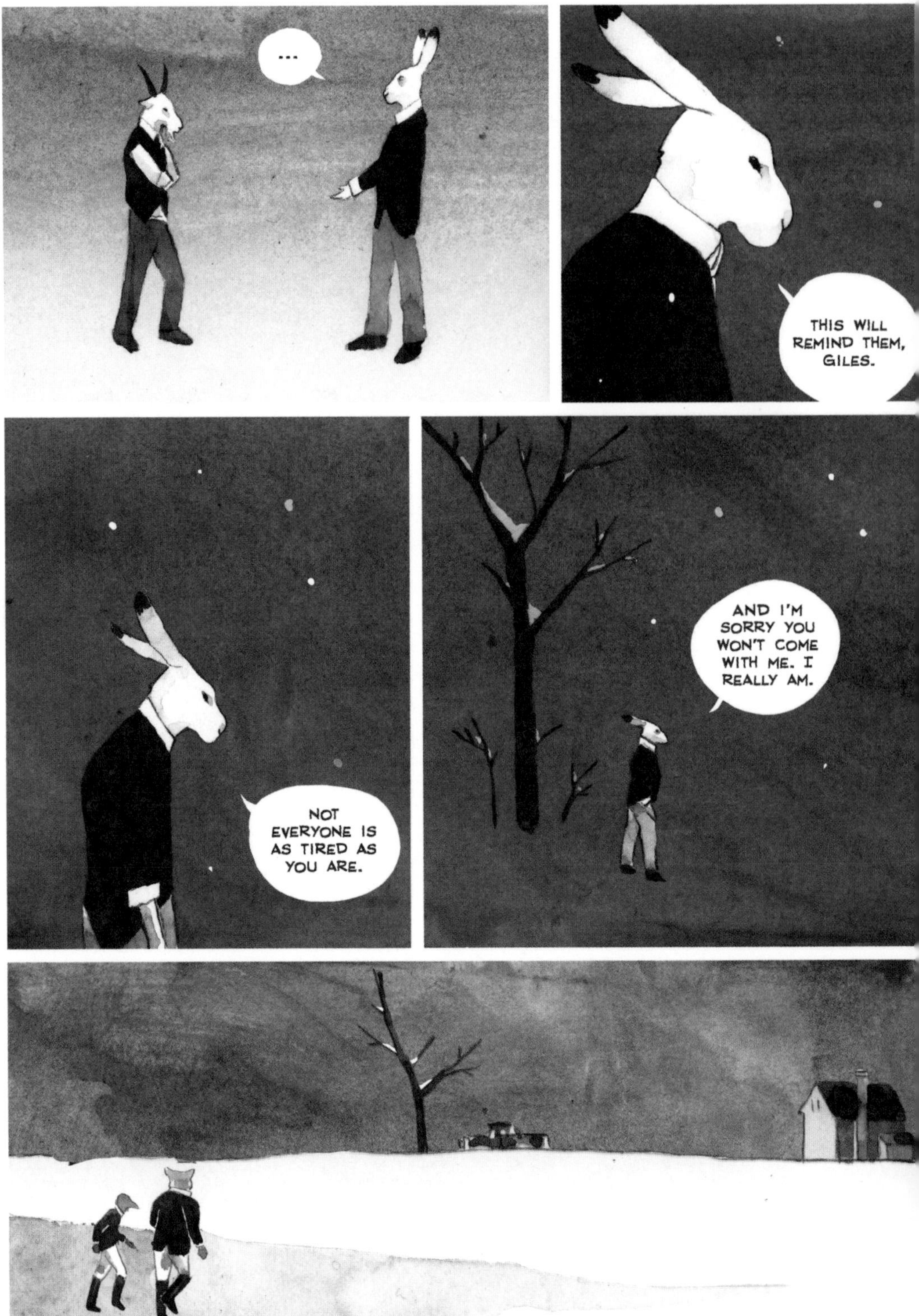
...
THIS WILL REMIND THEM, GILES.
NOT EVERYONE IS AS TIRED AS YOU ARE.
AND I'M SORRY YOU WON'T COME WITH ME. I REALLY AM.

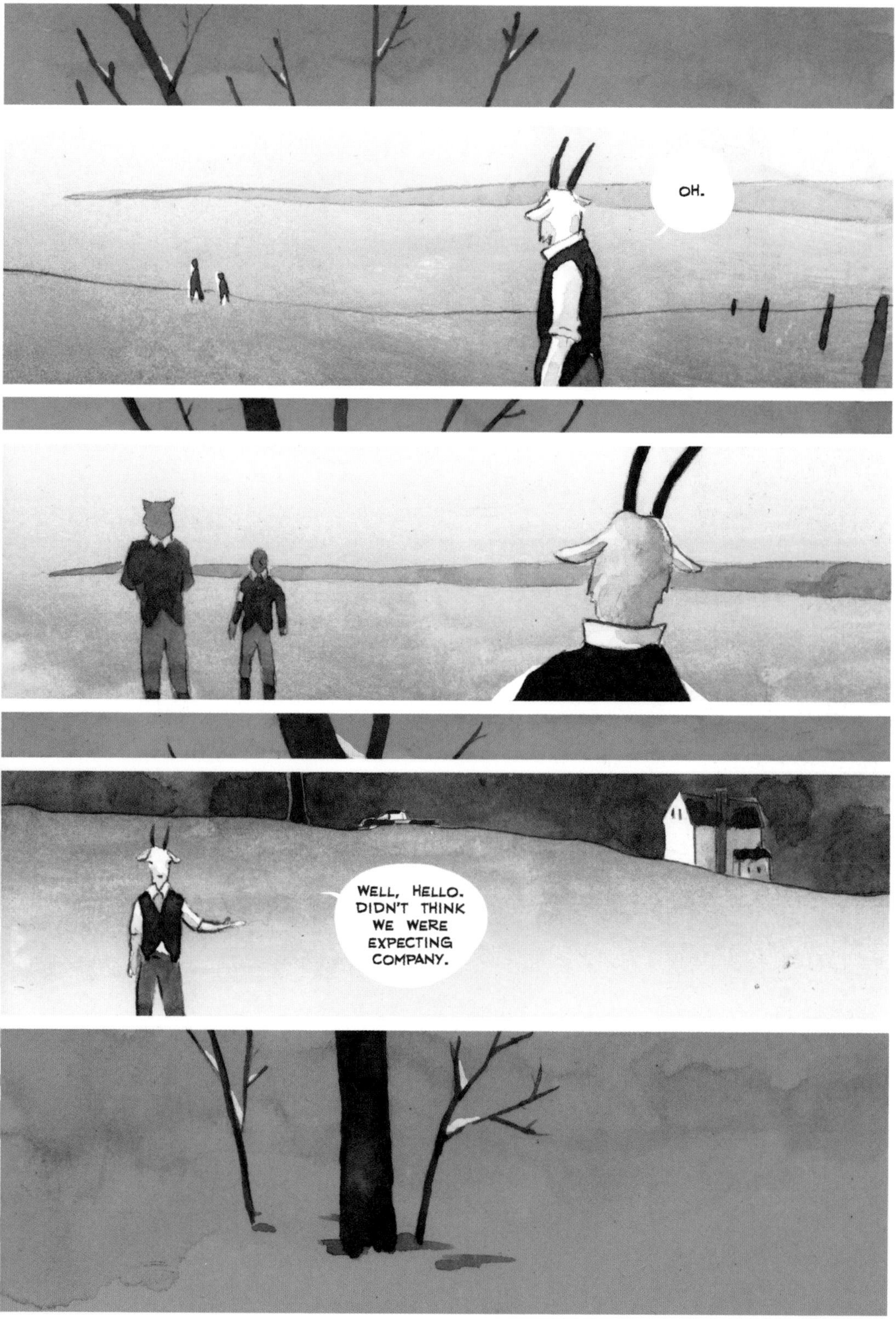
OH.
WELL, HELLO. DIDN'T THINK WE WERE EXPECTING COMPANY.

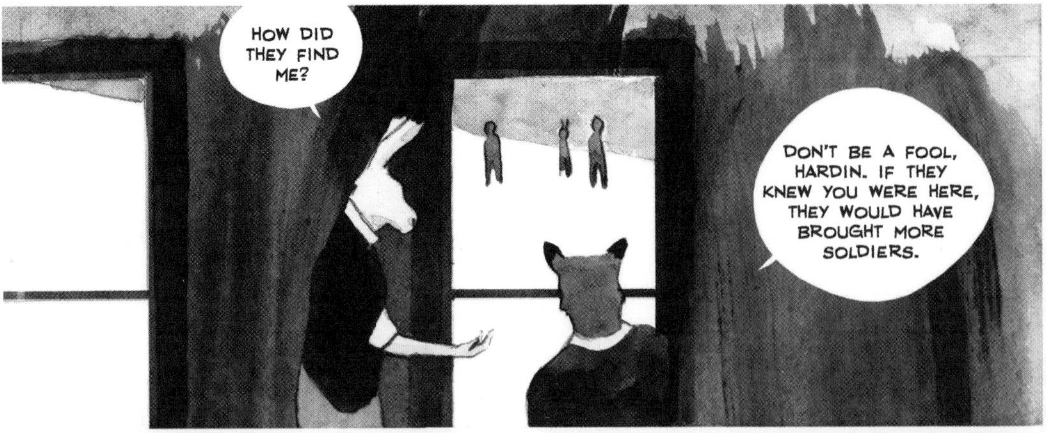
HOW DID THEY FIND ME?
DON'T BE A FOOL, HARDIN. IF THEY KNEW YOU WERE HERE, THEY WOULD HAVE BROUGHT MORE SOLDIERS.

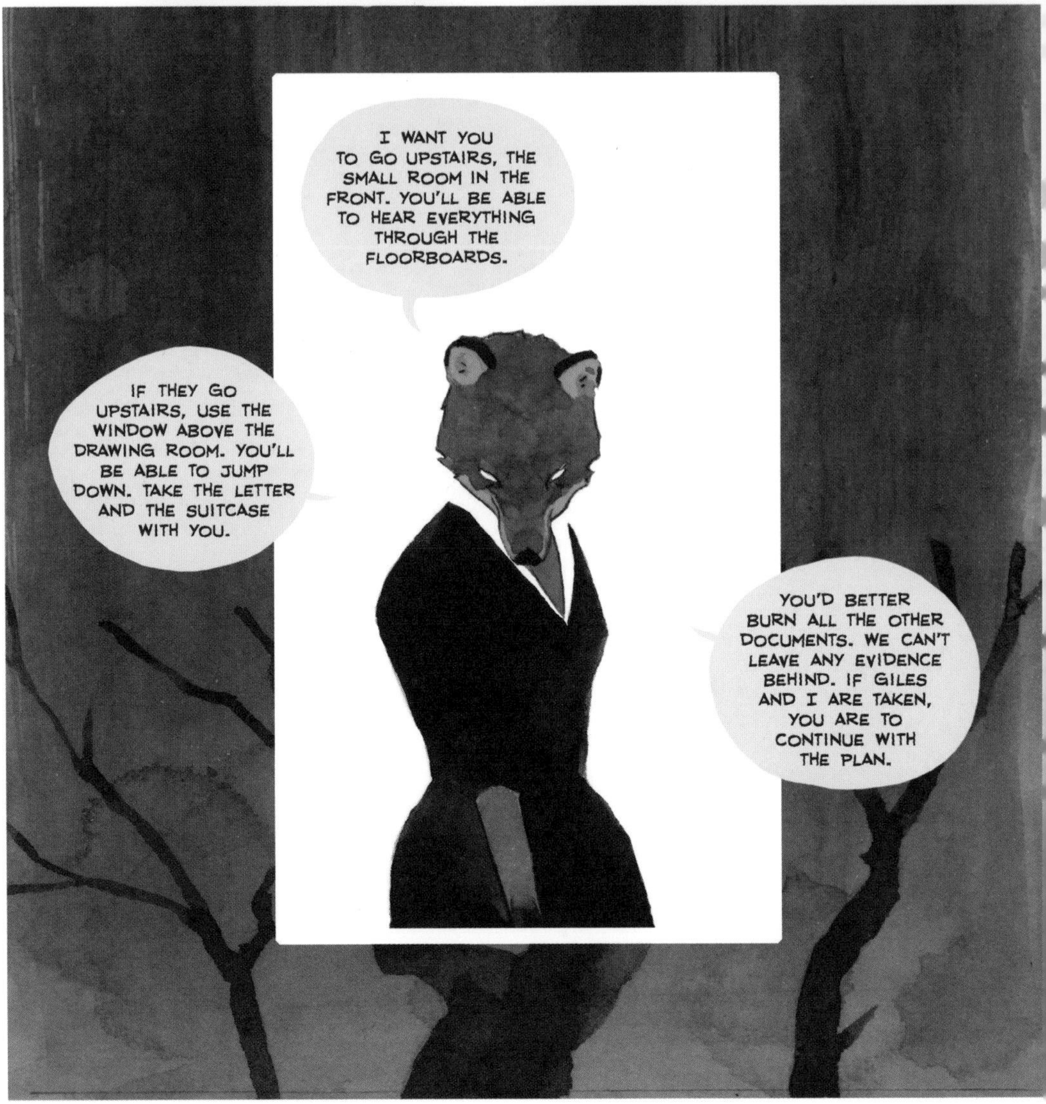
I WANT YOU TO GO UPSTAIRS, THE SMALL ROOM IN THE FRONT. YOU'LL BE ABLE TO HEAR EVERYTHING THROUGH THE FLOORBOARDS.
IF THEY GO UPSTAIRS, USE THE WINDOW ABOVE THE DRAWING ROOM. YOU'LL BE ABLE TO JUMP DOWN. TAKE THE LETTER AND THE SUITCASE WITH YOU.
YOU'D BETTER BURN ALL THE OTHER DOCUMENTS. WE CAN'T LEAVE ANY EVIDENCE BEHIND. IF GILES AND I ARE TAKEN, YOU ARE TO CONTINUE WITH THE PLAN.

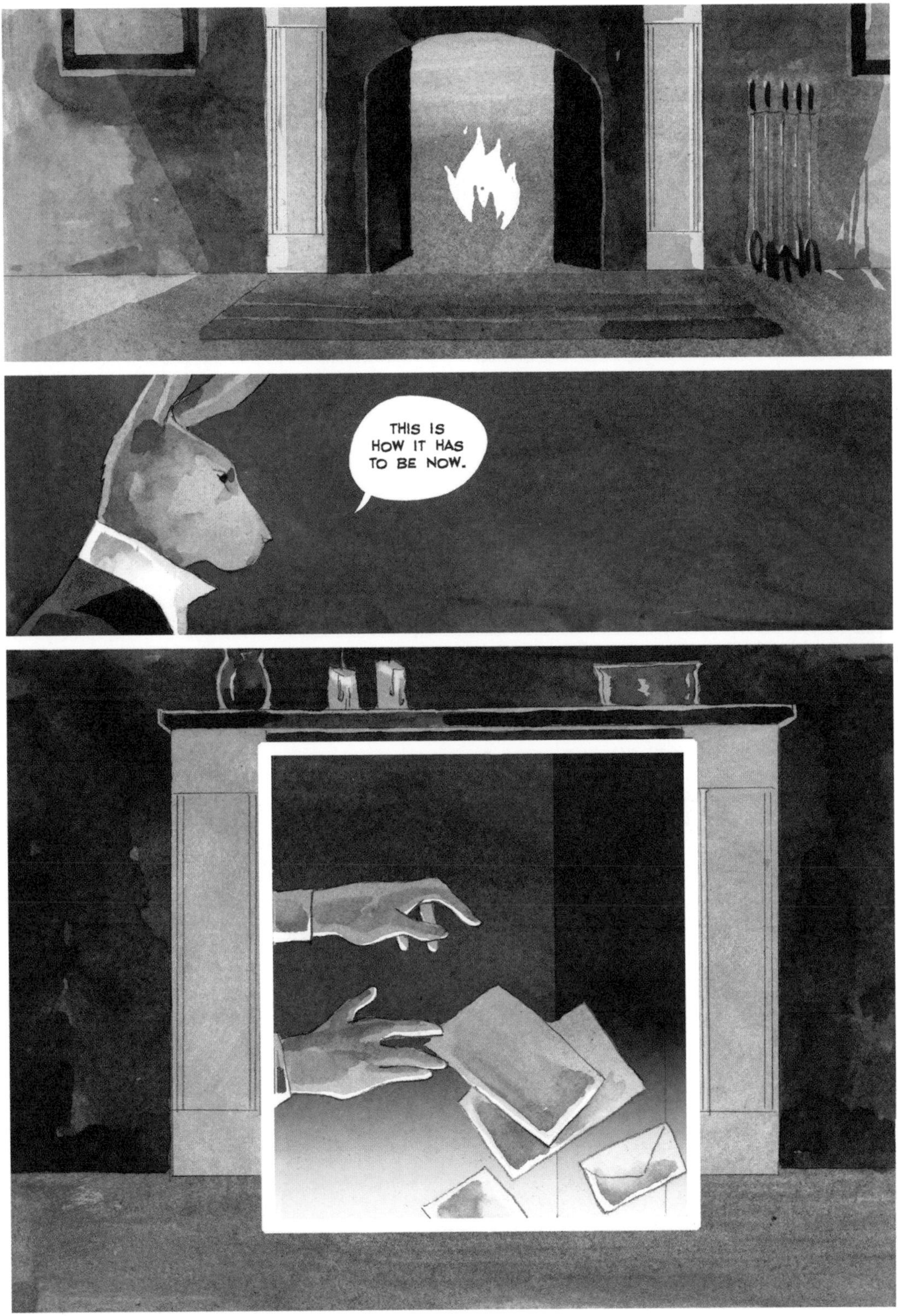
THIS IS
HOW IT HAS
TO BE NOW.

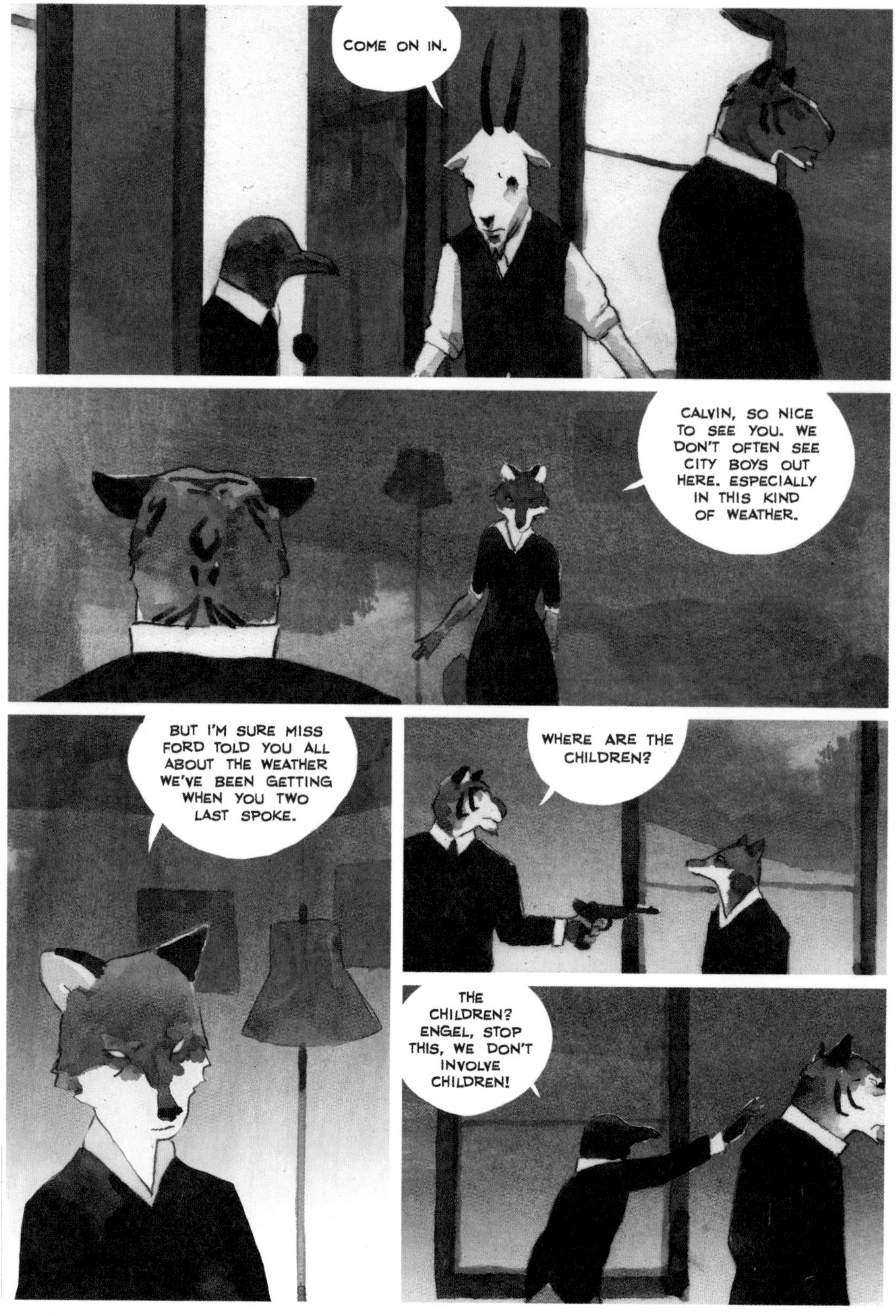
COME ON IN.
CALVIN, SO NICE TO SEE YOU. WE DON'T OFTEN SEE CITY BOYS OUT HERE. ESPECIALLY IN THIS KIND OF WEATHER.
BUT I'M SURE MISS FORD TOLD YOU ALL ABOUT THE WEATHER WE'VE BEEN GETTING WHEN YOU TWO LAST SPOKE.
WHERE ARE THE CHILDREN?
THE CHILDREN? ENGEL, STOP THIS, WE DON'T INVOLVE CHILDREN!

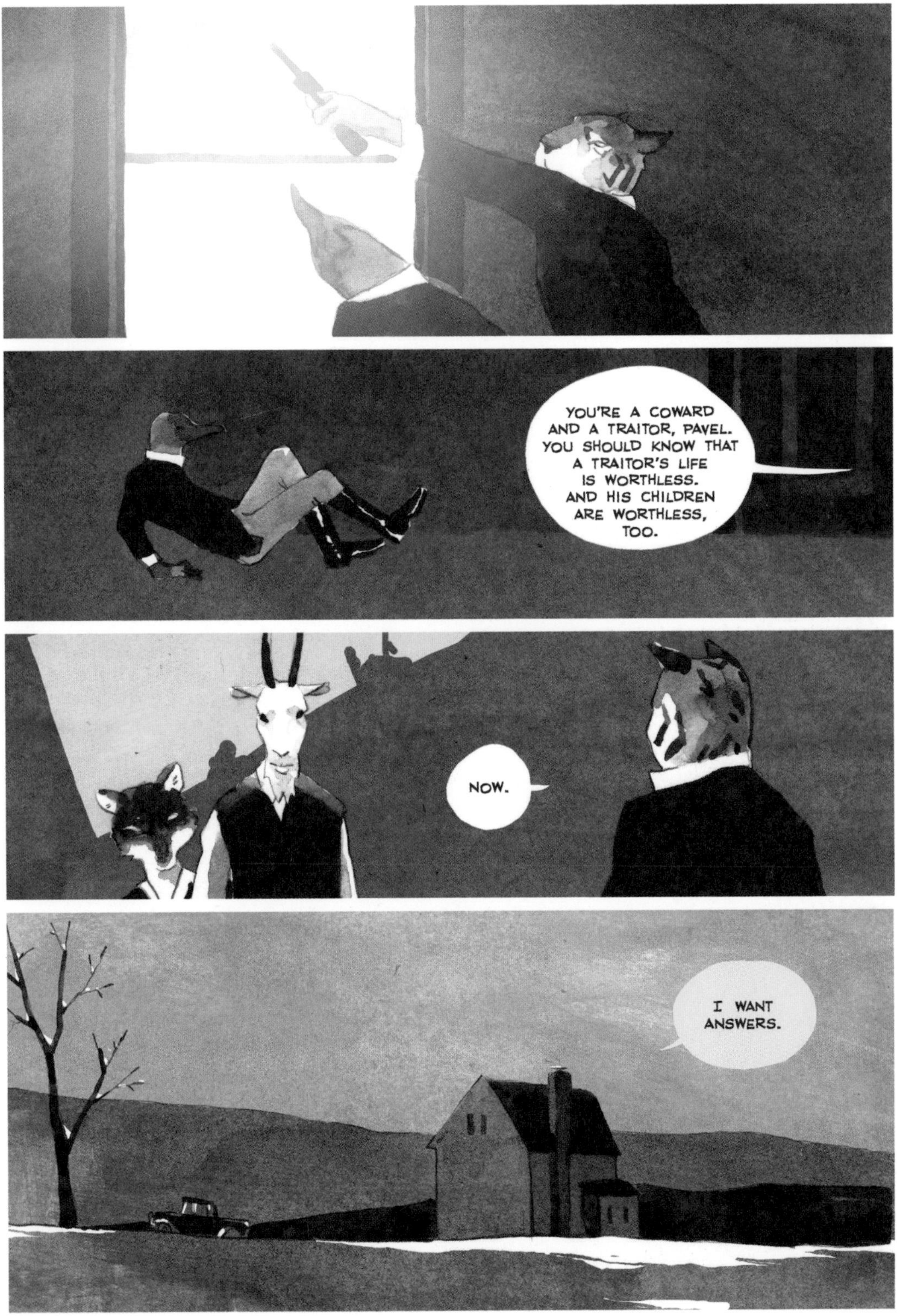
YOU'RE A COWARD AND A TRAITOR, PAVEL. YOU SHOULD KNOW THAT A TRAITOR'S LIFE IS WORTHLESS. AND HIS CHILDREN ARE WORTHLESS, TOO.
NOW.
I WANT ANSWERS.

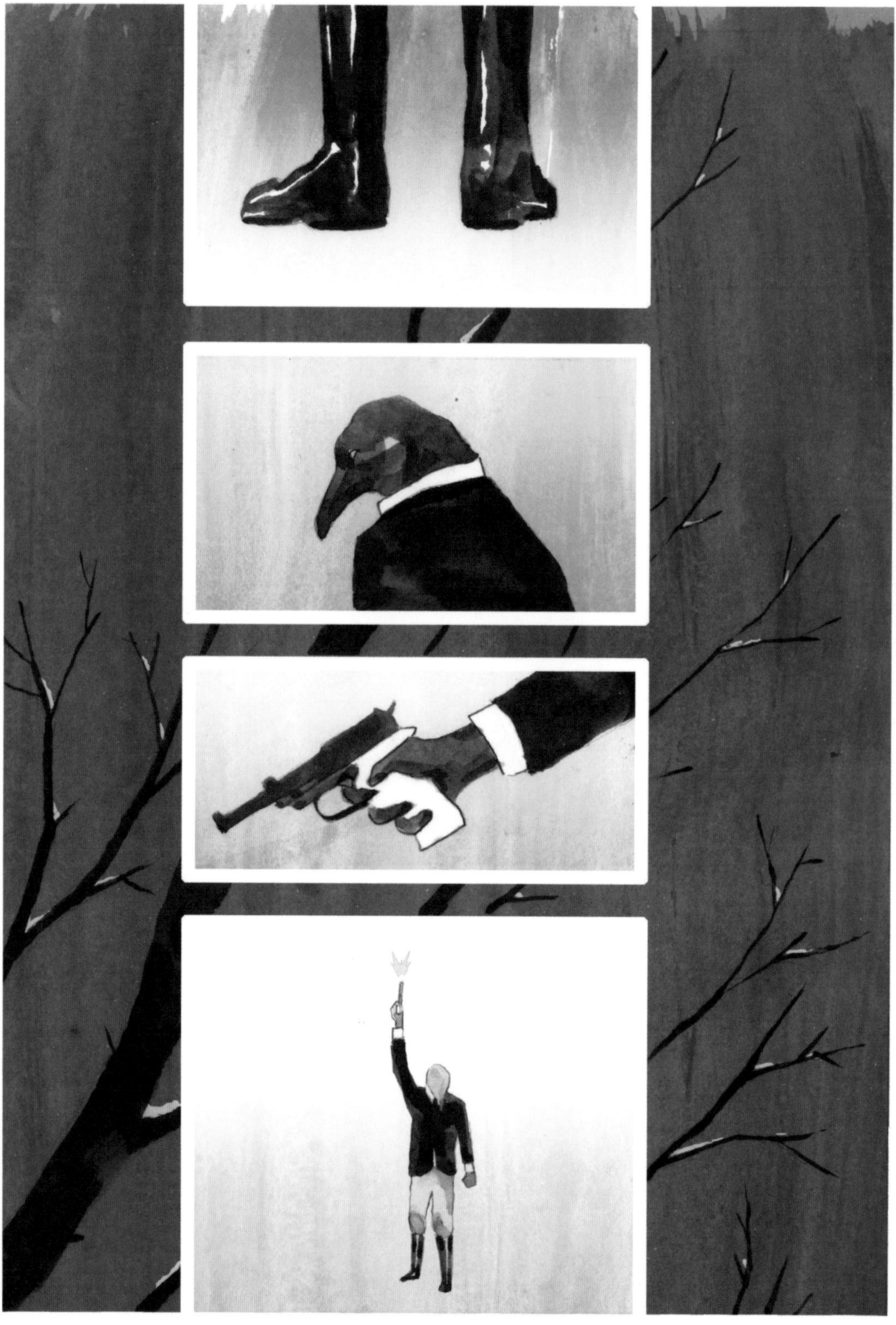

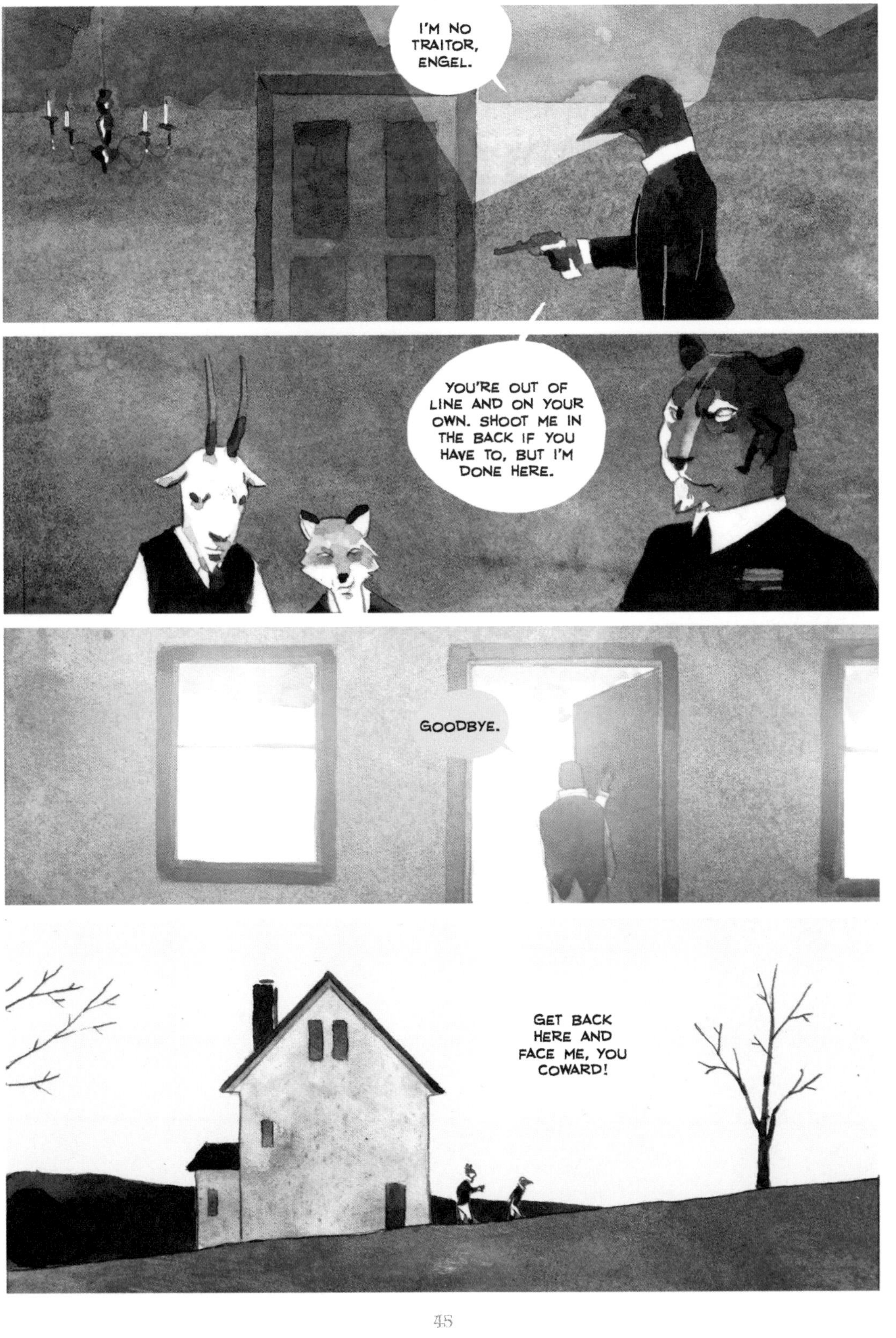
I'M NO TRAITOR, ENGEL.
YOU'RE OUT OF LINE AND ON YOUR OWN. SHOOT ME IN THE BACK IF YOU HAVE TO, BUT I'M DONE HERE.
GOODBYE.
GET BACK HERE AND FACE ME, YOU COWARD!

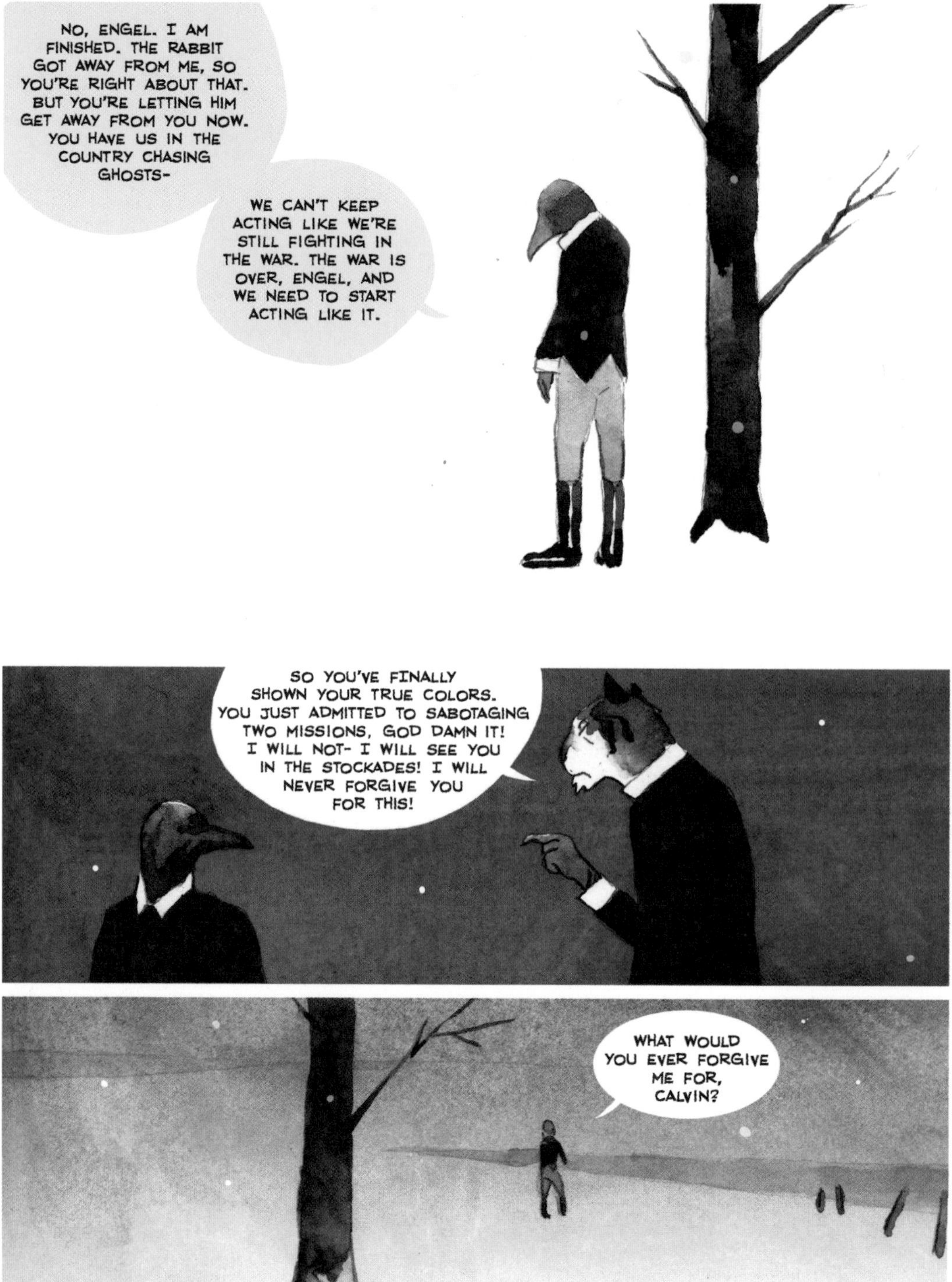
NO, ENGEL. I AM FINISHED. THE RABBIT GOT AWAY FROM ME, SO YOU'RE RIGHT ABOUT THAT. BUT YOU'RE LETTING HIM GET AWAY FROM YOU NOW. YOU HAVE US IN THE COUNTRY CHASING GHOSTS-
WE CAN'T KEEP ACTING LIKE WE'RE STILL FIGHTING IN THE WAR. THE WAR IS OVER, ENGEL, AND WE NEED TO START ACTING LIKE IT.
SO YOU'VE FINALLY SHOWN YOUR TRUE COLORS. YOU JUST ADMITTED TO SABOTAGING TWO MISSIONS, GOD DAMN IT! I WILL NOT- I WILL SEE YOU IN THE STOCKADES! I WILL NEVER FORGIVE YOU FOR THIS!
WHAT WOULD YOU EVER FORGIVE ME FOR, CALVIN?

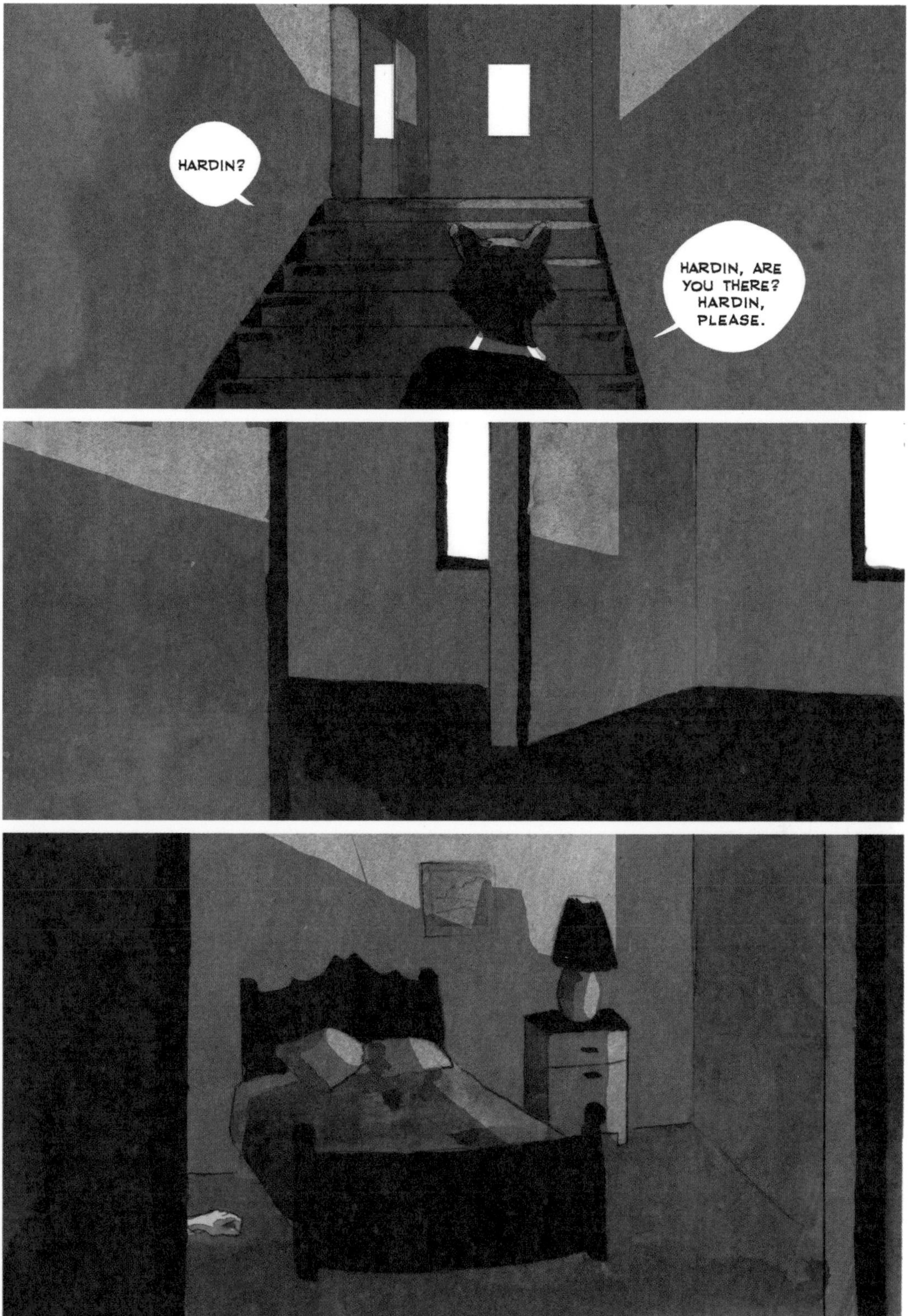
HARDIN?
HARDIN, ARE YOU THERE? HARDIN, PLEASE.

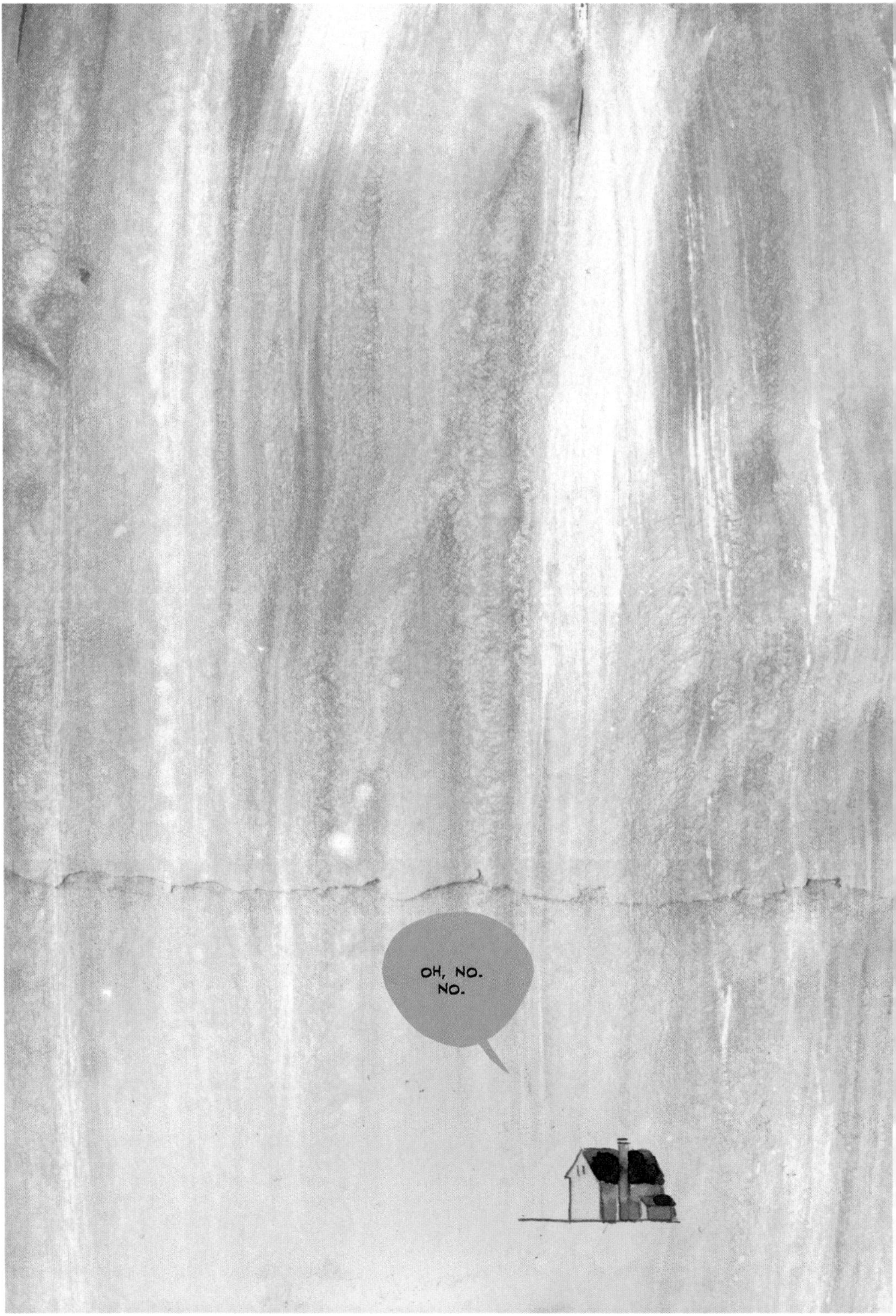
OH, NO.
NO.

Dear Tabitha,

I don't know if you got my last letter, or if you will get this one, but it is comforting to think that you will. This snow has been a godsend. It has hidden us, and it has almost halted the North's progress. Sometimes when I'm out on patrol, I put my hand in the snow, and if I lift up my sleeve it's almost as if I am disappearing.

I got your last letter, although it was so wet I could barely make out a word. Still, it was enough. I do wish I were home. Every day. But we have to finish what we set out to do. Giles has been invaluable to me here, and you were right in advising me to put my trust in him. With every rail line we disrupt I can buy us two more weeks. Two more weeks costs them money, and when the money runs out, the people in the North will rise up to join us. They are calling us now, so I must go.

Please give my love to the children. It has been ten months now since I have seen them. I have done things that I am not proud of, and other things that I hope will some day make them proud. Sometimes, after being out here so long, it gets hard to tell the difference. But all I need is the thought of you, and the children, to remember what needs to be done and how I will stop at nothing to see it through.

Your Husband,

James

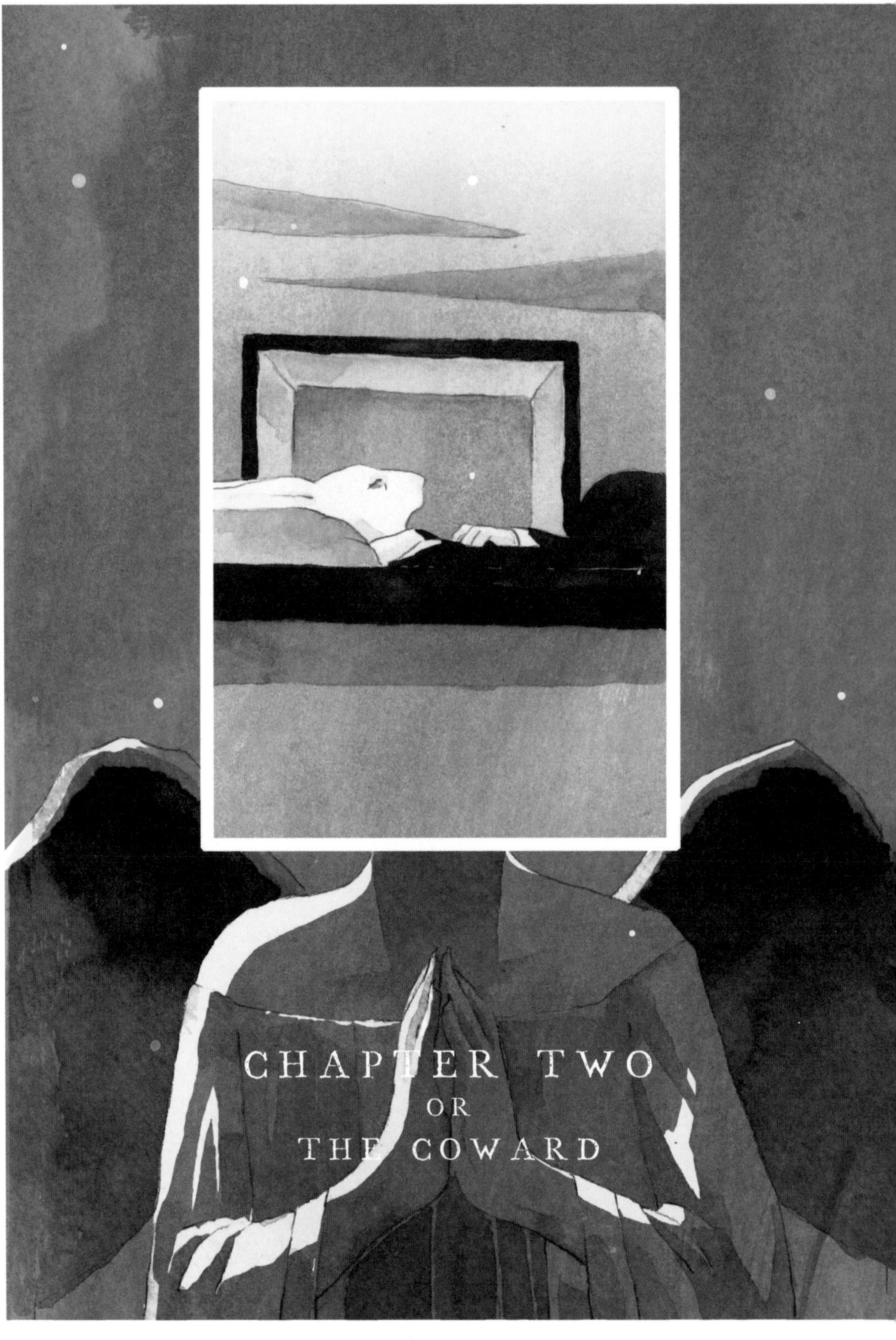
CHAPTER TWO
OR
THE COWARD

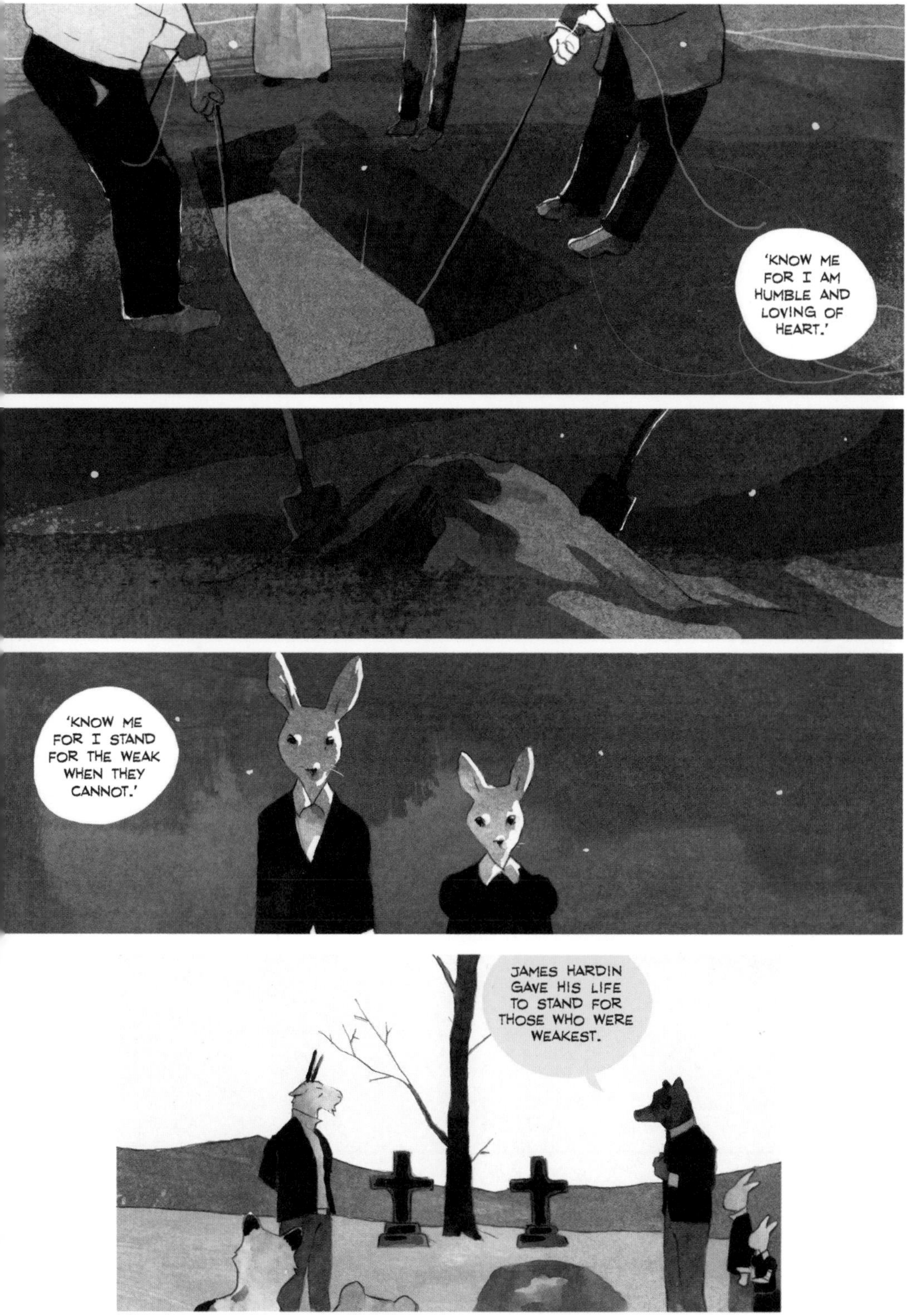
'KNOW ME
FOR I AM
HUMBLE AND
LOVING OF
HEART.'
'KNOW ME
FOR I STAND
FOR THE WEAK
WHEN THEY
CANNOT.'
JAMES HARDIN
GAVE HIS LIFE
TO STAND FOR
THOSE WHO WERE
WEAKEST.

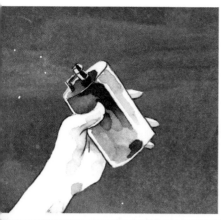

LISTEN—

I UNDERSTAND YOU'RE UPSET, BUT YOU CAN'T CRACK UP NOW. NOT WHEN WE'RE SO CLOSE. YOU'RE THE ONLY ONE LEFT WHO KNOWS HOW TO USE THE DEVICE. I CAN'T DO IT, SO I NEED YOU TO STEP UP, LIKE YOU USED TO.

IF WE STOP NOW, THEN WHAT WAS IT ALL FOR? JAMES GAVE HIS LIFE FOR THIS, GILES.

JAMES GAVE HIS LIFE FOR A STRAY BULLET. AND I'M NO MURDERER.

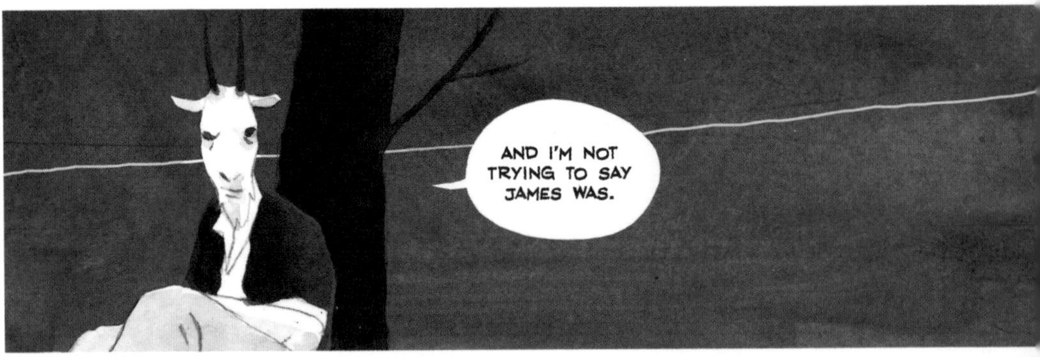
AND I'M NOT TRYING TO SAY JAMES WAS.

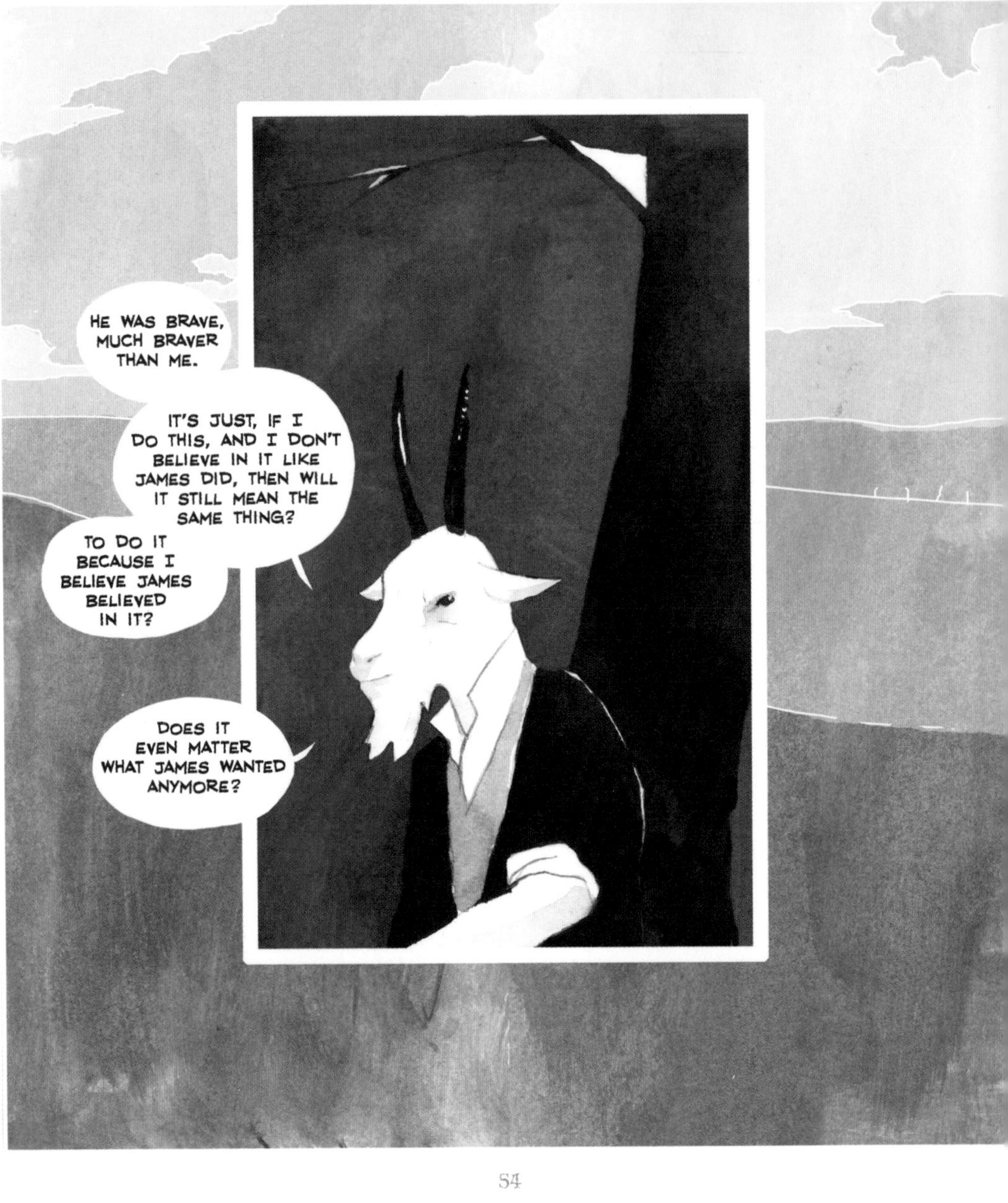
HE WAS BRAVE, MUCH BRAVER THAN ME.
IT'S JUST, IF I DO THIS, AND I DON'T BELIEVE IN IT LIKE JAMES DID, THEN WILL IT STILL MEAN THE SAME THING?
TO DO IT BECAUSE I BELIEVE JAMES BELIEVED IN IT?
DOES IT EVEN MATTER WHAT JAMES WANTED ANYMORE?

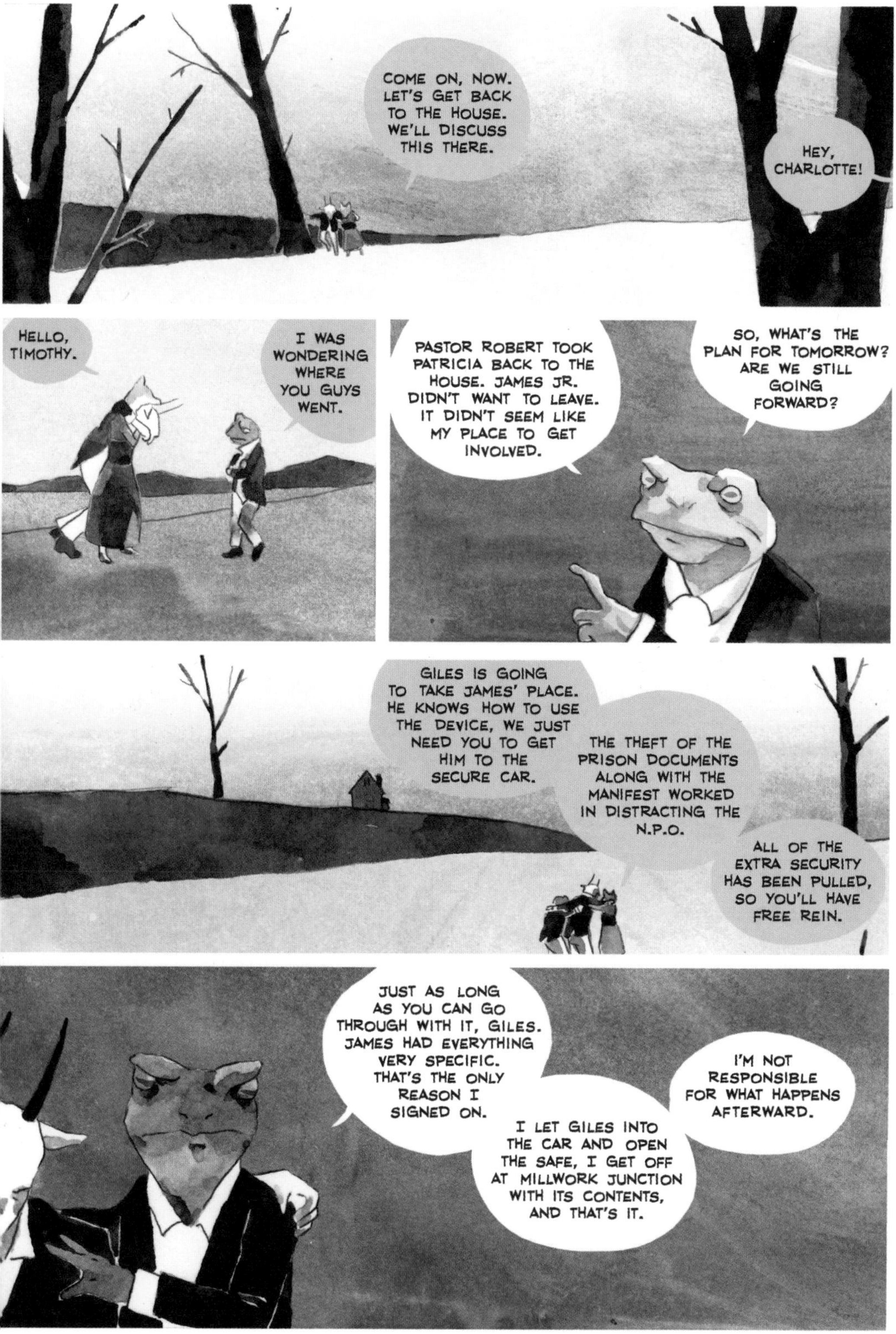
COME ON, NOW. LET'S GET BACK TO THE HOUSE. WE'LL DISCUSS THIS THERE.
HEY, CHARLOTTE!
HELLO, TIMOTHY.
I WAS WONDERING WHERE YOU GUYS WENT.
PASTOR ROBERT TOOK PATRICIA BACK TO THE HOUSE. JAMES JR. DIDN'T WANT TO LEAVE. IT DIDN'T SEEM LIKE MY PLACE TO GET INVOLVED.
SO, WHAT'S THE PLAN FOR TOMORROW? ARE WE STILL GOING FORWARD?
GILES IS GOING TO TAKE JAMES' PLACE. HE KNOWS HOW TO USE THE DEVICE, WE JUST NEED YOU TO GET HIM TO THE SECURE CAR.
THE THEFT OF THE PRISON DOCUMENTS ALONG WITH THE MANIFEST WORKED IN DISTRACTING THE N.P.O.
ALL OF THE EXTRA SECURITY HAS BEEN PULLED, SO YOU'LL HAVE FREE REIN.
JUST AS LONG AS YOU CAN GO THROUGH WITH IT, GILES. JAMES HAD EVERYTHING VERY SPECIFIC. THAT'S THE ONLY REASON I SIGNED ON.
I LET GILES INTO THE CAR AND OPEN THE SAFE, I GET OFF AT MILLWORK JUNCTION WITH ITS CONTENTS, AND THAT'S IT.
I'M NOT RESPONSIBLE FOR WHAT HAPPENS AFTERWARD.

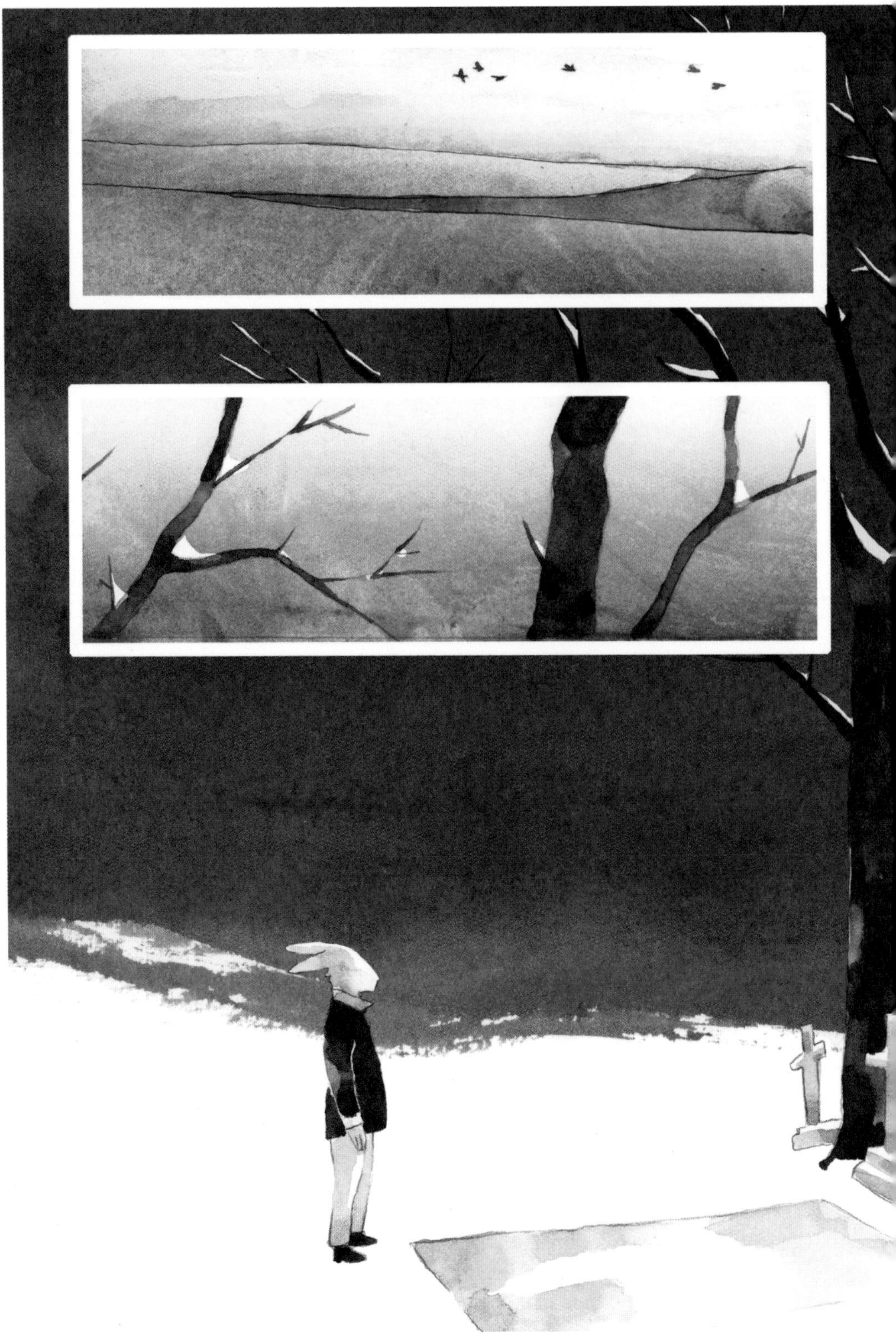

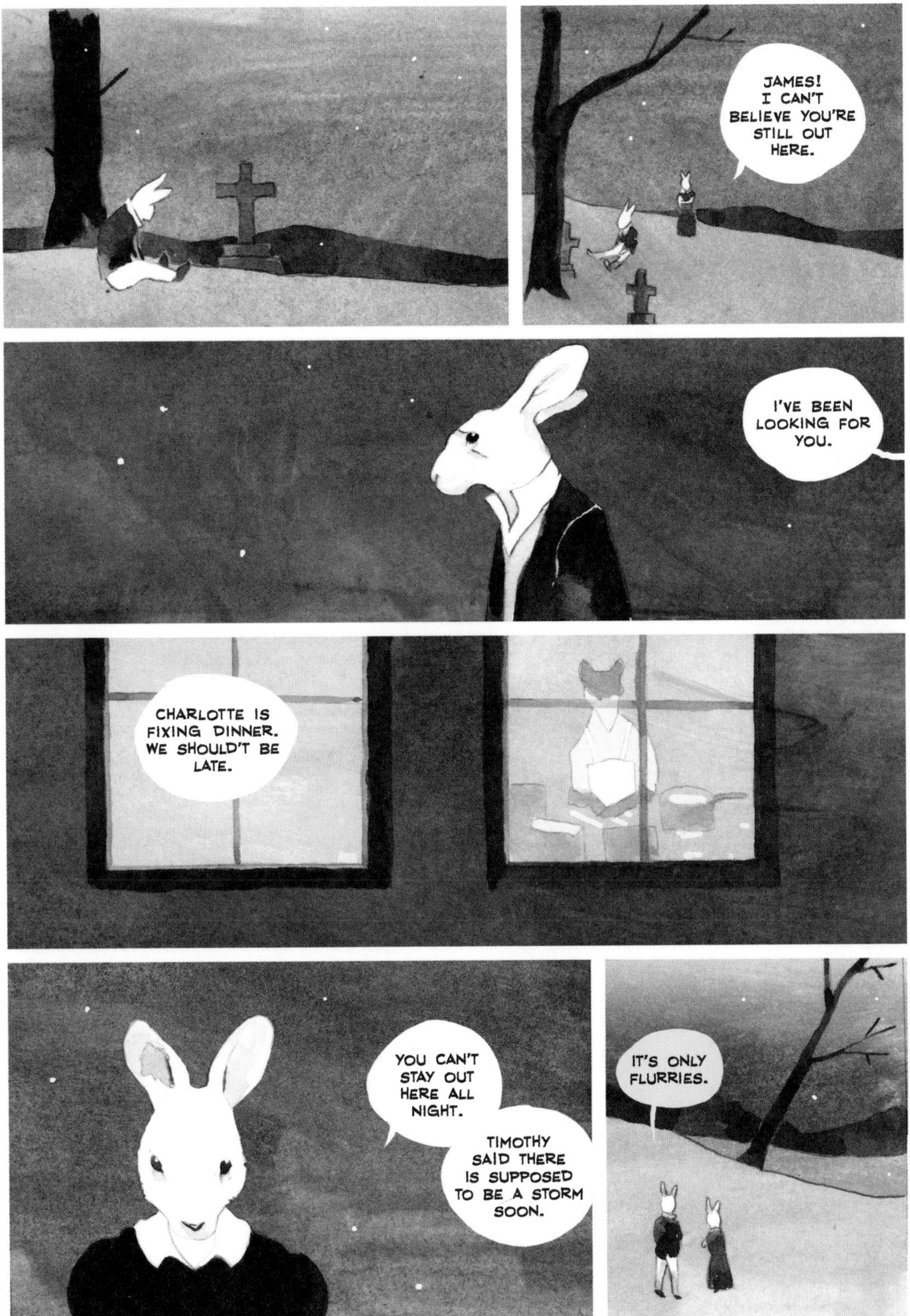
JAMES! I CAN'T BELIEVE YOU'RE STILL OUT HERE.
I'VE BEEN LOOKING FOR YOU.
CHARLOTTE IS FIXING DINNER. WE SHOULD'T BE LATE.
YOU CAN'T STAY OUT HERE ALL NIGHT.
TIMOTHY SAID THERE IS SUPPOSED TO BE A STORM SOON.
IT'S ONLY FLURRIES.

WAIT HERE.

YES, JAMES PICKED THE RIVER EAGLE BECAUSE ITS MANIFEST LISTS 'DOCUMENTS.'

IT HAS TO BE THIS TRAIN? I'M NOT SURE IF GILES IS READY.

JAMES' INFORMATION TELLS US THAT THESE WILL BE DOCUMENTS RELATED TO WEAPONRY AND SHIPPING MOVEMENTS.

THEY DON'T EVEN KNOW HOW VITAL THIS INFORMATION IS. WITH THE MILLWORK BRIDGE GONE, WE'LL BE ABLE TO CRIPPLE ALL OF THEIR OTHER ROUTES.

ALL I'M SAYING IS, GILES IS PASSED OUT UPSTAIRS.

CAN WE REALLY COUNT ON HIM?

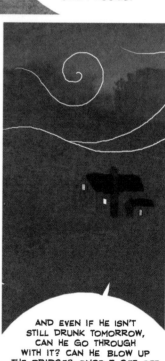

AND EVEN IF HE ISN'T STILL DRUNK TOMORROW, CAN HE GO THROUGH WITH IT? CAN HE BLOW UP THE BRIDGE? ONCE I GET OFF AT MILLWORK JUNCTION, IT WILL BE COMPLETELY UP TO HIM. JAMES WORKED SO HARD FOR THIS. IT WOULD BE A SHAME IF IT WAS ALL FOR NOTHING.

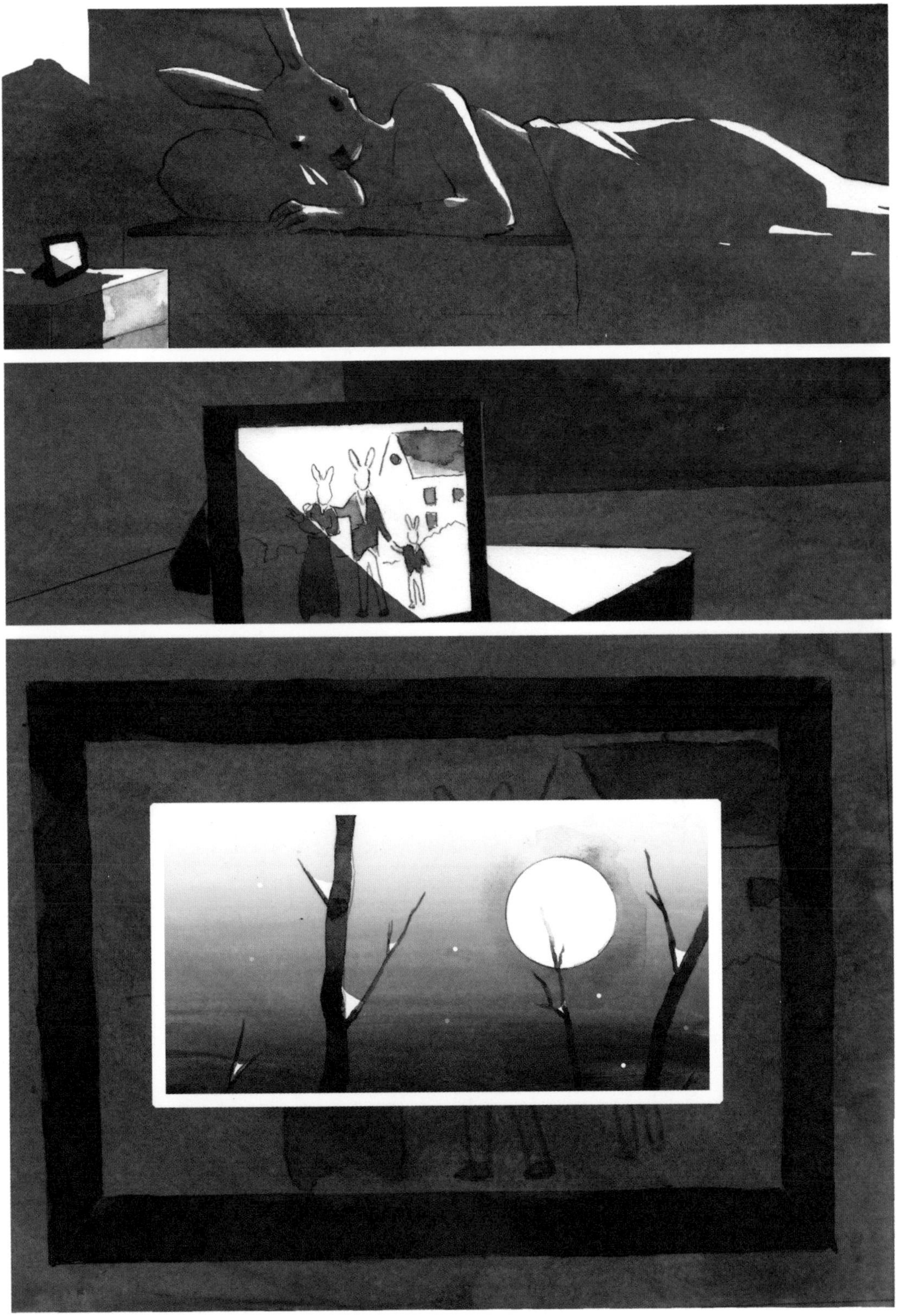

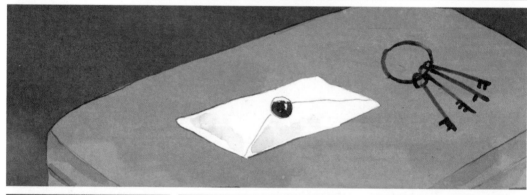

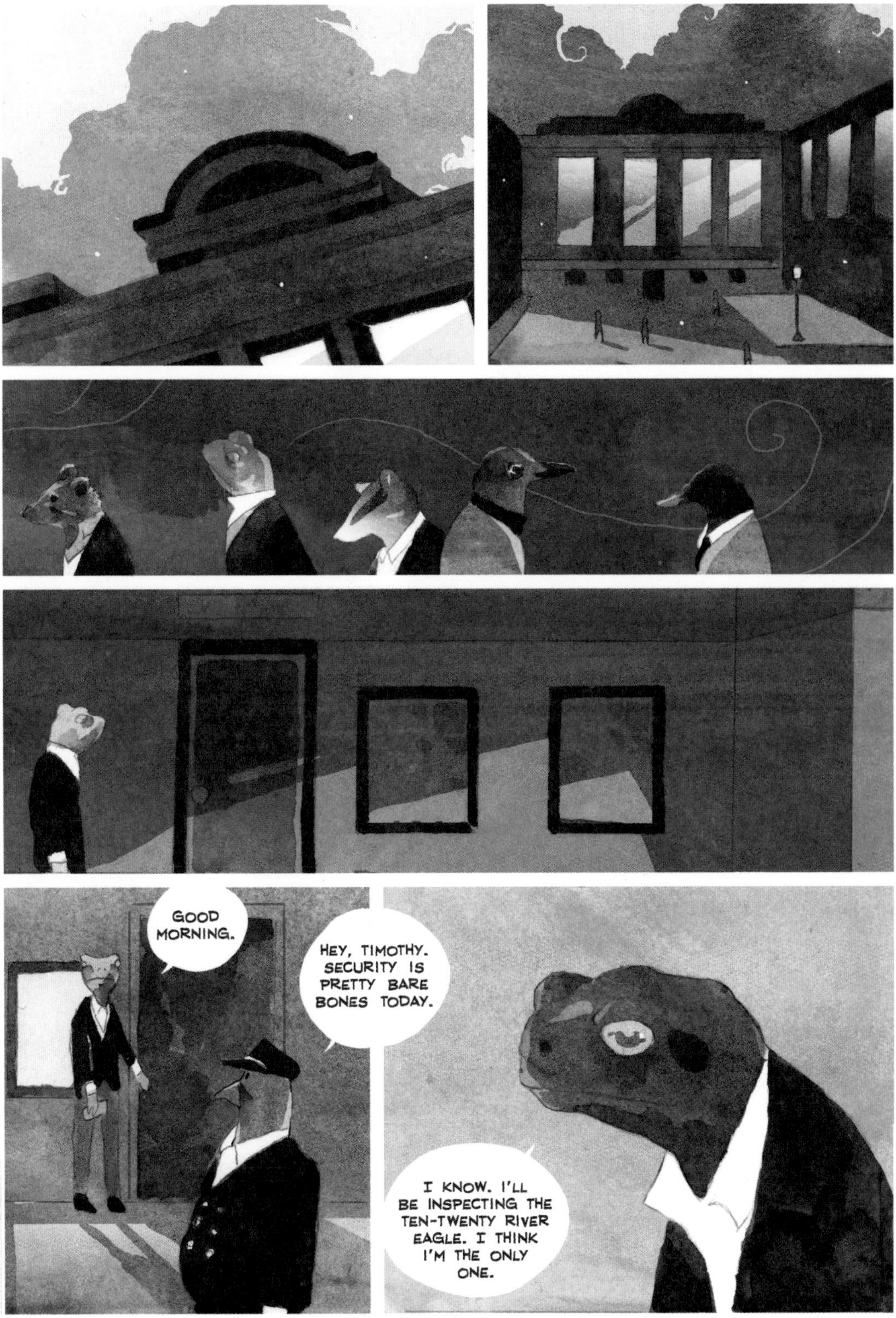
GOOD MORNING.
HEY, TIMOTHY. SECURITY IS PRETTY BARE BONES TODAY.
I KNOW. I'LL BE INSPECTING THE TEN-TWENTY RIVER EAGLE. I THINK I'M THE ONLY ONE.

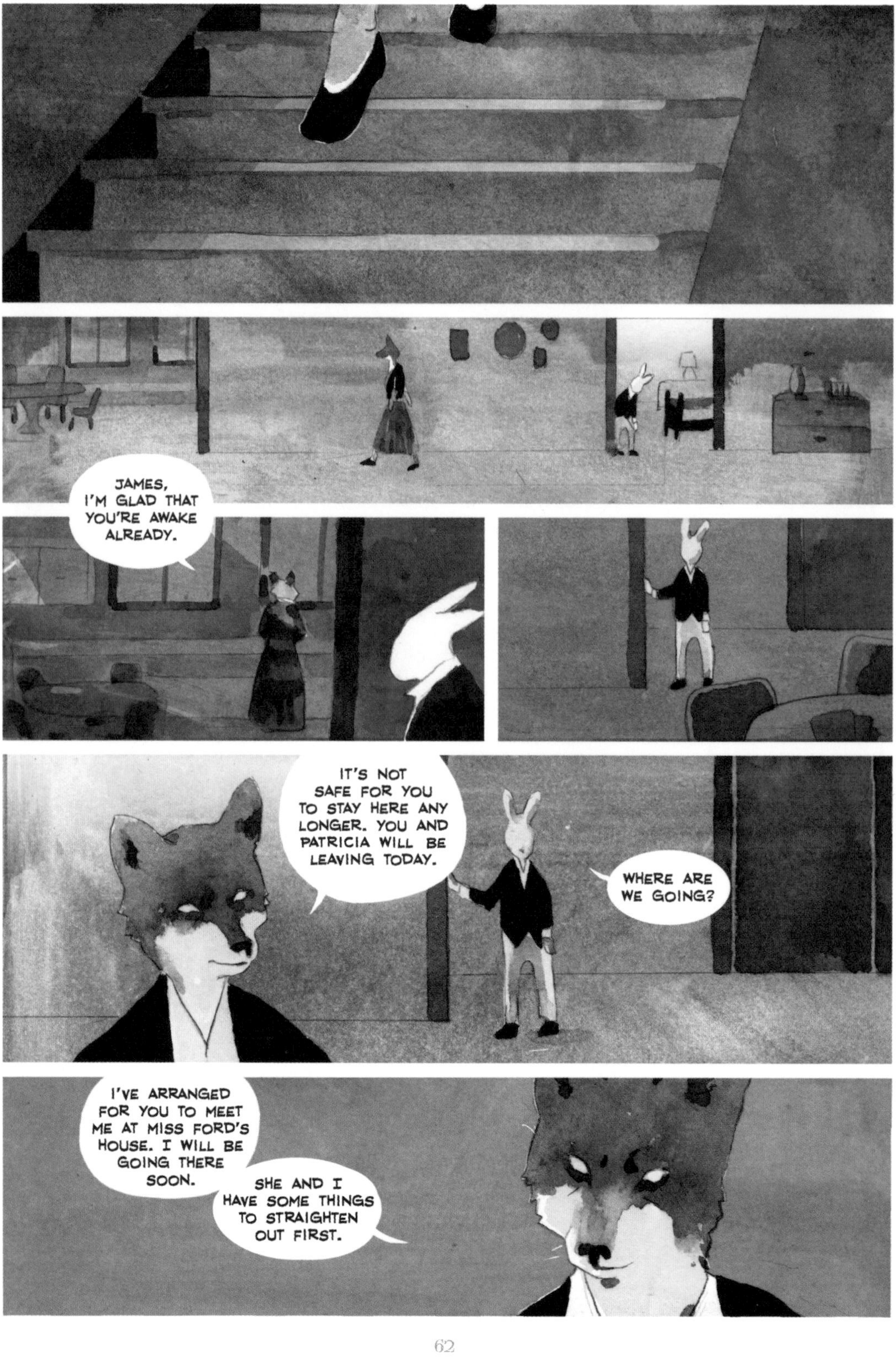
JAMES, I'M GLAD THAT YOU'RE AWAKE ALREADY.
IT'S NOT SAFE FOR YOU TO STAY HERE ANY LONGER. YOU AND PATRICIA WILL BE LEAVING TODAY.
WHERE ARE WE GOING?
I'VE ARRANGED FOR YOU TO MEET ME AT MISS FORD'S HOUSE. I WILL BE GOING THERE SOON.
SHE AND I HAVE SOME THINGS TO STRAIGHTEN OUT FIRST.

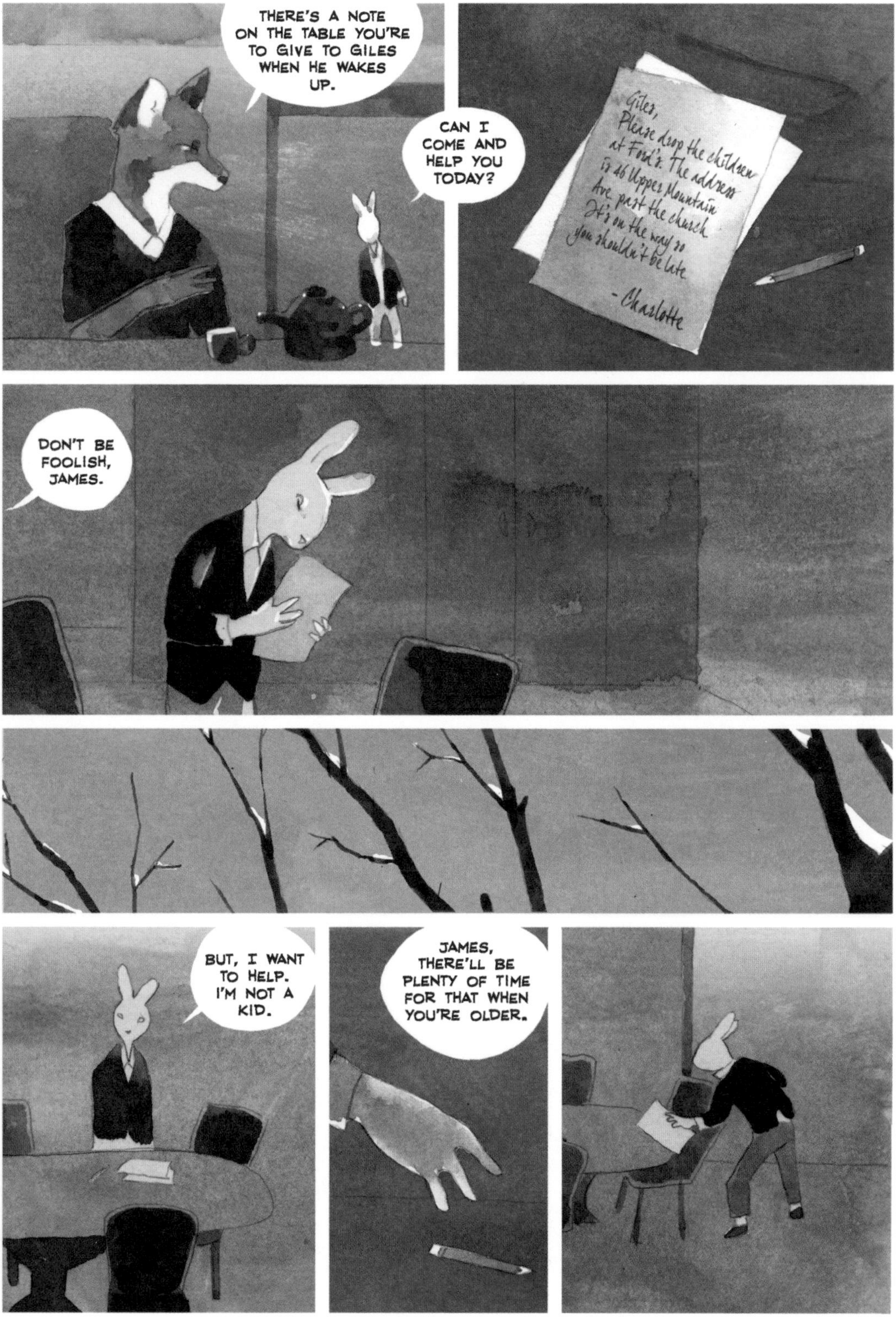
THERE'S A NOTE ON THE TABLE YOU'RE TO GIVE TO GILES WHEN HE WAKES UP.
CAN I COME AND HELP YOU TODAY?
Giles,
Please drop the children at Ford's. The address is 46 Upper Mountain Ave. past the church
It's on the way so you shouldn't be late
- Charlotte
DON'T BE FOOLISH, JAMES.
BUT, I WANT TO HELP. I'M NOT A KID.
JAMES, THERE'LL BE PLENTY OF TIME FOR THAT WHEN YOU'RE OLDER.

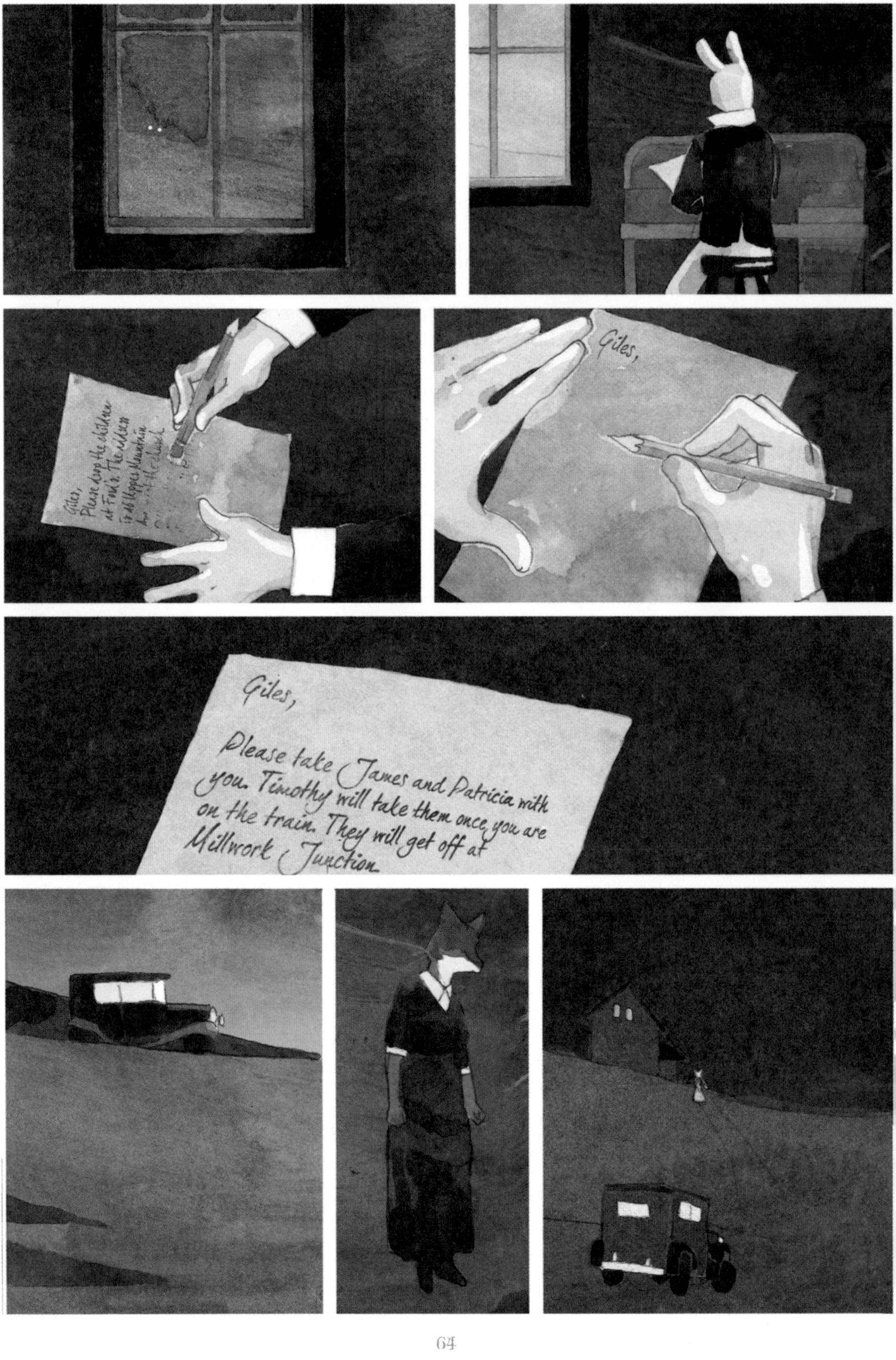
Giles,
Giles,
Please take James and Patricia with you. Timothy will take them once you are on the train. They will get off at Millwork Junction

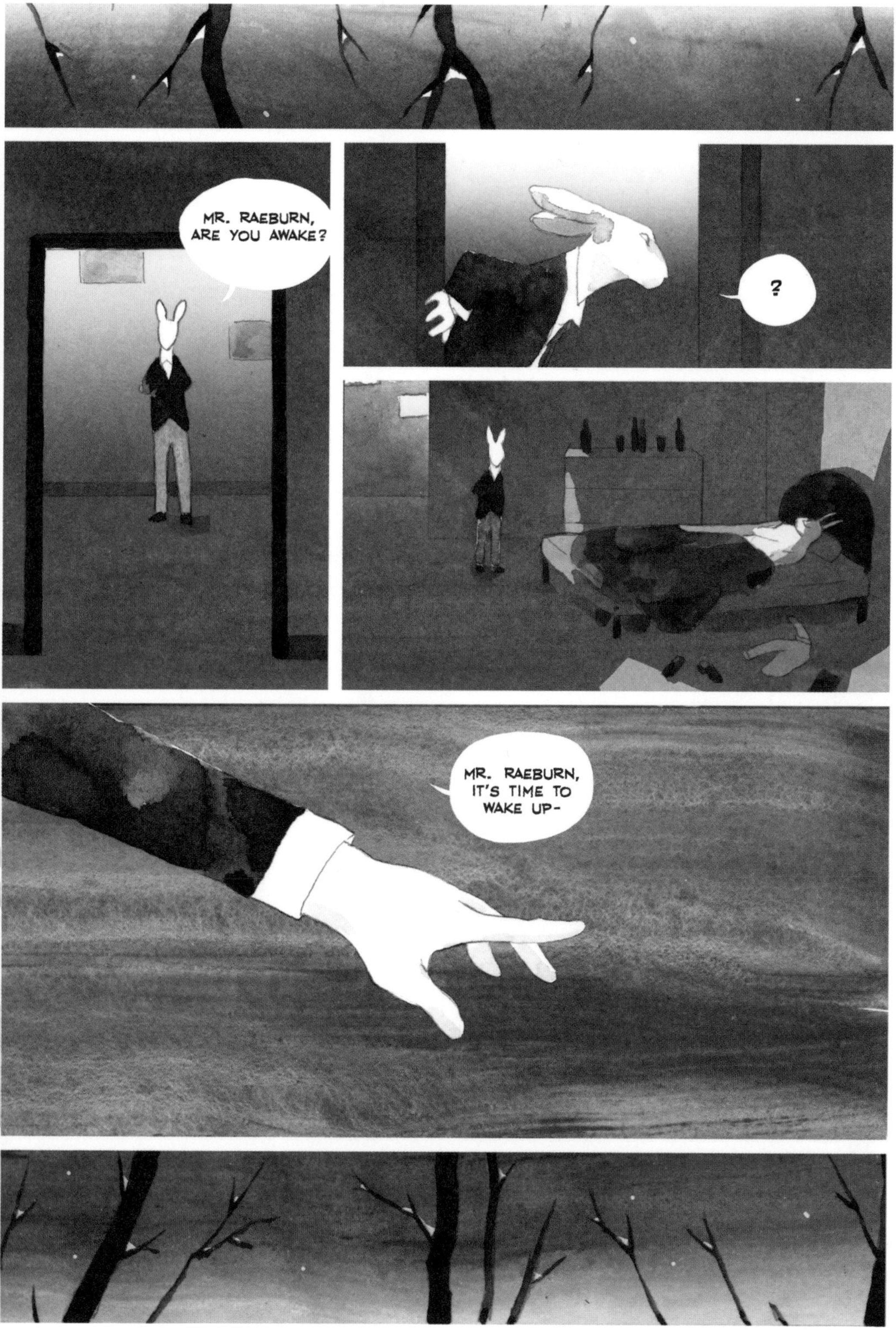
MR. RAEBURN, ARE YOU AWAKE?
?
MR. RAEBURN, IT'S TIME TO WAKE UP-

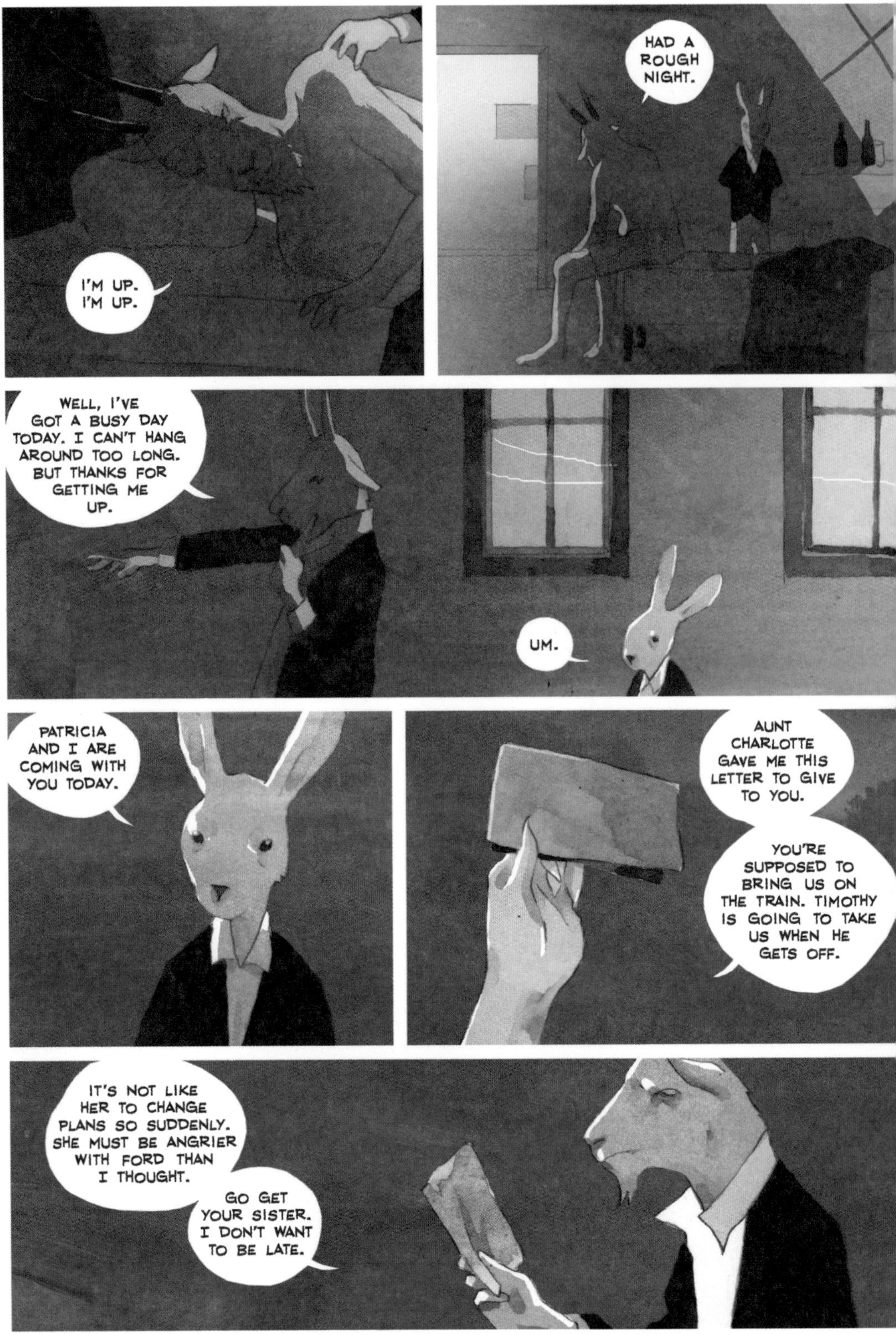
I'M UP. I'M UP.
HAD A ROUGH NIGHT.
WELL, I'VE GOT A BUSY DAY TODAY. I CAN'T HANG AROUND TOO LONG. BUT THANKS FOR GETTING ME UP.
UM.
PATRICIA AND I ARE COMING WITH YOU TODAY.
AUNT CHARLOTTE GAVE ME THIS LETTER TO GIVE TO YOU.
YOU'RE SUPPOSED TO BRING US ON THE TRAIN. TIMOTHY IS GOING TO TAKE US WHEN HE GETS OFF.
IT'S NOT LIKE HER TO CHANGE PLANS SO SUDDENLY. SHE MUST BE ANGRIER WITH FORD THAN I THOUGHT.
GO GET YOUR SISTER. I DON'T WANT TO BE LATE.

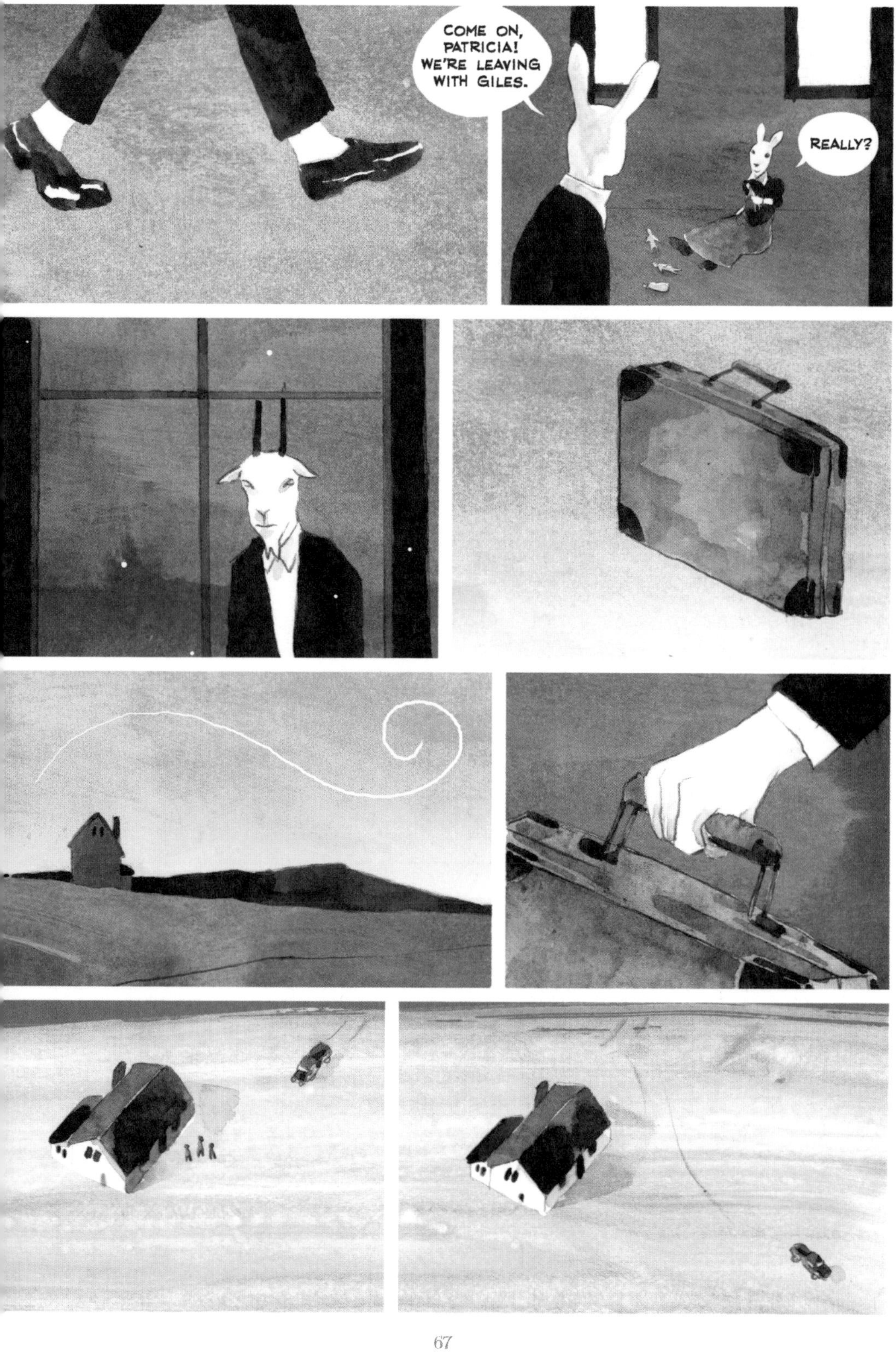
COME ON, PATRICIA! WE'RE LEAVING WITH GILES.
REALLY?

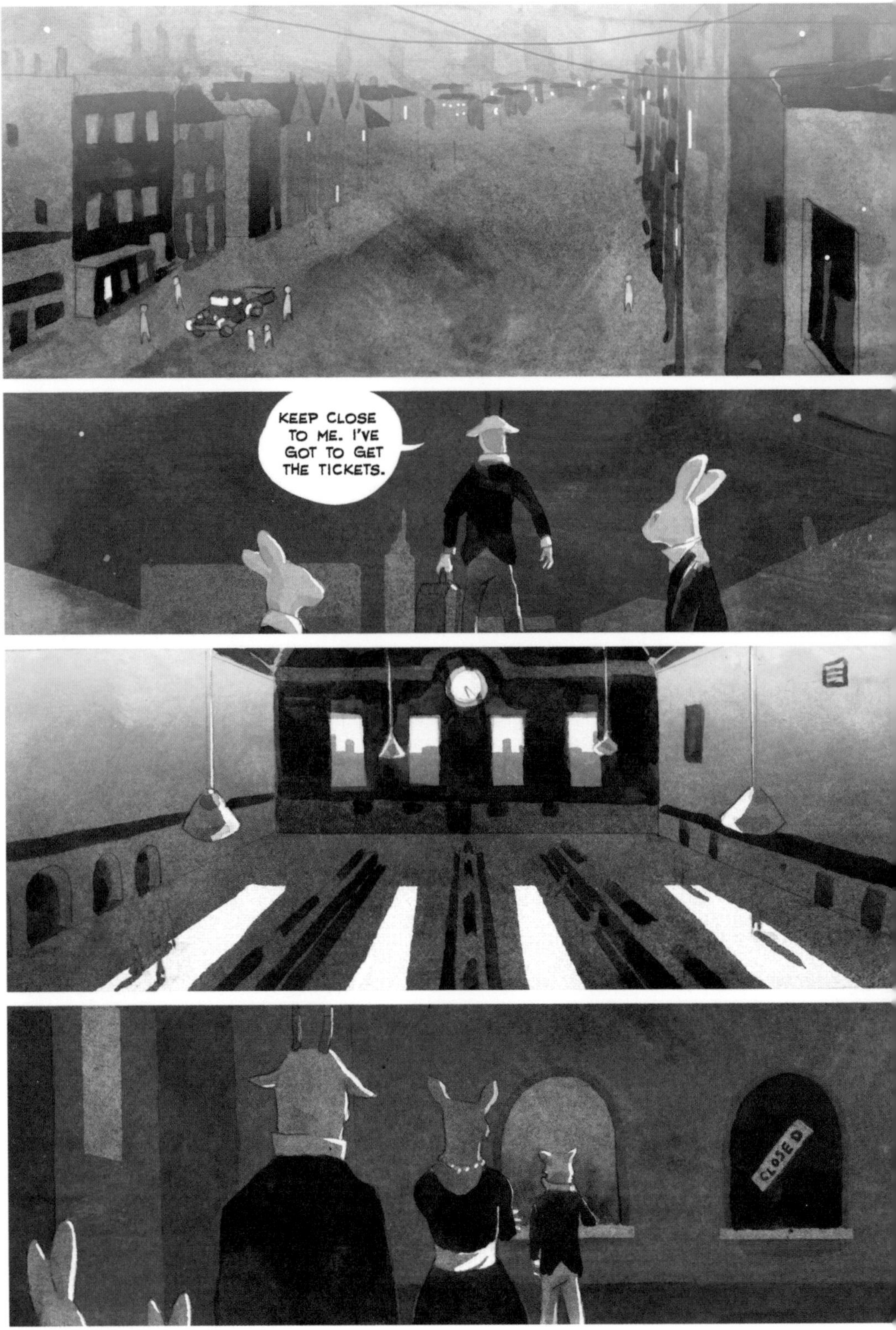
KEEP CLOSE TO ME. I'VE GOT TO GET THE TICKETS.
CLOSED

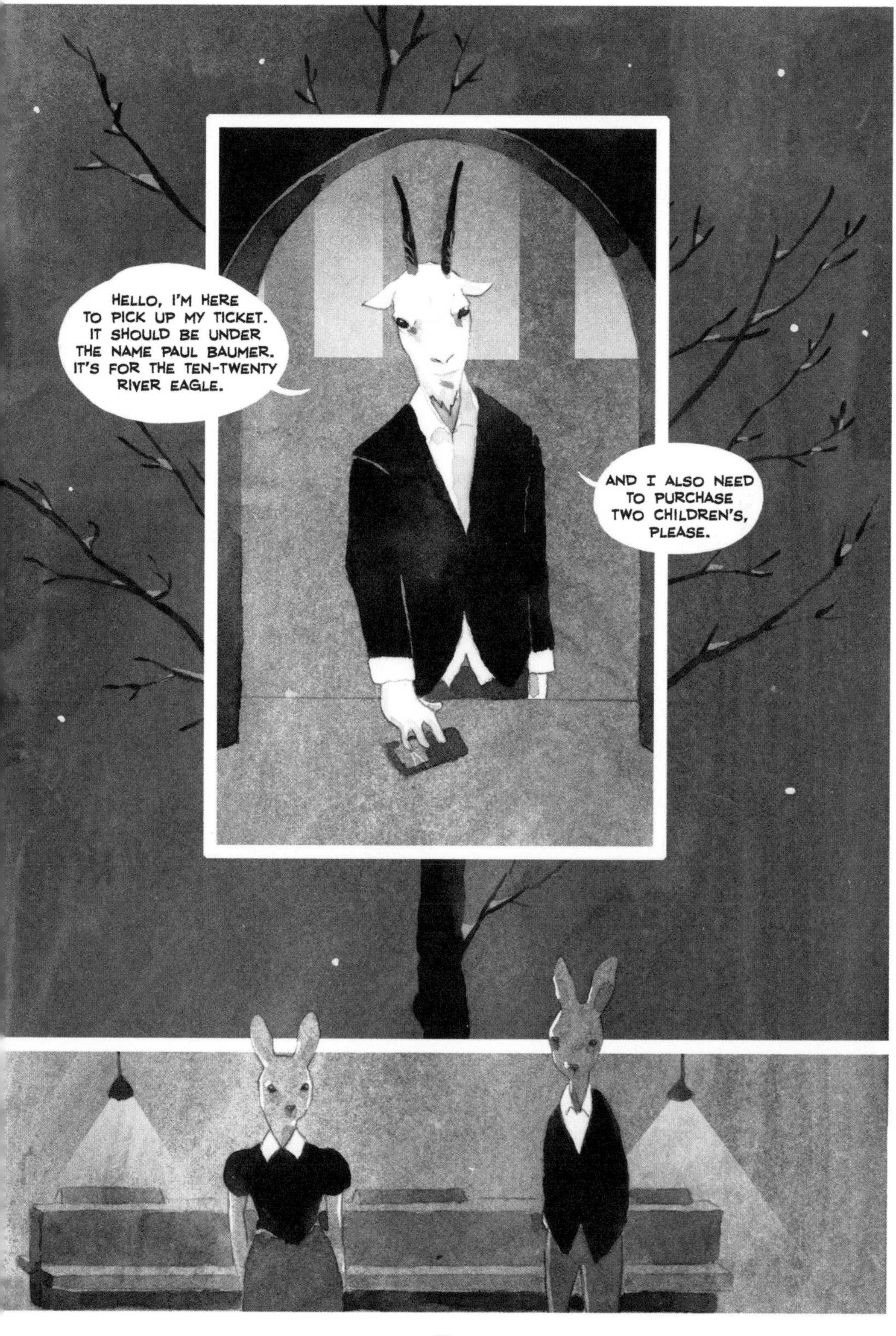
HELLO, I'M HERE TO PICK UP MY TICKET. IT SHOULD BE UNDER THE NAME PAUL BAUMER. IT'S FOR THE TEN-TWENTY RIVER EAGLE.
AND I ALSO NEED TO PURCHASE TWO CHILDREN'S, PLEASE.

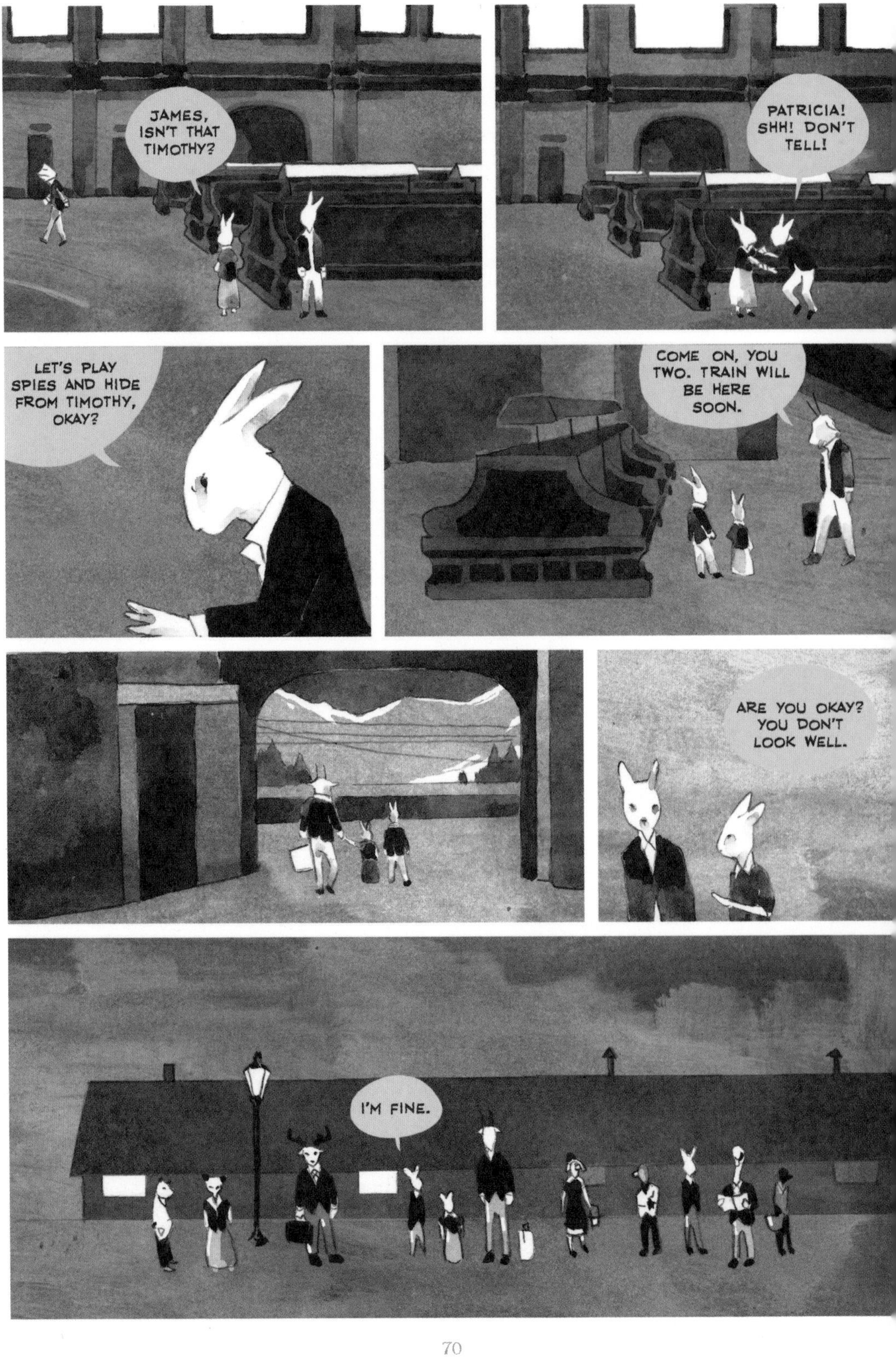
JAMES, ISN'T THAT TIMOTHY?
PATRICIA! SHH! DON'T TELL!
LET'S PLAY SPIES AND HIDE FROM TIMOTHY, OKAY?
COME ON, YOU TWO. TRAIN WILL BE HERE SOON.
ARE YOU OKAY? YOU DON'T LOOK WELL.
I'M FINE.

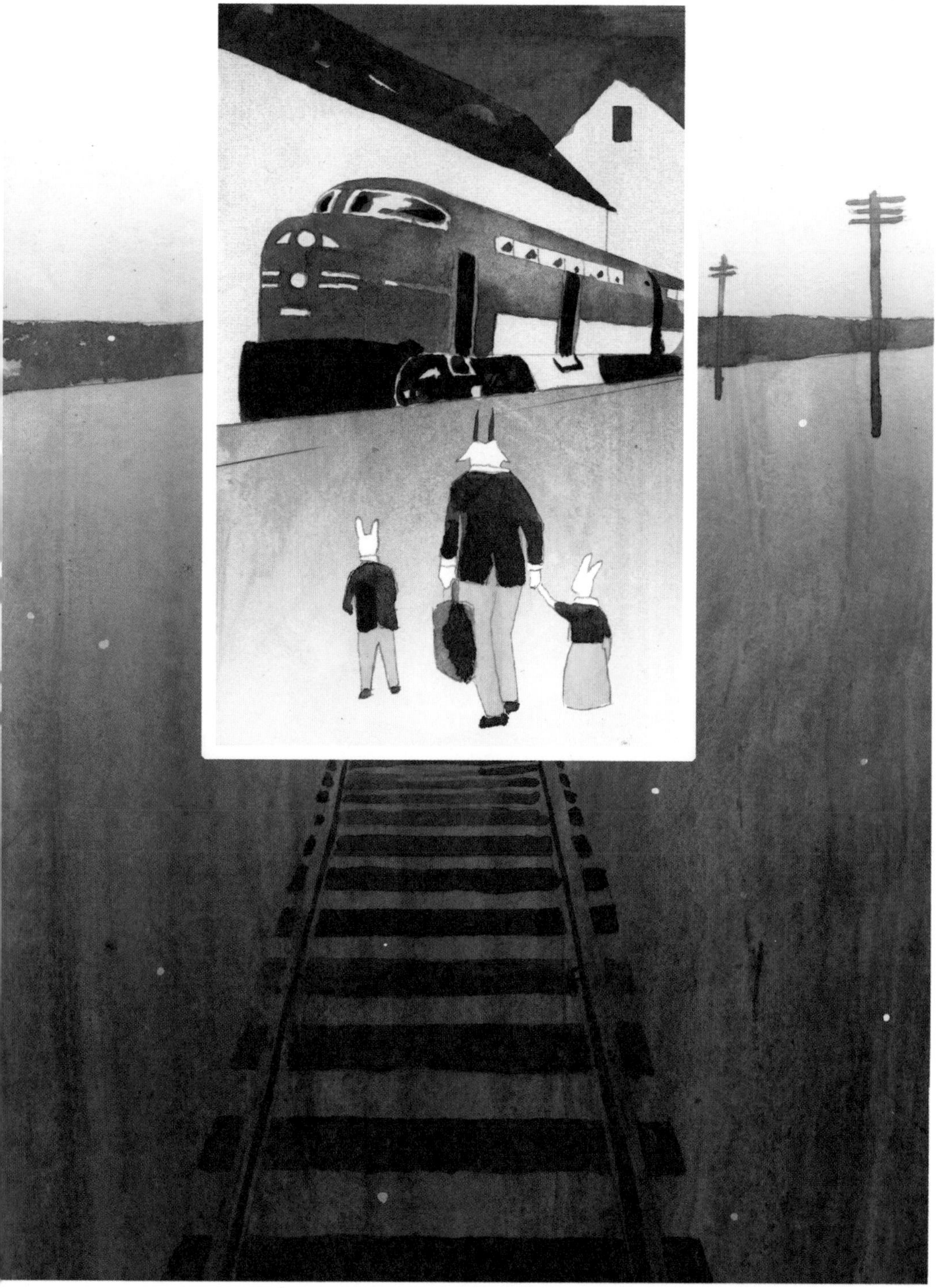

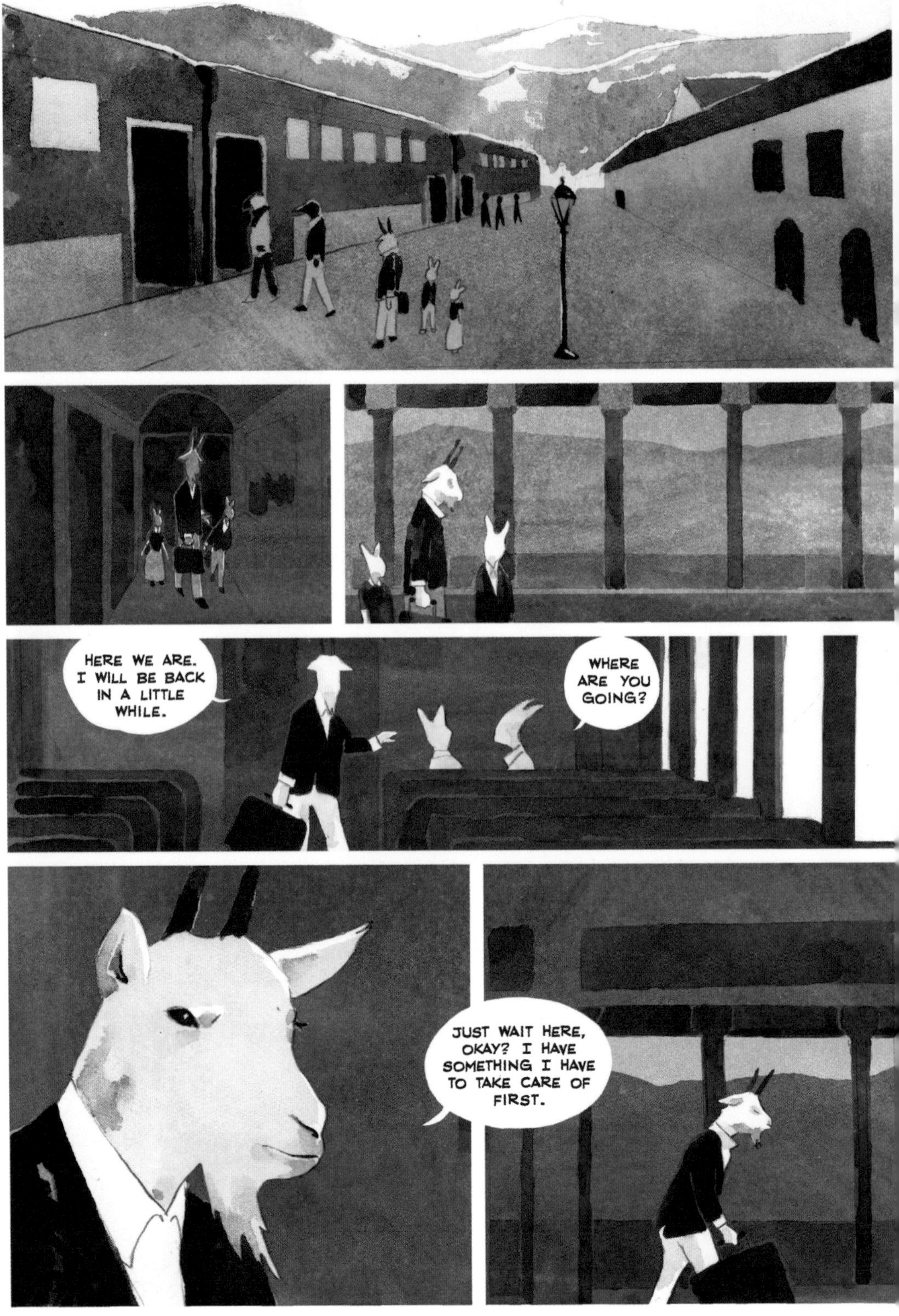
HERE WE ARE. I WILL BE BACK IN A LITTLE WHILE.
WHERE ARE YOU GOING?
JUST WAIT HERE, OKAY? I HAVE SOMETHING I HAVE TO TAKE CARE OF FIRST.

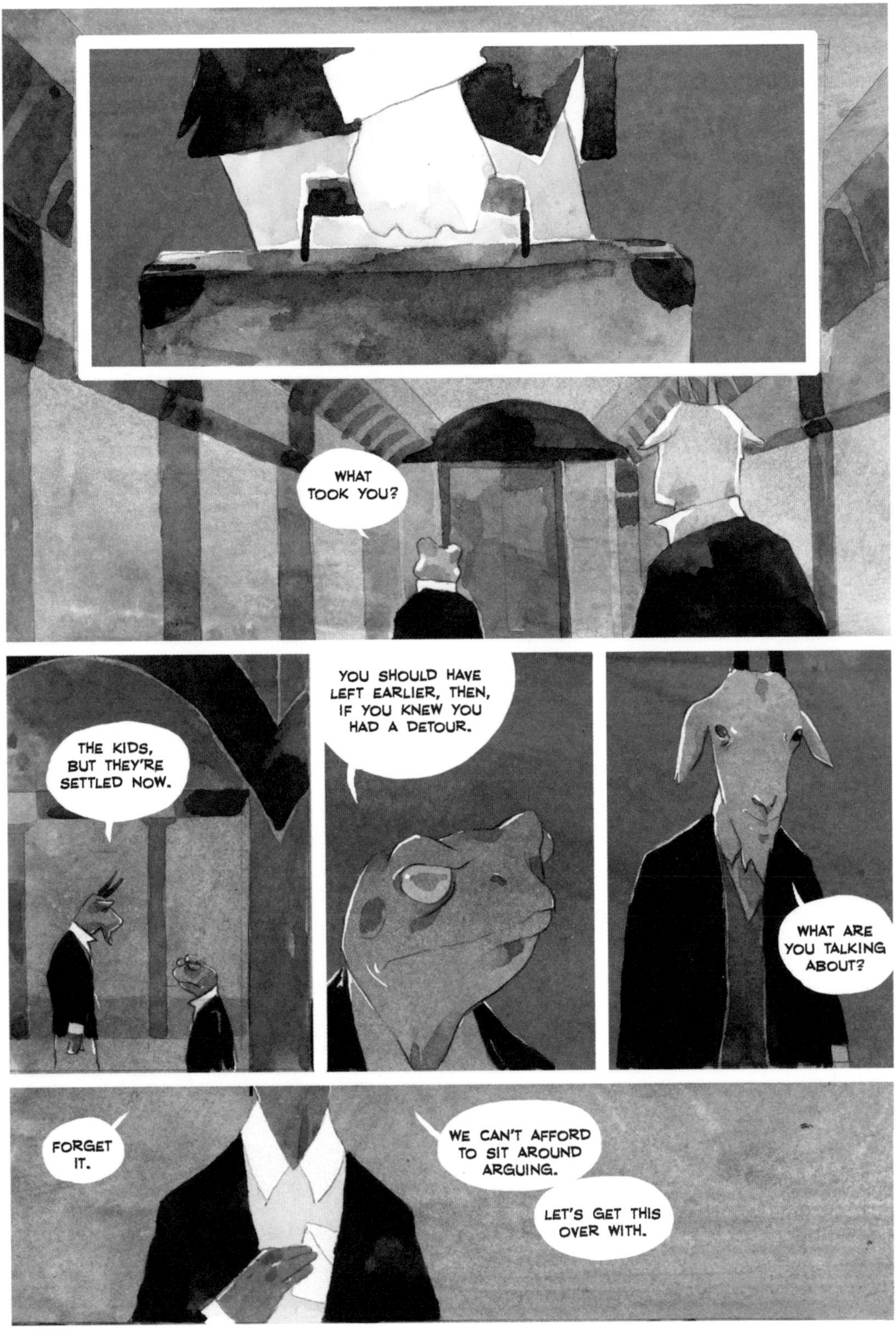
WHAT TOOK YOU?
THE KIDS, BUT THEY'RE SETTLED NOW.
YOU SHOULD HAVE LEFT EARLIER, THEN, IF YOU KNEW YOU HAD A DETOUR.
WHAT ARE YOU TALKING ABOUT?
FORGET IT.
WE CAN'T AFFORD TO SIT AROUND ARGUING.
LET'S GET THIS OVER WITH.

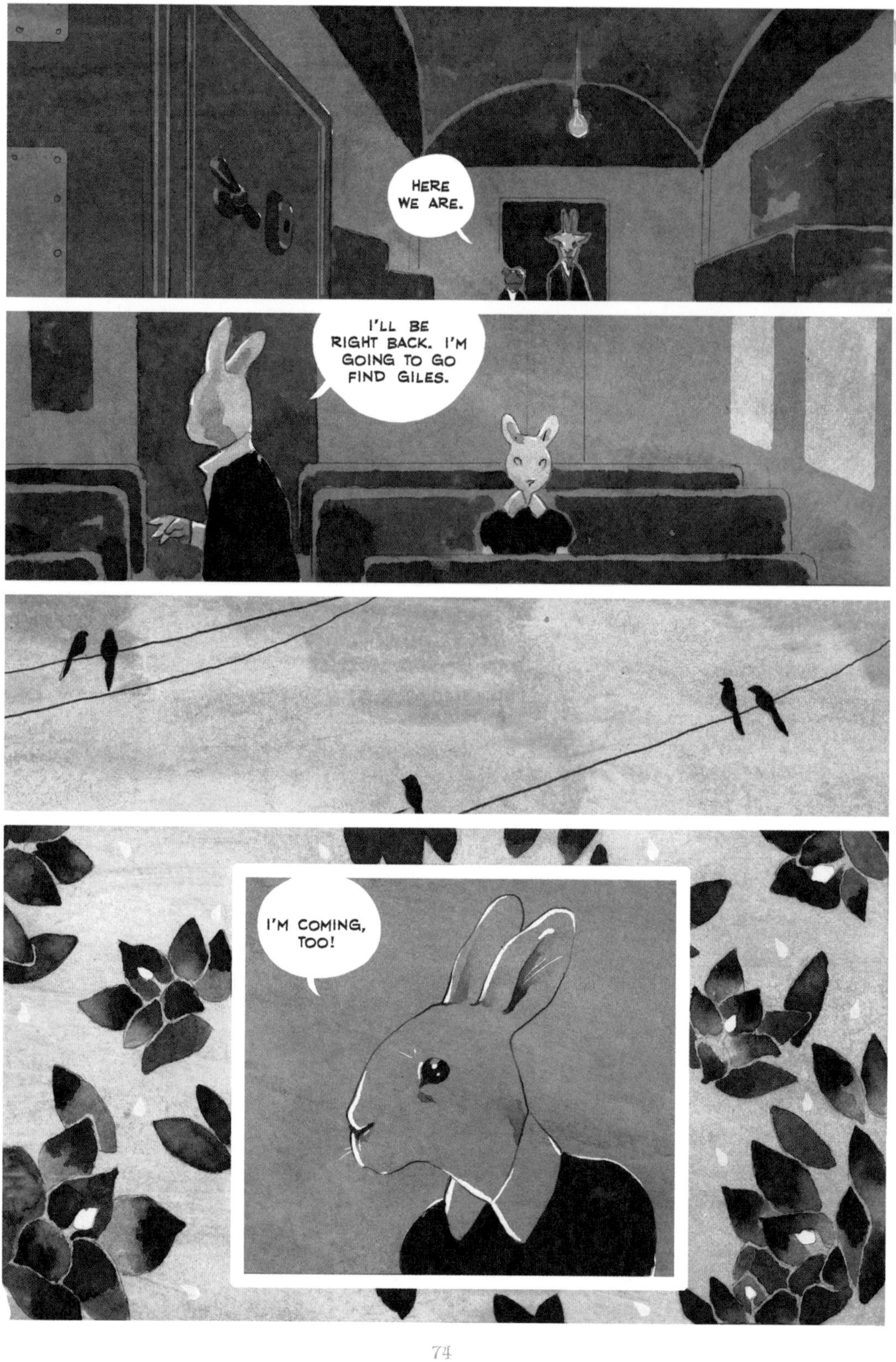
HERE WE ARE.
I'LL BE RIGHT BACK. I'M GOING TO GO FIND GILES.
I'M COMING, TOO!

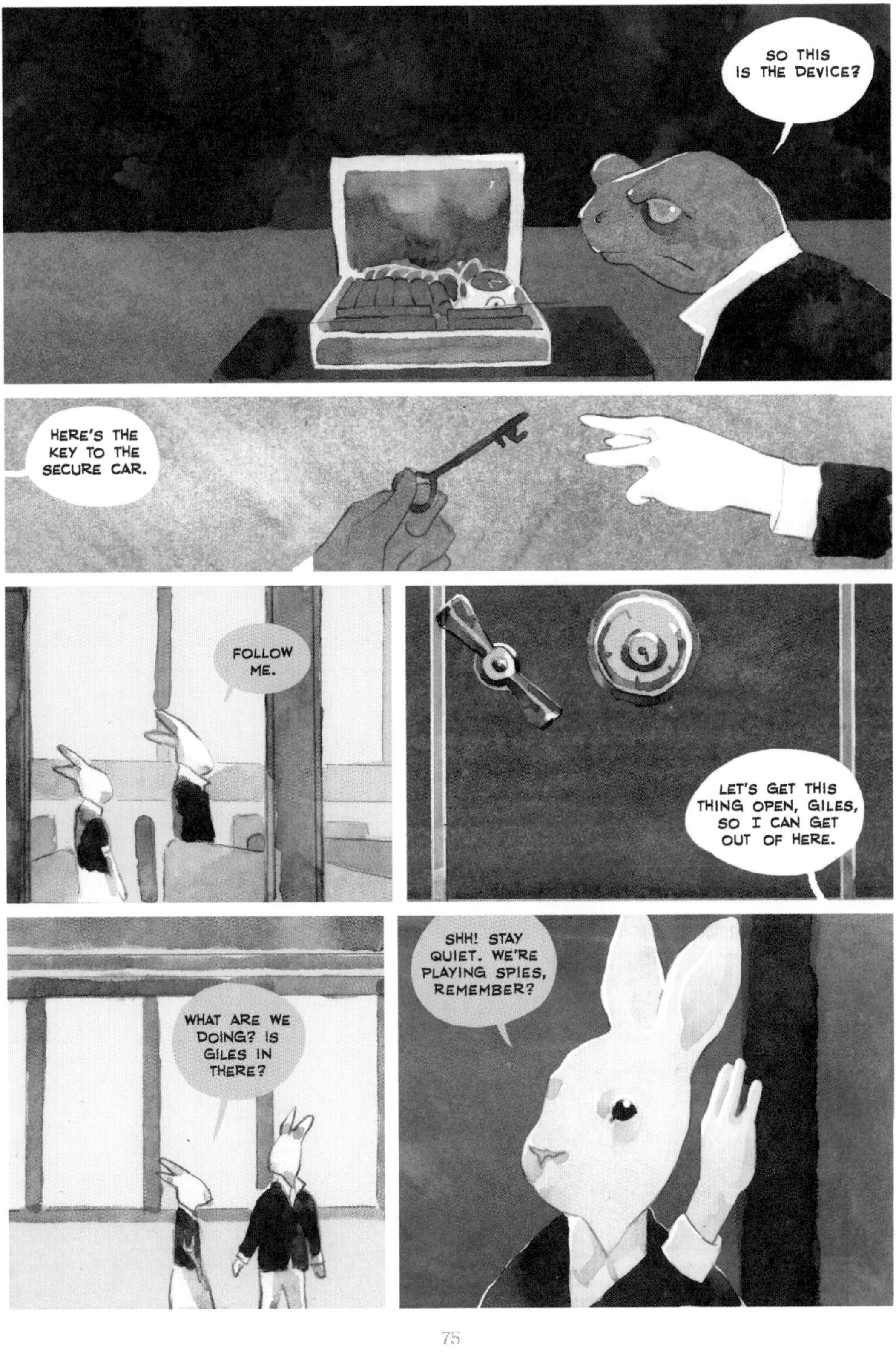
SO THIS IS THE DEVICE?
HERE'S THE KEY TO THE SECURE CAR.
FOLLOW ME.
LET'S GET THIS THING OPEN, GILES, SO I CAN GET OUT OF HERE.
WHAT ARE WE DOING? IS GILES IN THERE?
SHH! STAY QUIET. WE'RE PLAYING SPIES, REMEMBER?

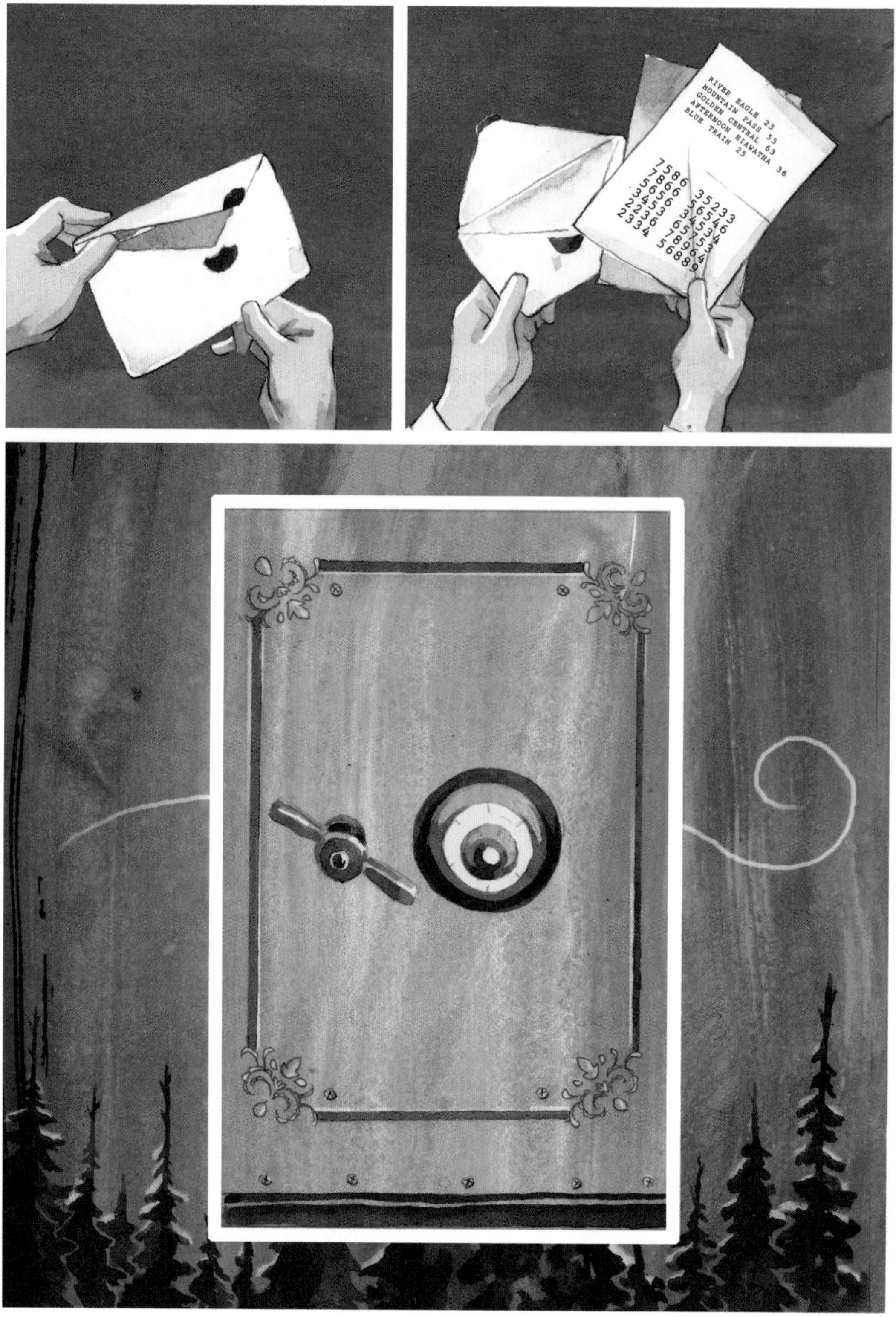
RIVER EAGLE 23
MOUNTAIN PASS 55
GOLDEN CENTRAL 63
AFTERNOON HIAWATHA 36
BLUE TRAIN 25
7586 35233
7866 65546
5656 34534
3453 65753
2236 78964
2334 56889

ONCE YOU GET OFF AT MILLWORK JUNCTION, I'VE GOT TO COME BACK HERE AND TRIGGER THE DEVICE.

ONCE I OPEN THIS, MY JOB IS DONE. CHARLOTTE TOLD YOU WHAT TO DO, RIGHT?

I HAVE TO TRIGGER IT AT THE PRECISE MOMENT SO THAT IT DETONATES OVER THE BRIDGE.

I'LL HAVE FIVE MINUTES TO JUMP. EVERYONE ELSE, WELL—

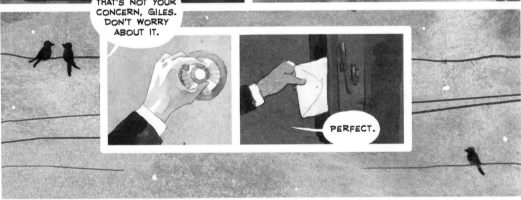

THAT'S NOT YOUR CONCERN, GILES. DON'T WORRY ABOUT IT.

PERFECT.

ALL RIGHT, ALL THE DOCUMENTS ARE HERE. LEAVE THE SUITCASE, GILES. WE'LL LOCK THE DOOR. IT WILL BE SAFE.

WHERE ARE WE GOING NOW?

COME ON.

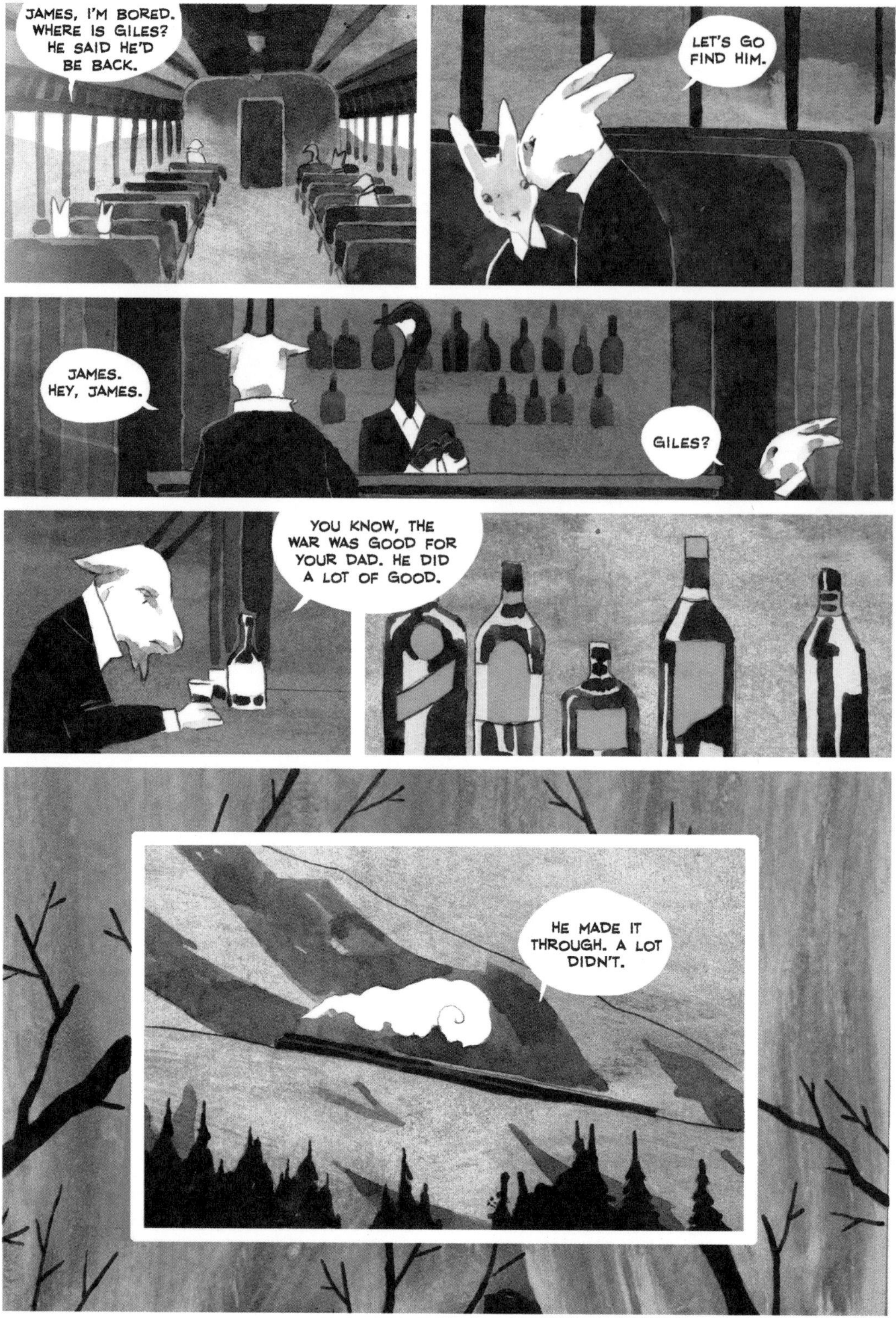
JAMES, I'M BORED. WHERE IS GILES? HE SAID HE'D BE BACK.
LET'S GO FIND HIM.
JAMES. HEY, JAMES.
GILES?
YOU KNOW, THE WAR WAS GOOD FOR YOUR DAD. HE DID A LOT OF GOOD.
HE MADE IT THROUGH. A LOT DIDN'T.

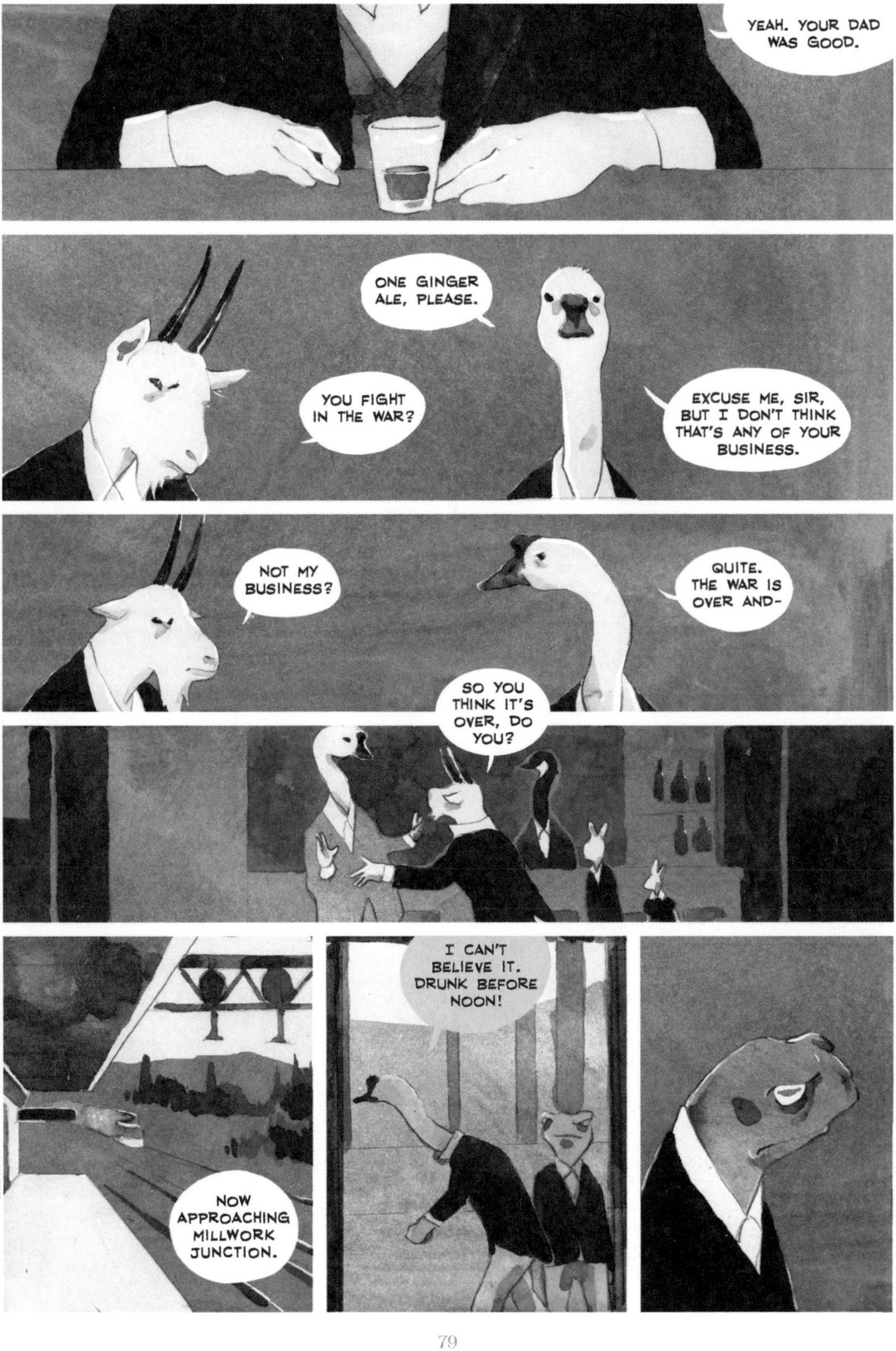
YEAH. YOUR DAD WAS GOOD.
ONE GINGER ALE, PLEASE.
YOU FIGHT IN THE WAR?
EXCUSE ME, SIR, BUT I DON'T THINK THAT'S ANY OF YOUR BUSINESS.
NOT MY BUSINESS?
QUITE. THE WAR IS OVER AND-
SO YOU THINK IT'S OVER, DO YOU?
NOW APPROACHING MILLWORK JUNCTION.
I CAN'T BELIEVE IT. DRUNK BEFORE NOON!

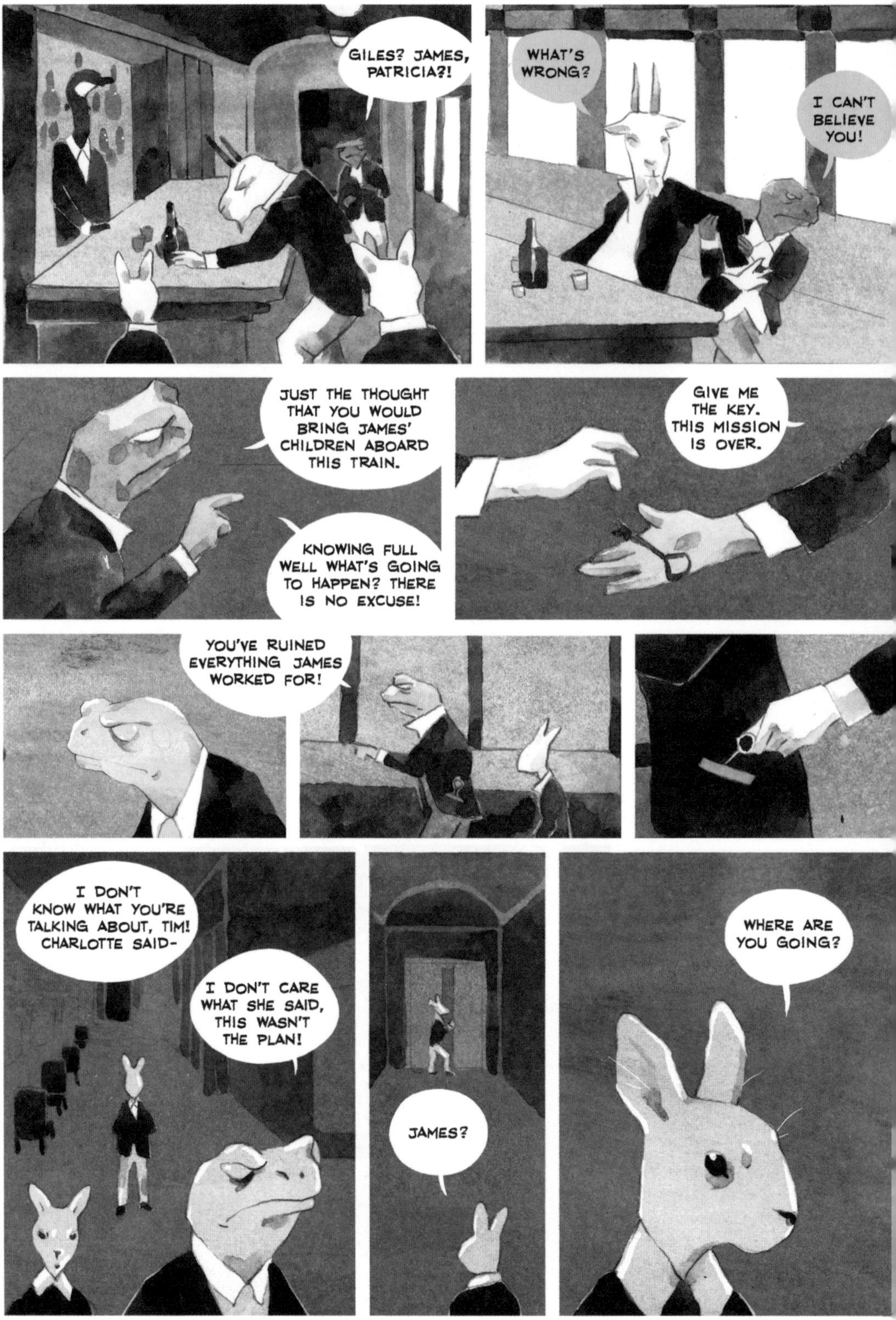
GILES? JAMES, PATRICIA?!
WHAT'S WRONG?
I CAN'T BELIEVE YOU!
JUST THE THOUGHT THAT YOU WOULD BRING JAMES' CHILDREN ABOARD THIS TRAIN.
KNOWING FULL WELL WHAT'S GOING TO HAPPEN? THERE IS NO EXCUSE!
GIVE ME THE KEY. THIS MISSION IS OVER.
YOU'VE RUINED EVERYTHING JAMES WORKED FOR!
I DON'T KNOW WHAT YOU'RE TALKING ABOUT, TIM! CHARLOTTE SAID-
I DON'T CARE WHAT SHE SAID, THIS WASN'T THE PLAN!
JAMES?
WHERE ARE YOU GOING?

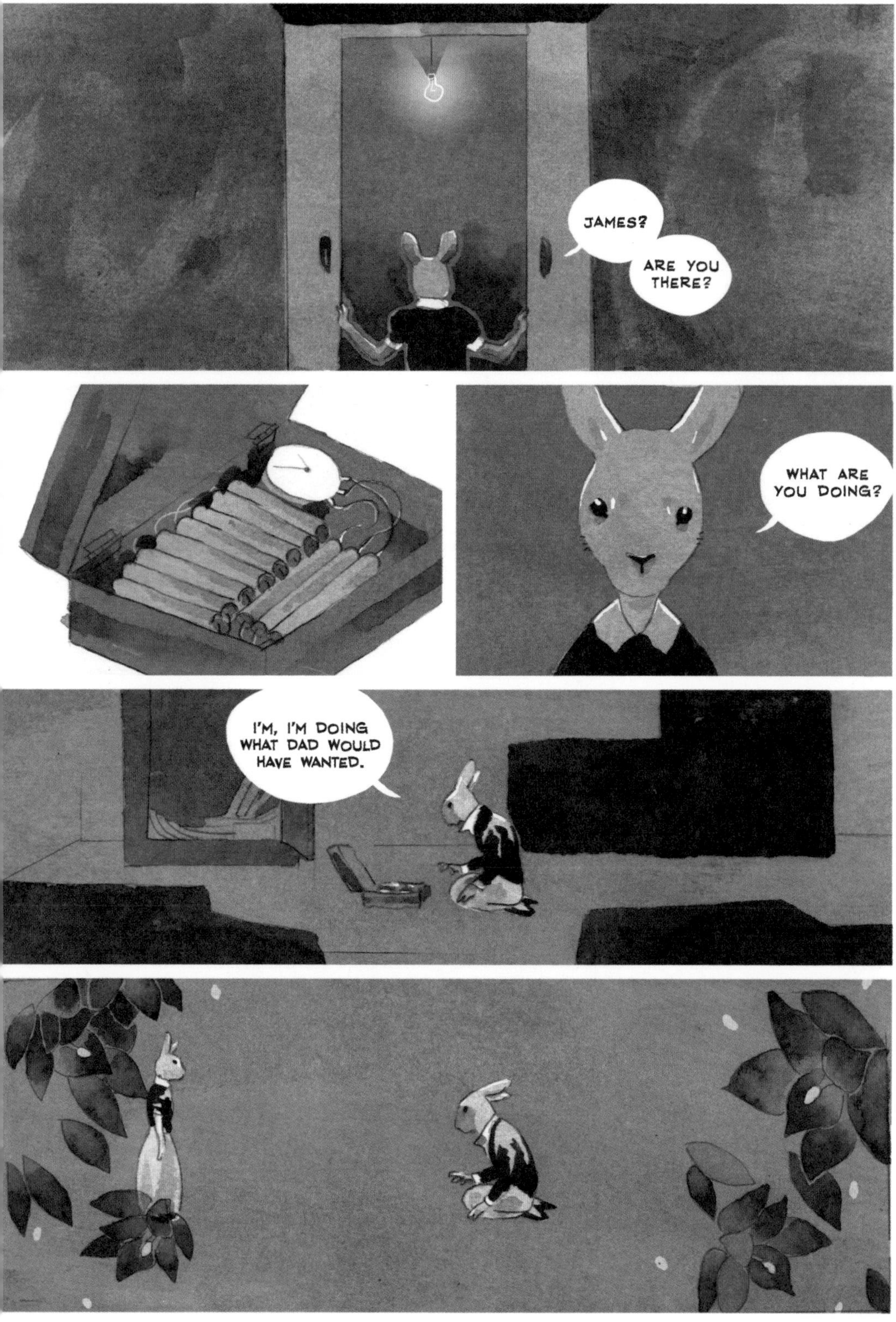
JAMES?
ARE YOU THERE?
WHAT ARE YOU DOING?
I'M, I'M DOING WHAT DAD WOULD HAVE WANTED.

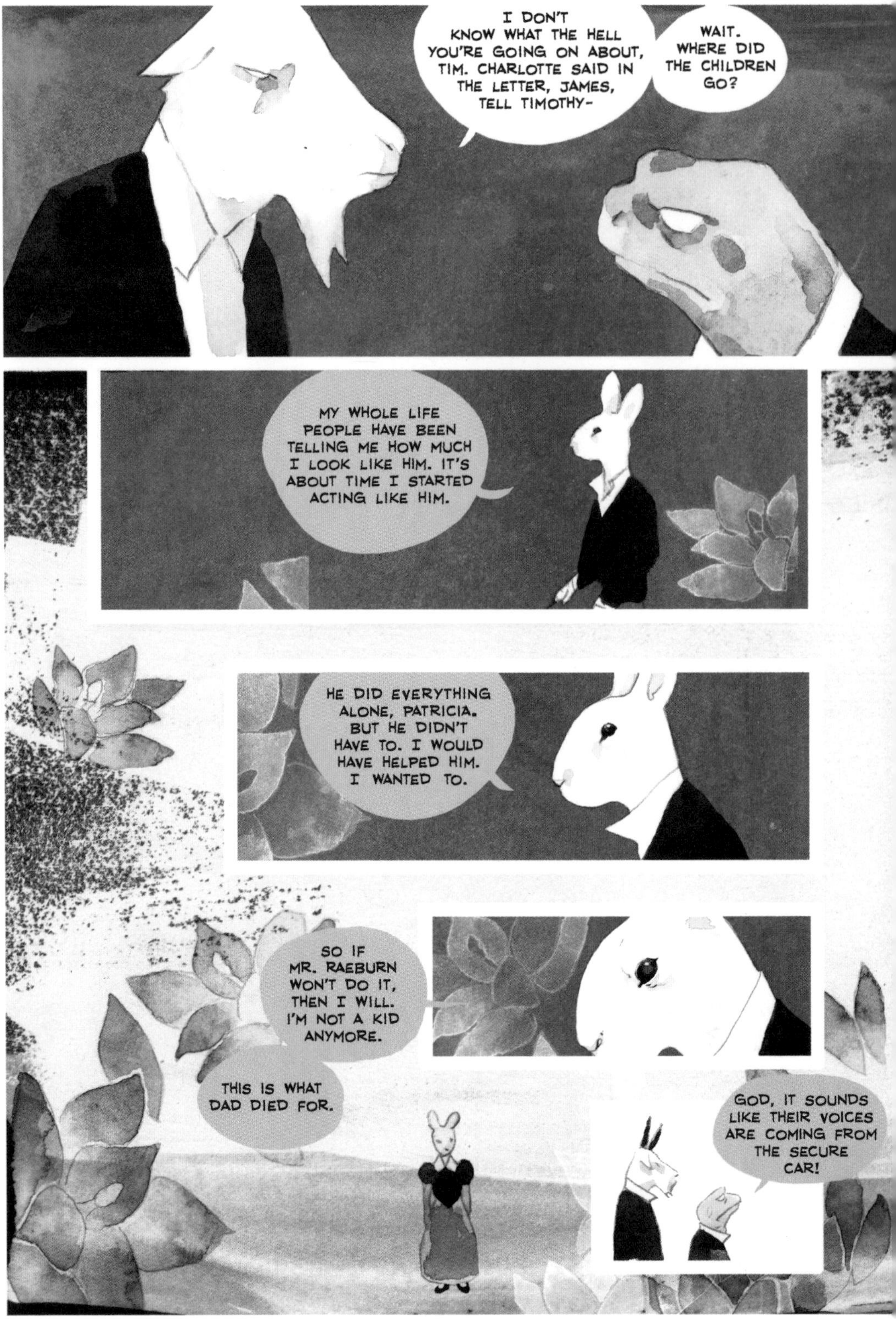
I DON'T KNOW WHAT THE HELL YOU'RE GOING ON ABOUT, TIM. CHARLOTTE SAID IN THE LETTER, JAMES, TELL TIMOTHY-
WAIT. WHERE DID THE CHILDREN GO?
MY WHOLE LIFE PEOPLE HAVE BEEN TELLING ME HOW MUCH I LOOK LIKE HIM. IT'S ABOUT TIME I STARTED ACTING LIKE HIM.
HE DID EVERYTHING ALONE, PATRICIA. BUT HE DIDN'T HAVE TO. I WOULD HAVE HELPED HIM. I WANTED TO.
SO IF MR. RAEBURN WON'T DO IT, THEN I WILL. I'M NOT A KID ANYMORE.
THIS IS WHAT DAD DIED FOR.
GOD, IT SOUNDS LIKE THEIR VOICES ARE COMING FROM THE SECURE CAR!

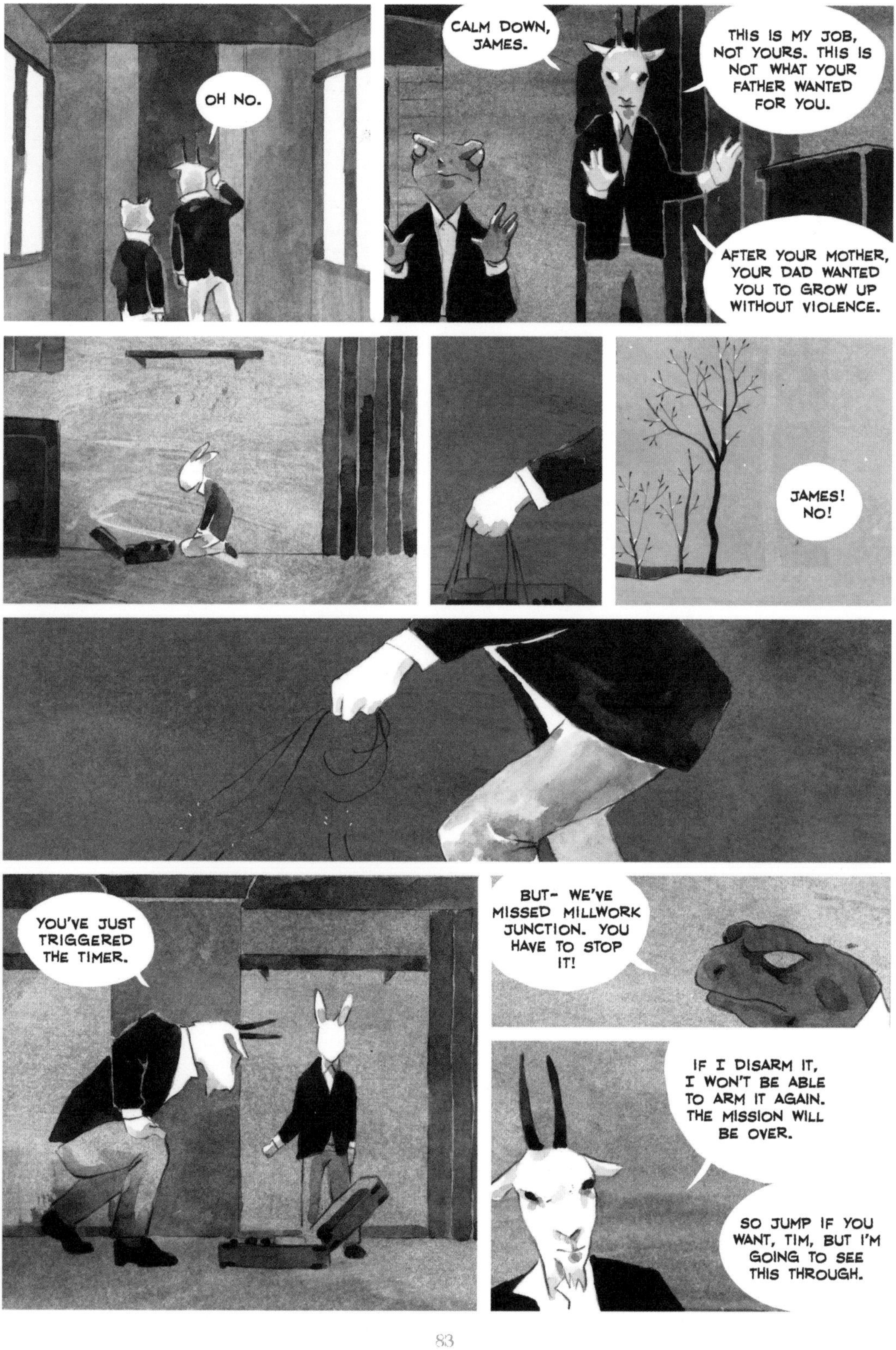
OH NO.
CALM DOWN, JAMES.
THIS IS MY JOB, NOT YOURS. THIS IS NOT WHAT YOUR FATHER WANTED FOR YOU.
AFTER YOUR MOTHER, YOUR DAD WANTED YOU TO GROW UP WITHOUT VIOLENCE.
JAMES! NO!
YOU'VE JUST TRIGGERED THE TIMER.
BUT- WE'VE MISSED MILLWORK JUNCTION. YOU HAVE TO STOP IT!
IF I DISARM IT, I WON'T BE ABLE TO ARM IT AGAIN. THE MISSION WILL BE OVER.
SO JUMP IF YOU WANT, TIM, BUT I'M GOING TO SEE THIS THROUGH.

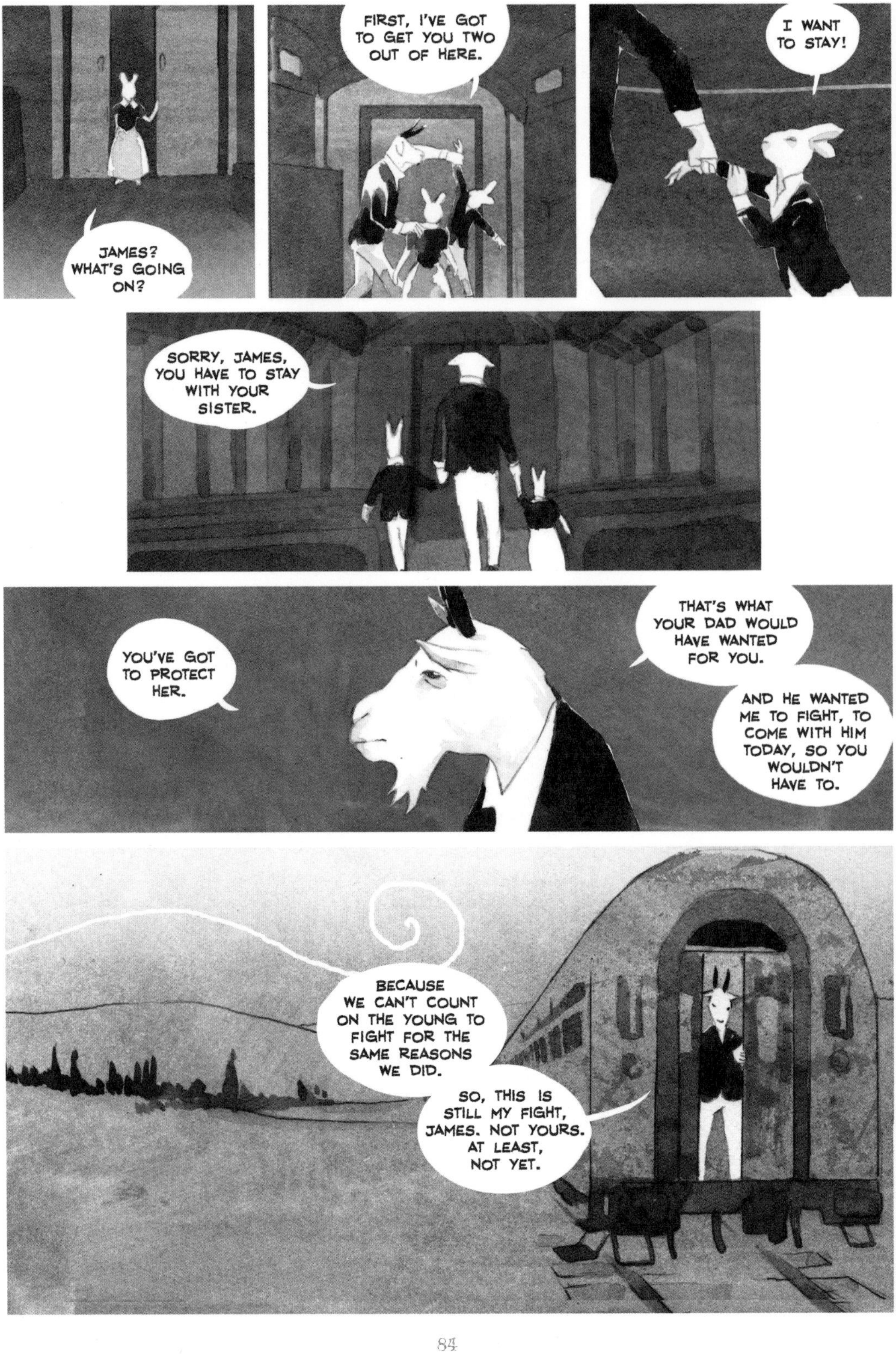
JAMES? WHAT'S GOING ON?
FIRST, I'VE GOT TO GET YOU TWO OUT OF HERE.
I WANT TO STAY!
SORRY, JAMES, YOU HAVE TO STAY WITH YOUR SISTER.
YOU'VE GOT TO PROTECT HER.
THAT'S WHAT YOUR DAD WOULD HAVE WANTED FOR YOU.
AND HE WANTED ME TO FIGHT, TO COME WITH HIM TODAY, SO YOU WOULDN'T HAVE TO.
BECAUSE WE CAN'T COUNT ON THE YOUNG TO FIGHT FOR THE SAME REASONS WE DID.
SO, THIS IS STILL MY FIGHT, JAMES. NOT YOURS. AT LEAST, NOT YET.

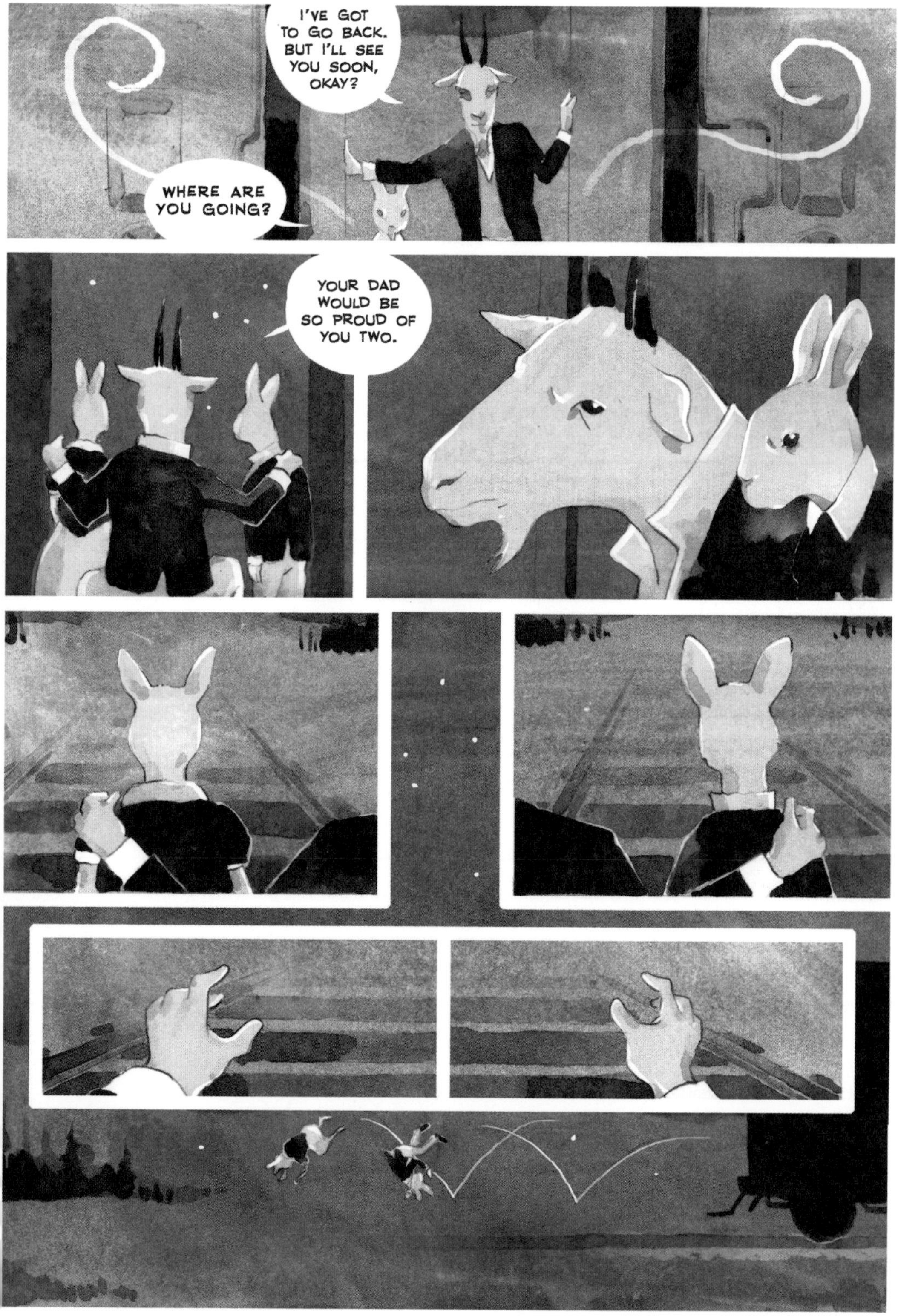
I'VE GOT TO GO BACK. BUT I'LL SEE YOU SOON, OKAY?
WHERE ARE YOU GOING?
YOUR DAD WOULD BE SO PROUD OF YOU TWO.

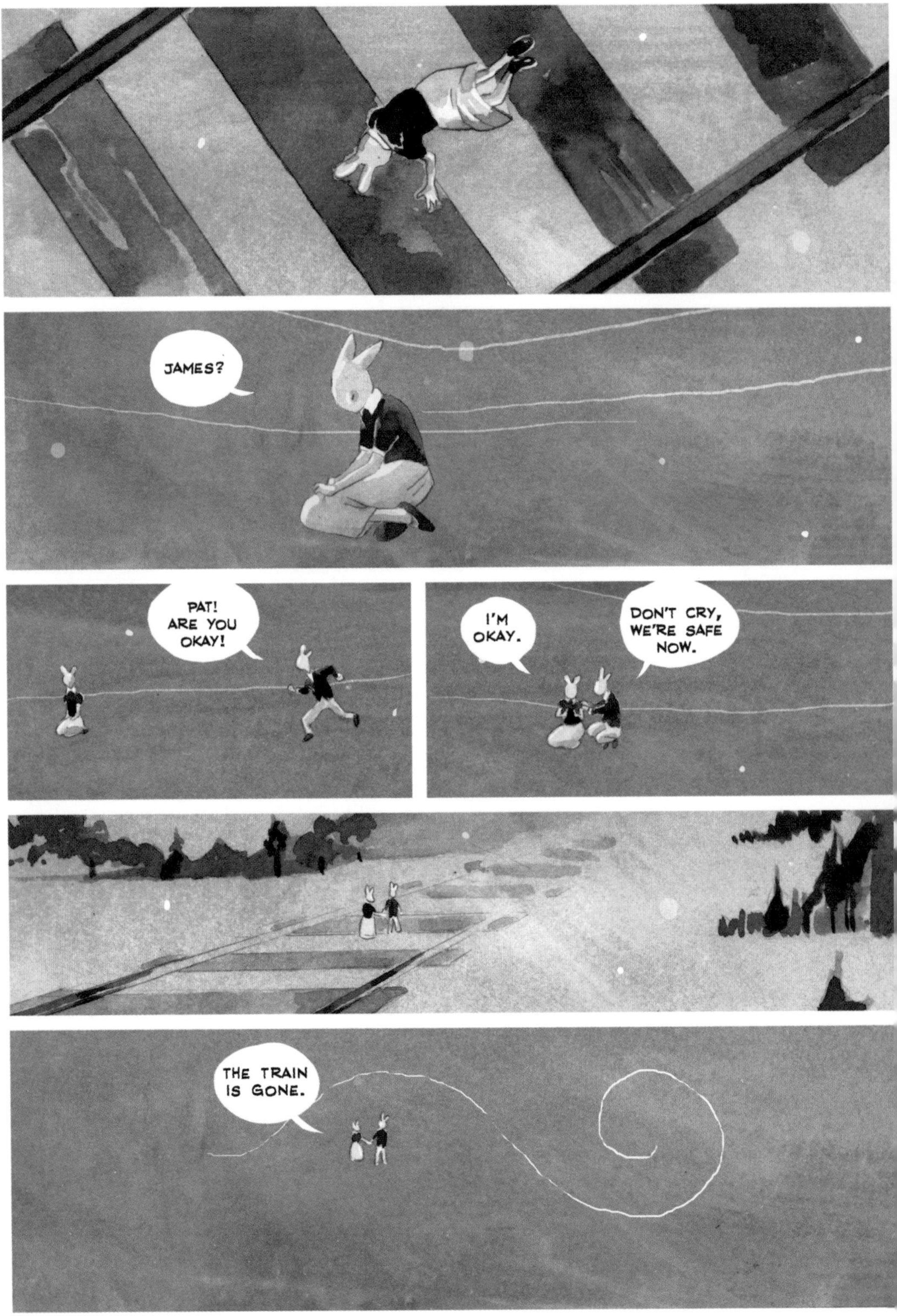
JAMES?
PAT! ARE YOU OKAY!
I'M OKAY.
DON'T CRY, WE'RE SAFE NOW.
THE TRAIN IS GONE.

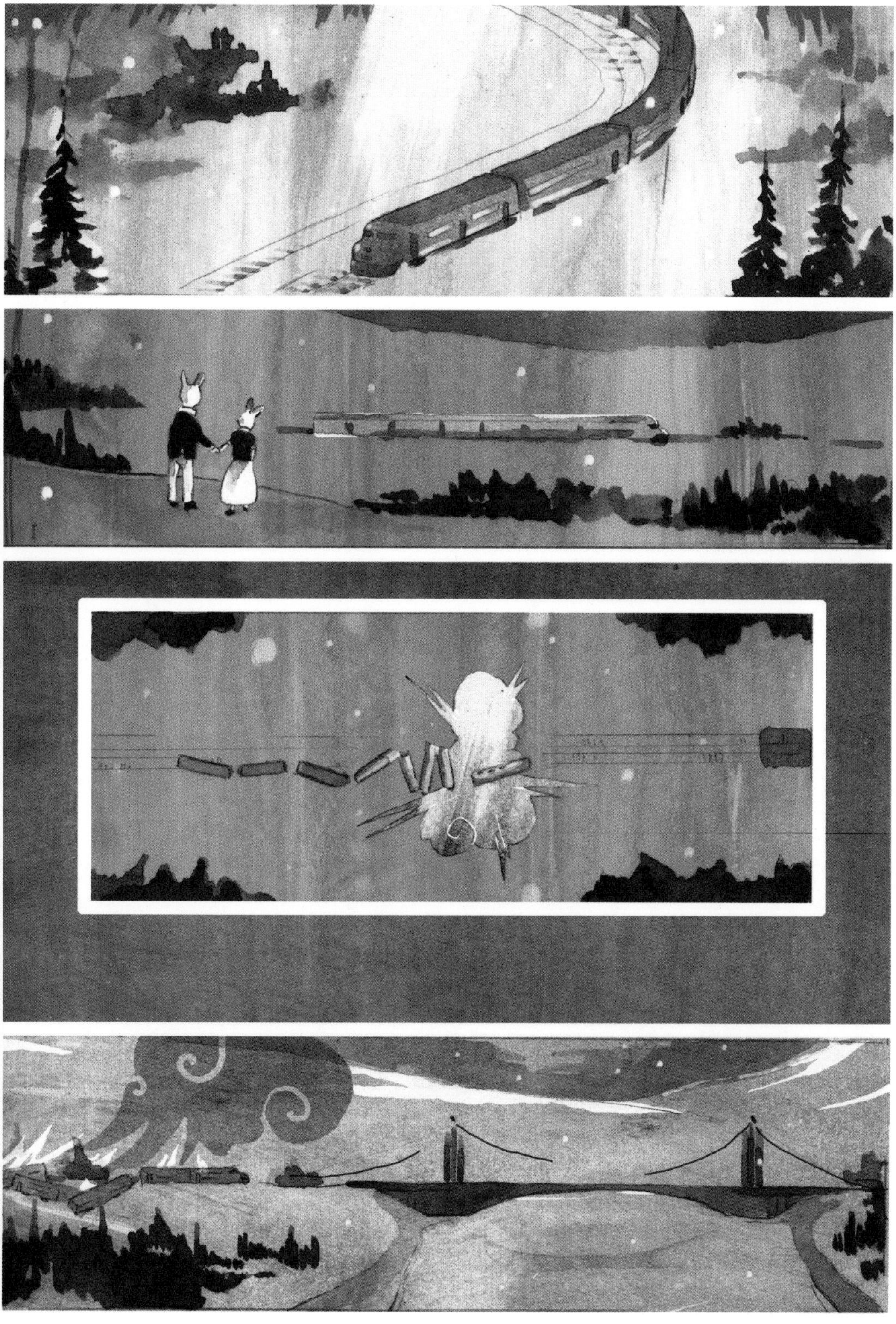

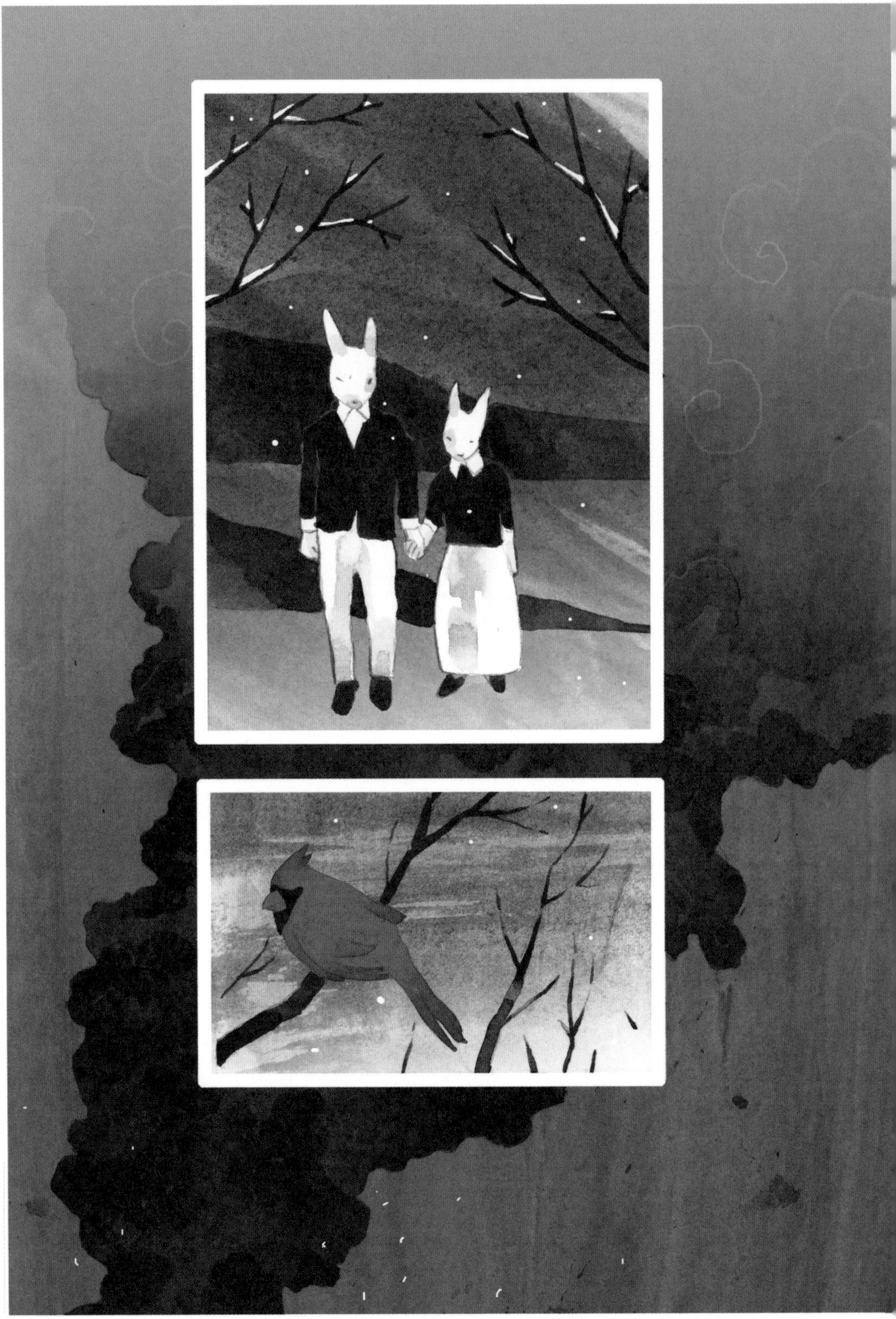

Tab,

Many years ago, when I was just a boy, I believed it was my duty to my country to fight. Everyone was so proud as all of us young boys left for the North during the Old War. We looked sharp. They even held a parade for us and called us 'The Iron Youth.' James was too young to fight then, but I think he would have done well. He and Charlotte are such a great team. She comes up with all of these wild ideas and somehow he gets them all done. It's like magic. But it leaves me feeling a bit out of place.

Maybe it's just because I've been here before, like some terrible case of déjà vu. It seems like there are the same faces around me talking, laughing, and dying. And once again we're out-gunned. But I trust James, and as long as he keeps fighting, so will I. I will try my best to keep him safe, because he's the one who reminds me that there are still things worth fighting for. If it were up to me we'd all just drop our guns. But what good would that do in the end?

Yours,

Giles

89

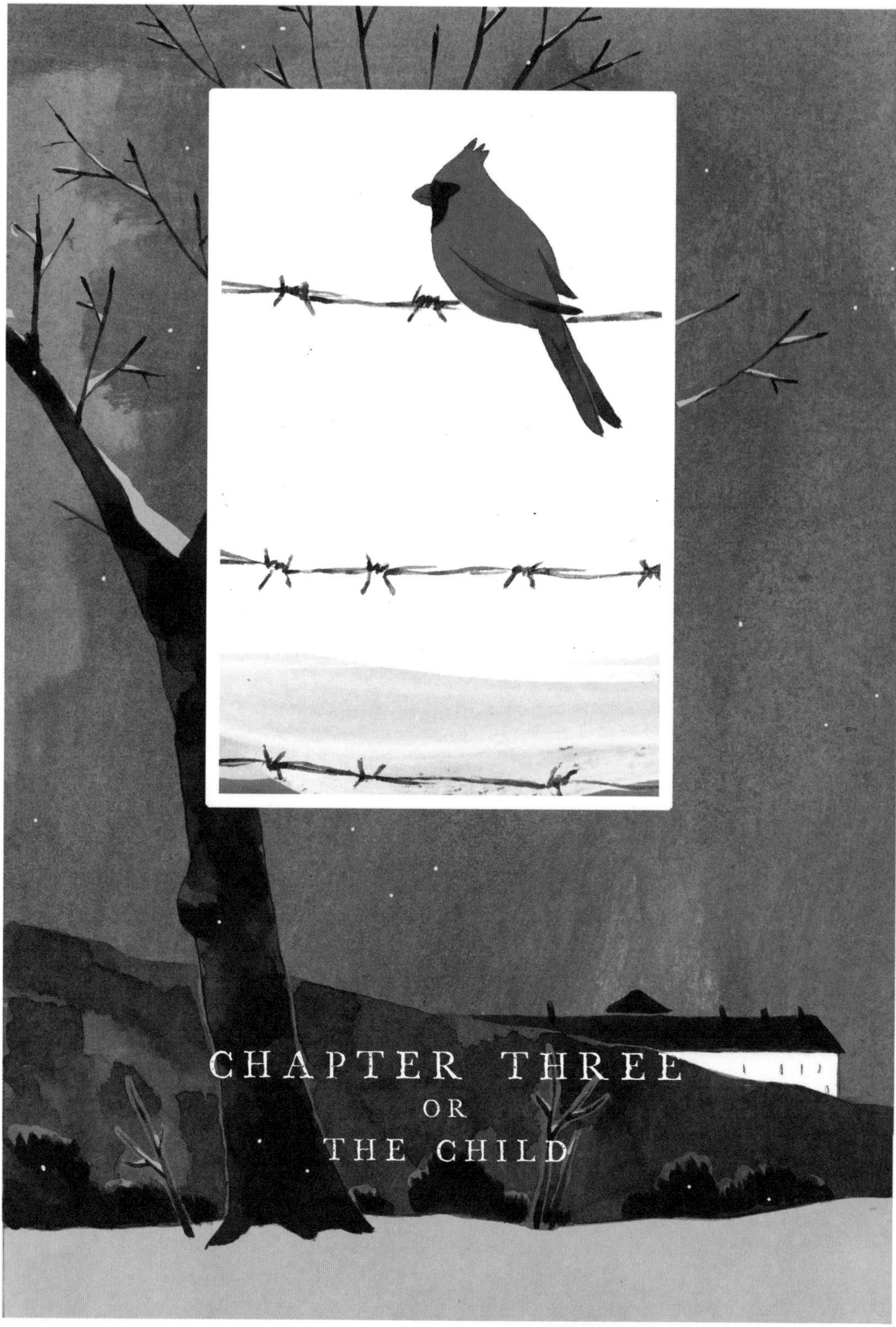

CHAPTER THREE OR THE CHILD

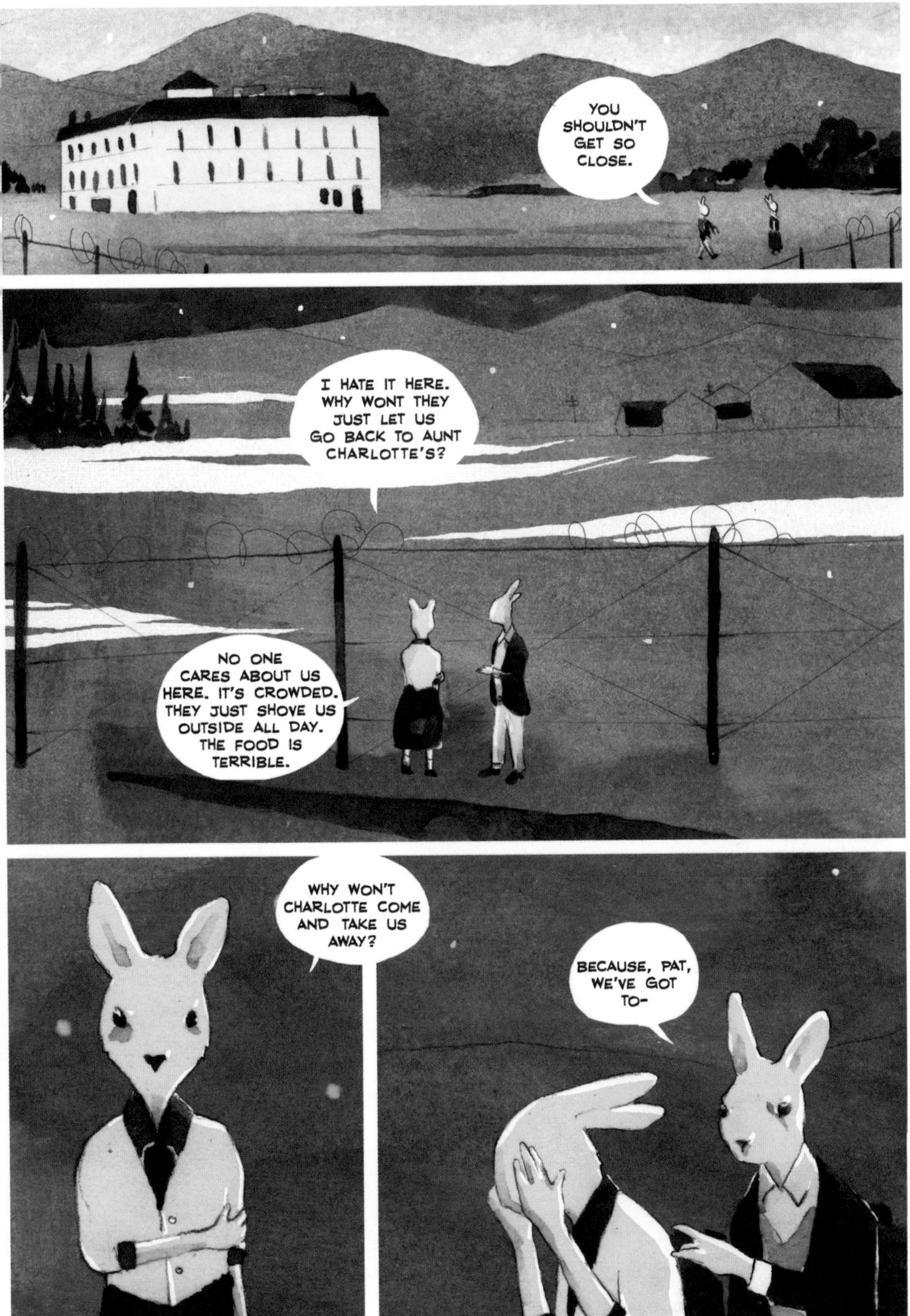
YOU SHOULDN'T GET SO CLOSE.
I HATE IT HERE. WHY WONT THEY JUST LET US GO BACK TO AUNT CHARLOTTE'S?
NO ONE CARES ABOUT US HERE. IT'S CROWDED. THEY JUST SHOVE US OUTSIDE ALL DAY. THE FOOD IS TERRIBLE.
WHY WON'T CHARLOTTE COME AND TAKE US AWAY?
BECAUSE, PAT, WE'VE GOT TO-

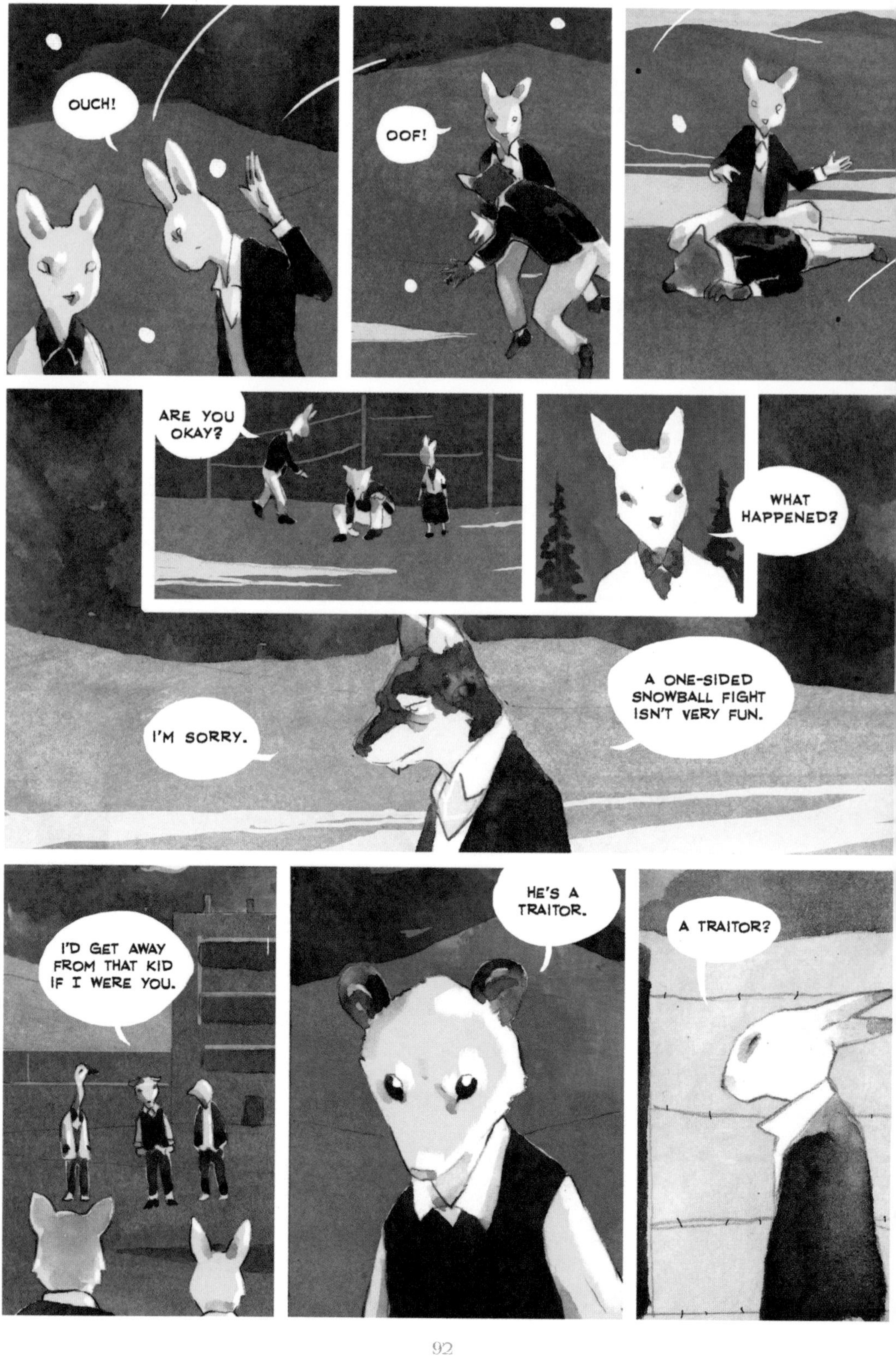
OUCH!
OOF!
ARE YOU OKAY?
WHAT HAPPENED?
I'M SORRY.
A ONE-SIDED SNOWBALL FIGHT ISN'T VERY FUN.
I'D GET AWAY FROM THAT KID IF I WERE YOU.
HE'S A TRAITOR.
A TRAITOR?

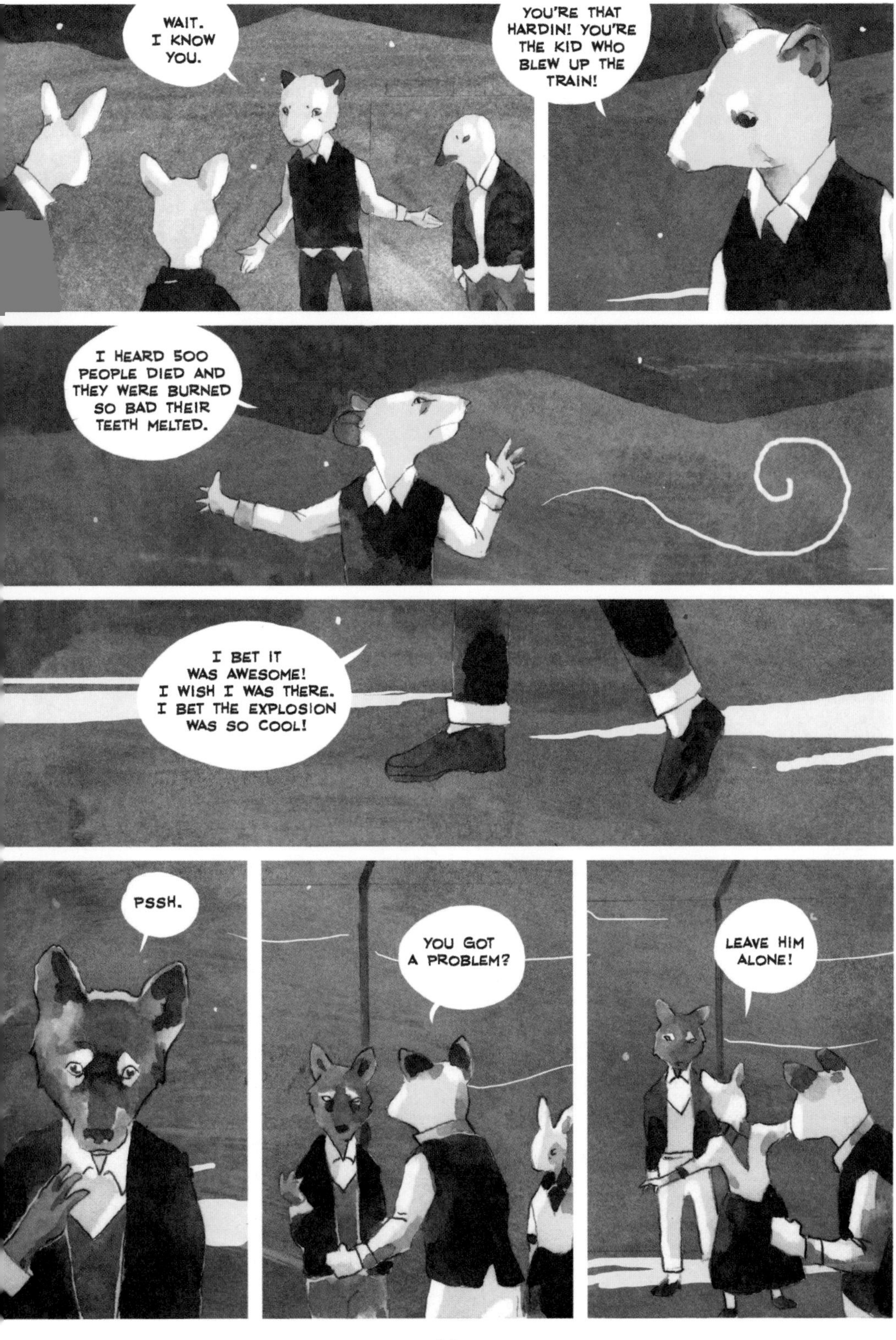
WAIT. I KNOW YOU.
YOU'RE THAT HARDIN! YOU'RE THE KID WHO BLEW UP THE TRAIN!
I HEARD 500 PEOPLE DIED AND THEY WERE BURNED SO BAD THEIR TEETH MELTED.
I BET IT WAS AWESOME! I WISH I WAS THERE. I BET THE EXPLOSION WAS SO COOL!
PSSH.
YOU GOT A PROBLEM?
LEAVE HIM ALONE!

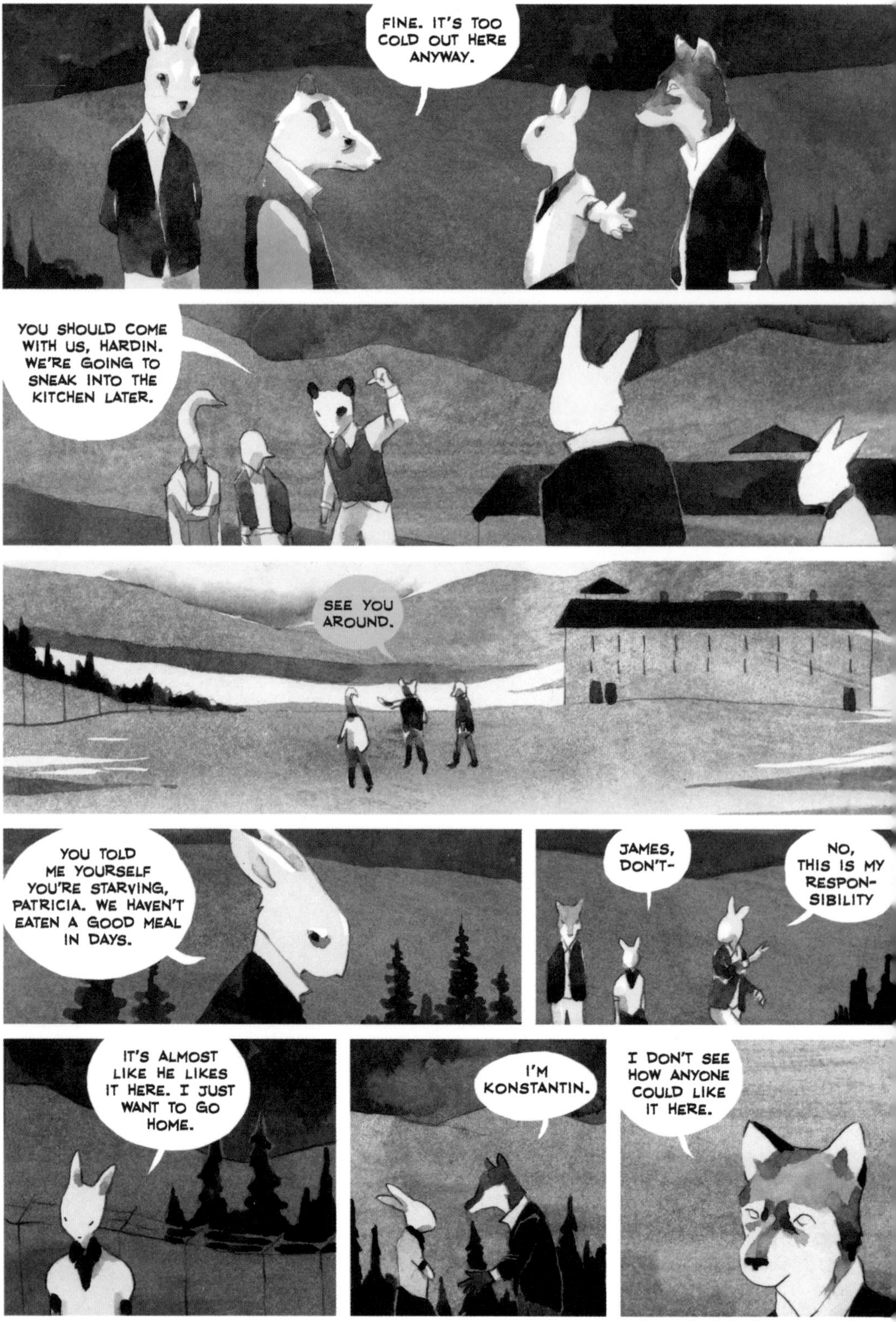
FINE. IT'S TOO COLD OUT HERE ANYWAY.
YOU SHOULD COME WITH US, HARDIN. WE'RE GOING TO SNEAK INTO THE KITCHEN LATER.
SEE YOU AROUND.
YOU TOLD ME YOURSELF YOU'RE STARVING, PATRICIA. WE HAVEN'T EATEN A GOOD MEAL IN DAYS.
JAMES, DON'T-
NO, THIS IS MY RESPON-SIBILITY
IT'S ALMOST LIKE HE LIKES IT HERE. I JUST WANT TO GO HOME.
I'M KONSTANTIN.
I DON'T SEE HOW ANYONE COULD LIKE IT HERE.

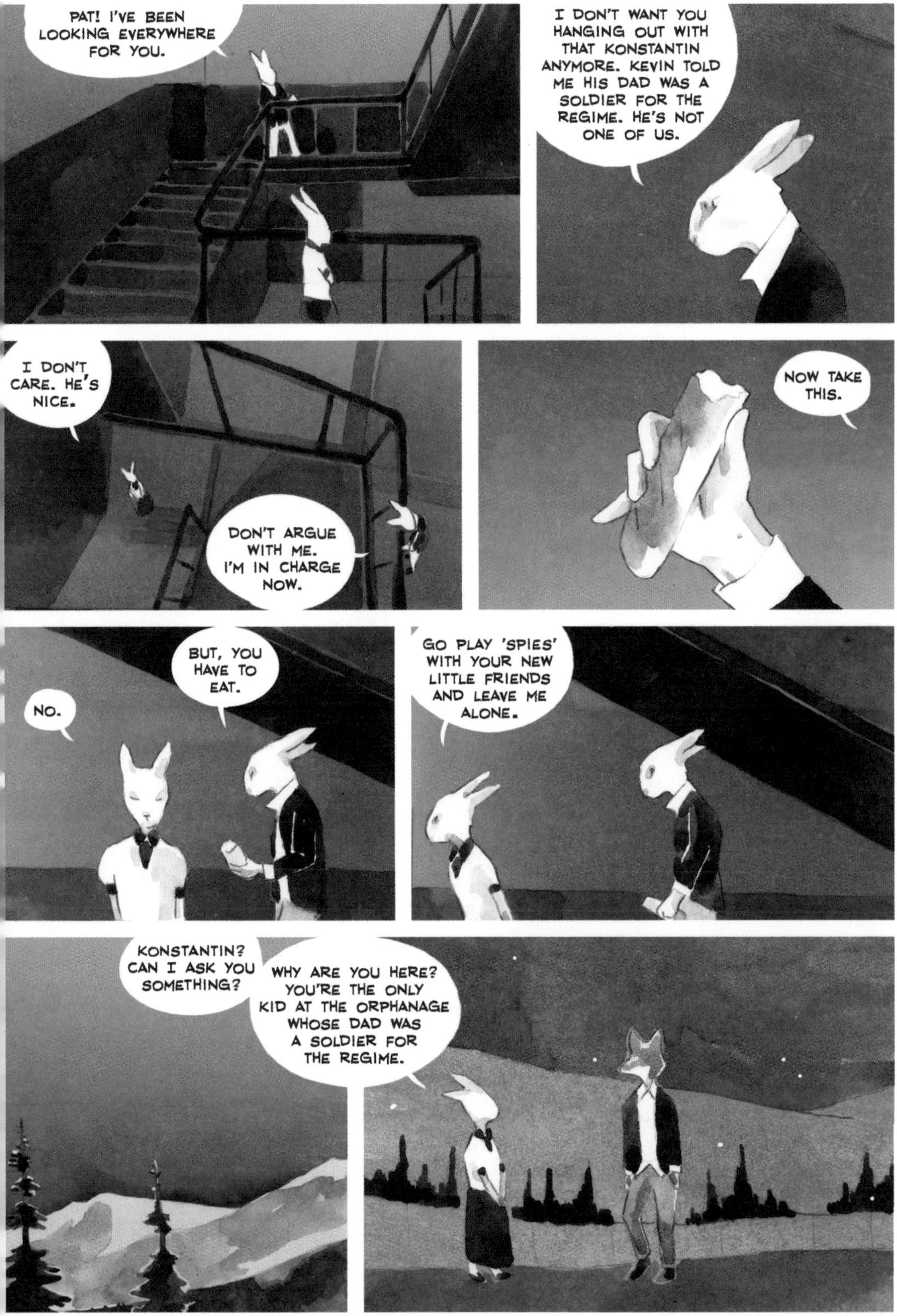
PAT! I'VE BEEN LOOKING EVERYWHERE FOR YOU.
I DON'T WANT YOU HANGING OUT WITH THAT KONSTANTIN ANYMORE. KEVIN TOLD ME HIS DAD WAS A SOLDIER FOR THE REGIME. HE'S NOT ONE OF US.
I DON'T CARE. HE'S NICE.
DON'T ARGUE WITH ME. I'M IN CHARGE NOW.
NOW TAKE THIS.
NO.
BUT, YOU HAVE TO EAT.
GO PLAY 'SPIES' WITH YOUR NEW LITTLE FRIENDS AND LEAVE ME ALONE.
KONSTANTIN? CAN I ASK YOU SOMETHING?
WHY ARE YOU HERE? YOU'RE THE ONLY KID AT THE ORPHANAGE WHOSE DAD WAS A SOLDIER FOR THE REGIME.

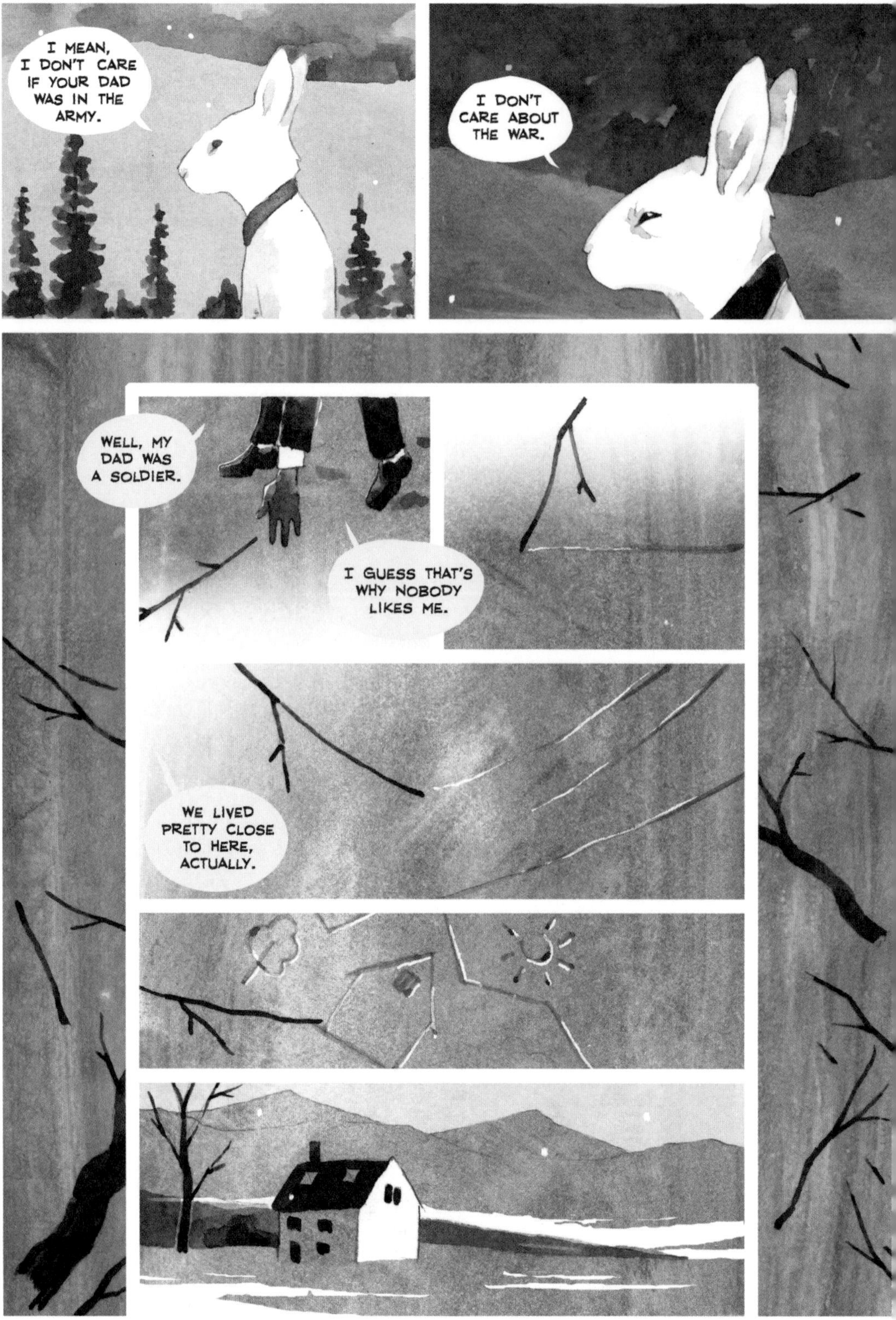
I MEAN, I DON'T CARE IF YOUR DAD WAS IN THE ARMY.
I DON'T CARE ABOUT THE WAR.
WELL, MY DAD WAS A SOLDIER.
I GUESS THAT'S WHY NOBODY LIKES ME.
WE LIVED PRETTY CLOSE TO HERE, ACTUALLY.

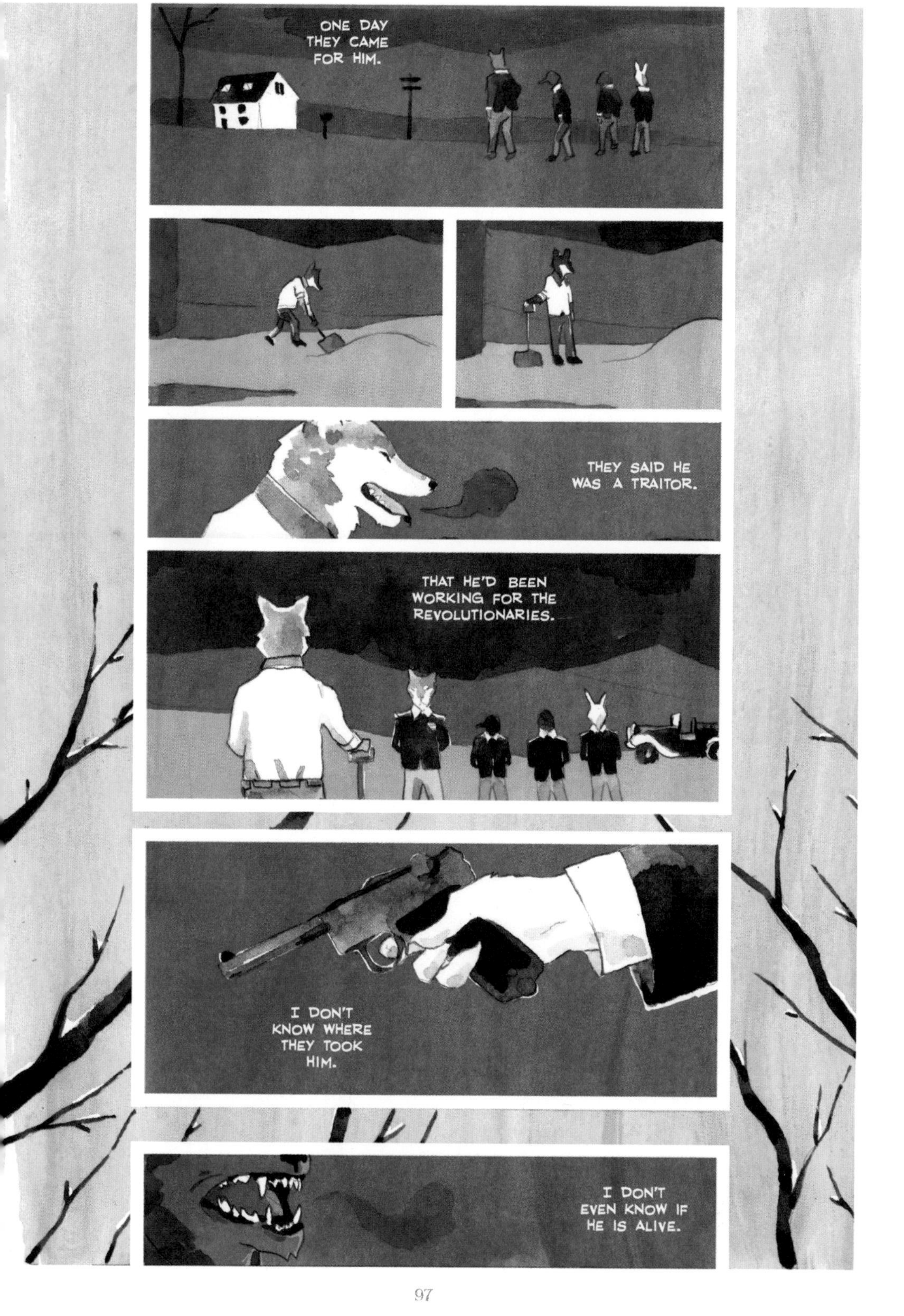
ONE DAY THEY CAME FOR HIM.
THEY SAID HE WAS A TRAITOR.
THAT HE'D BEEN WORKING FOR THE REVOLUTIONARIES.
I DON'T KNOW WHERE THEY TOOK HIM.
I DON'T EVEN KNOW IF HE IS ALIVE.

AND SO I ENDED UP HERE. I DIDN'T HAVE ANY OTHER FAMILY.

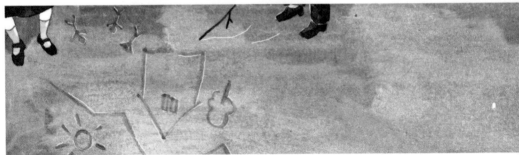

WELL, MY DAD IS DEAD. SO IS MY MOM.

BUT I HAVE AN AUNT, AND SHE'S REALLY NICE.

I WISH I COULD GO BACK THERE.

YOU REALLY WANT TO LEAVE?

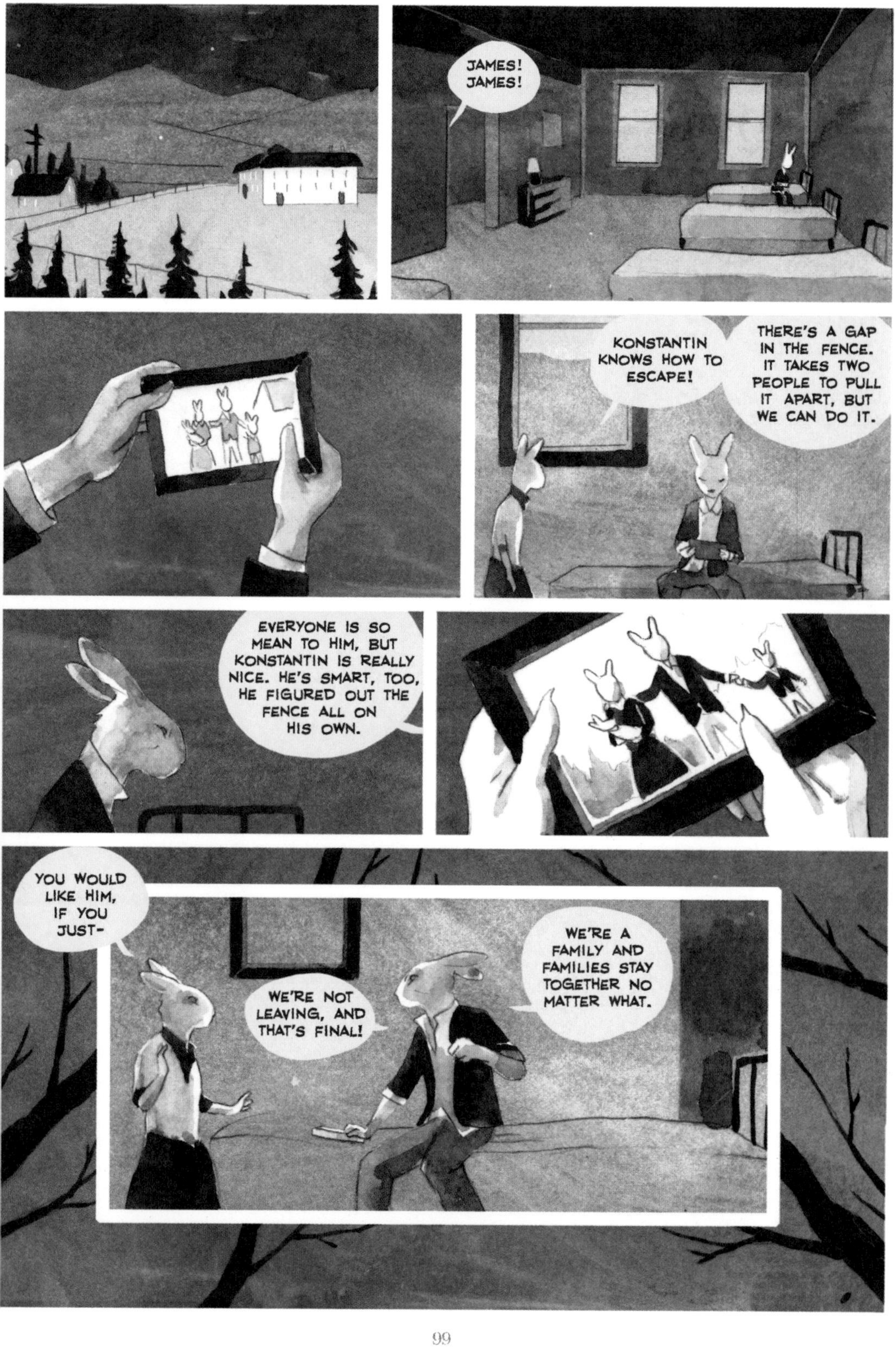
JAMES!
JAMES!
KONSTANTIN KNOWS HOW TO ESCAPE!
THERE'S A GAP IN THE FENCE. IT TAKES TWO PEOPLE TO PULL IT APART, BUT WE CAN DO IT.
EVERYONE IS SO MEAN TO HIM, BUT KONSTANTIN IS REALLY NICE. HE'S SMART, TOO, HE FIGURED OUT THE FENCE ALL ON HIS OWN.
YOU WOULD LIKE HIM, IF YOU JUST-
WE'RE NOT LEAVING, AND THAT'S FINAL!
WE'RE A FAMILY AND FAMILIES STAY TOGETHER NO MATTER WHAT.

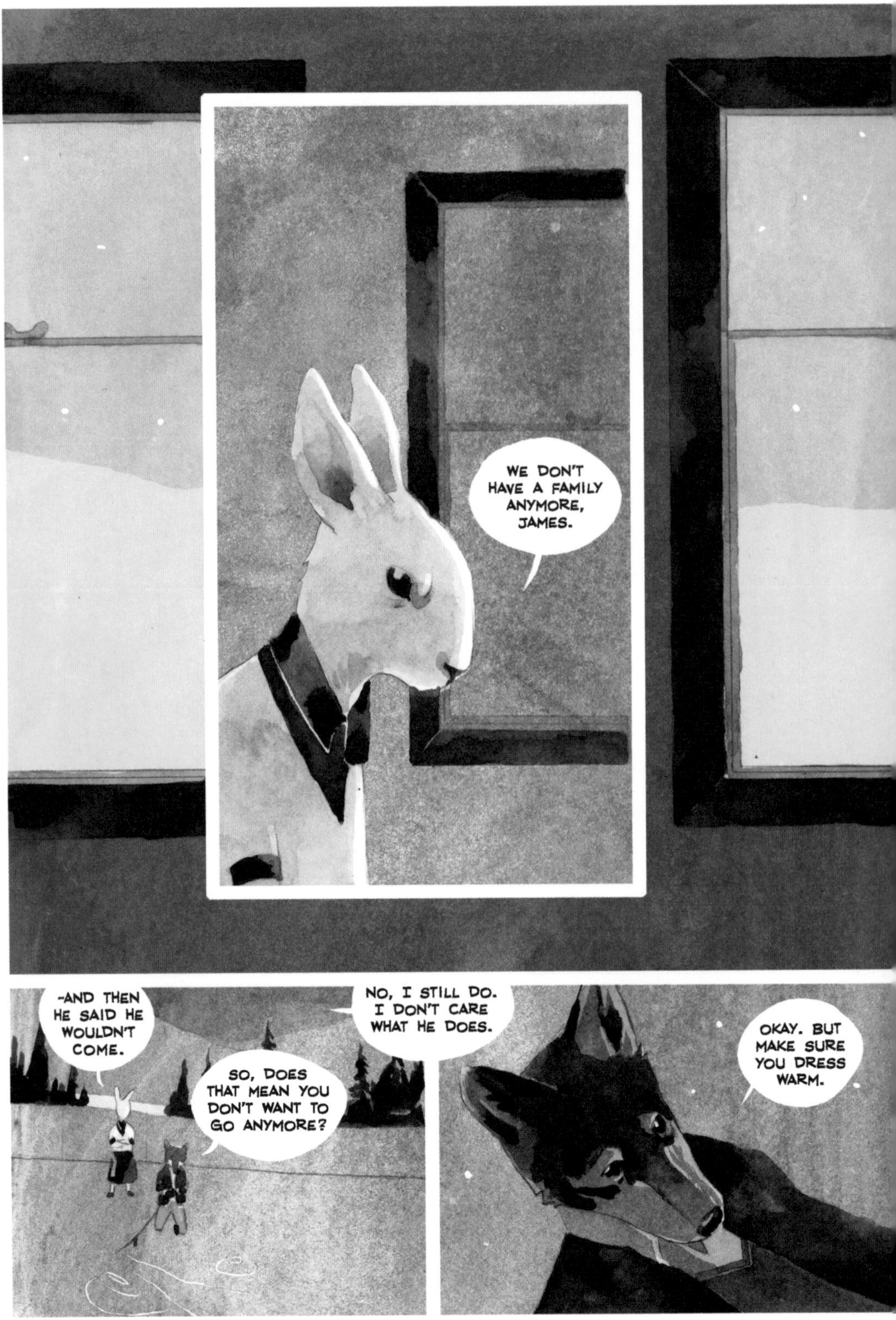

WE DON'T HAVE A FAMILY ANYMORE, JAMES.
-AND THEN HE SAID HE WOULDN'T COME.
SO, DOES THAT MEAN YOU DON'T WANT TO GO ANYMORE?
NO, I STILL DO. I DON'T CARE WHAT HE DOES.
OKAY. BUT MAKE SURE YOU DRESS WARM.

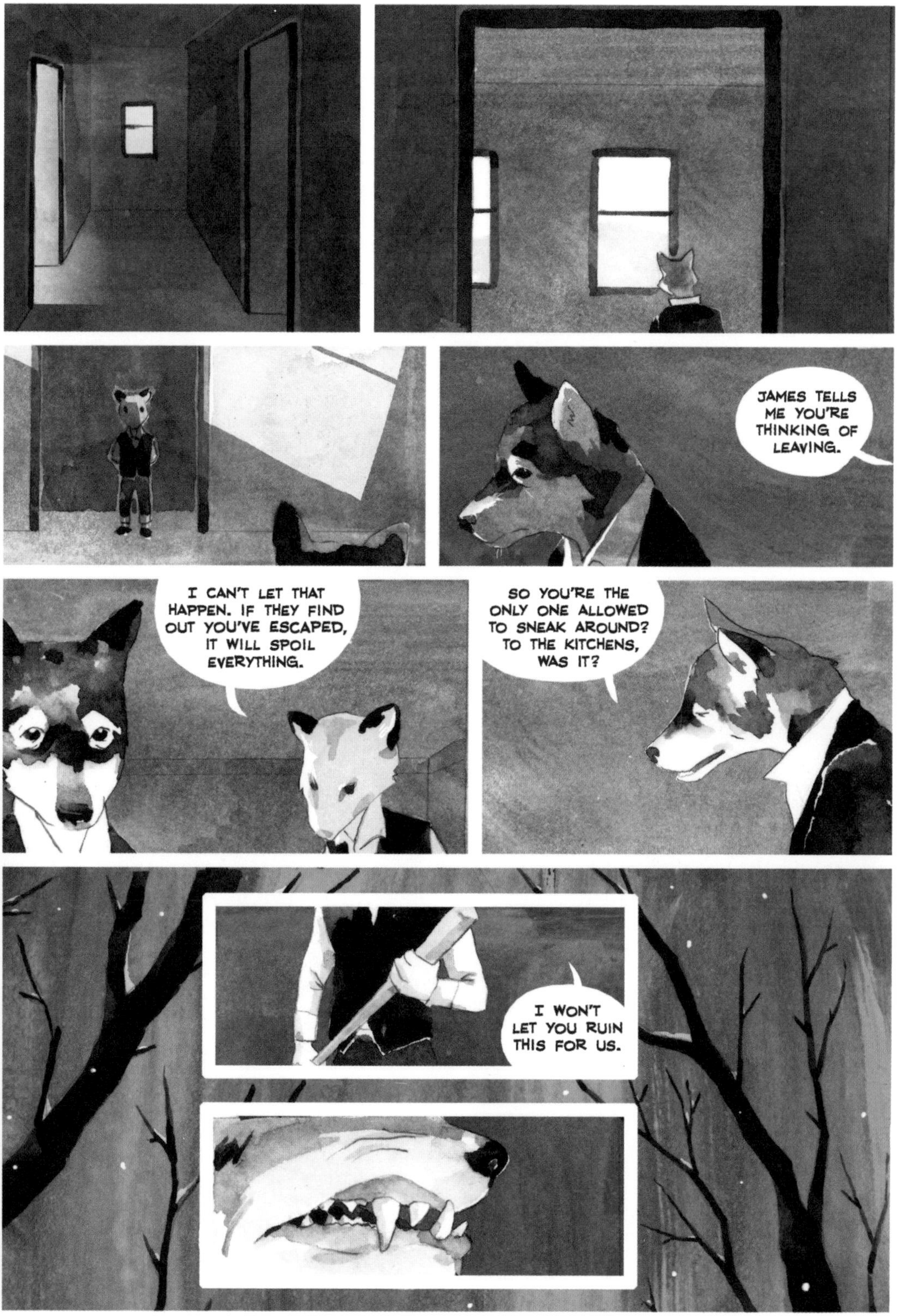
JAMES TELLS ME YOU'RE THINKING OF LEAVING.
I CAN'T LET THAT HAPPEN. IF THEY FIND OUT YOU'VE ESCAPED, IT WILL SPOIL EVERYTHING.
SO YOU'RE THE ONLY ONE ALLOWED TO SNEAK AROUND? TO THE KITCHENS, WAS IT?
I WON'T LET YOU RUIN THIS FOR US.

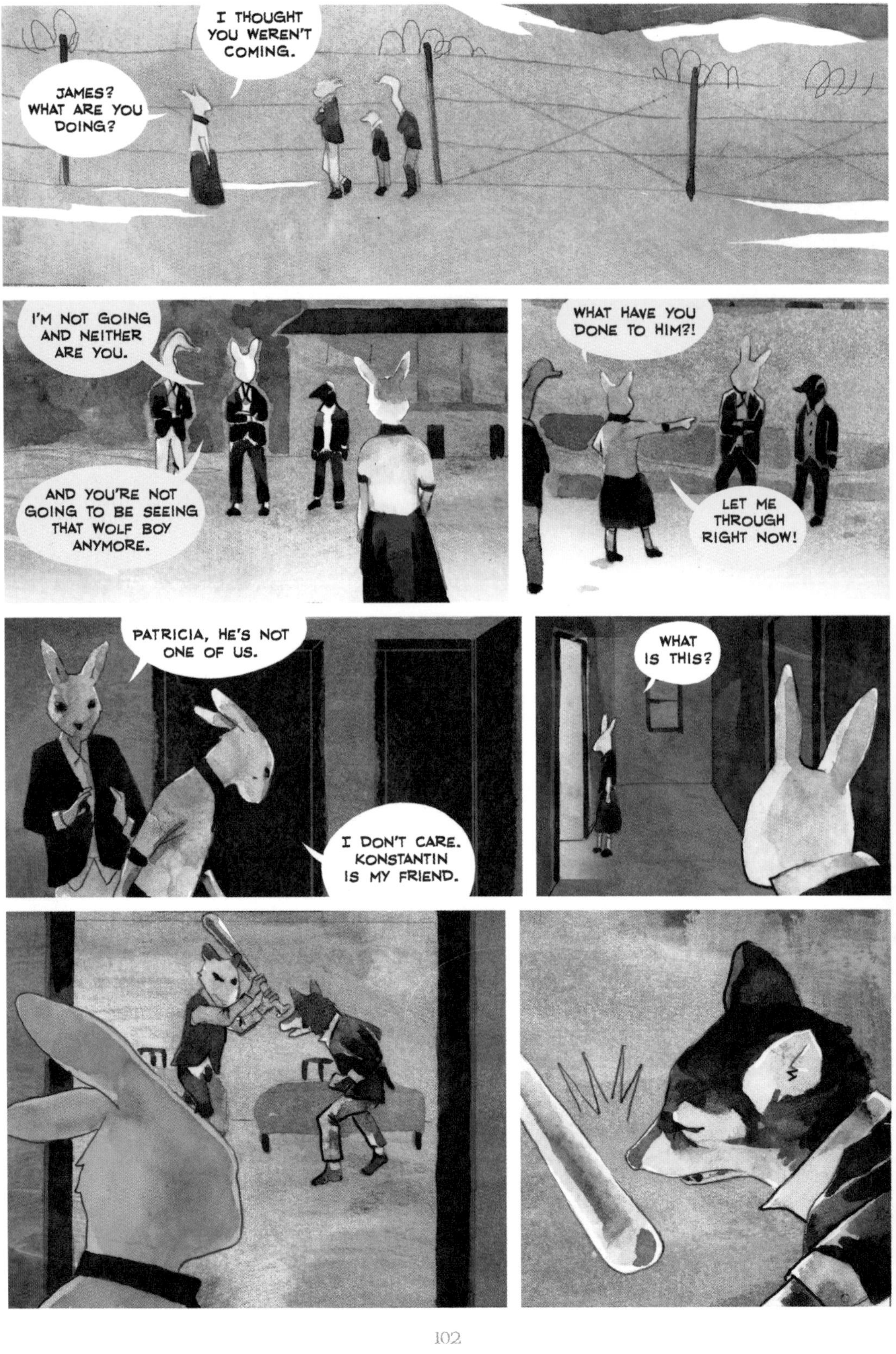
JAMES? WHAT ARE YOU DOING?
I THOUGHT YOU WEREN'T COMING.
I'M NOT GOING AND NEITHER ARE YOU.
AND YOU'RE NOT GOING TO BE SEEING THAT WOLF BOY ANYMORE.
WHAT HAVE YOU DONE TO HIM?!
LET ME THROUGH RIGHT NOW!
PATRICIA, HE'S NOT ONE OF US.
I DON'T CARE. KONSTANTIN IS MY FRIEND.
WHAT IS THIS?

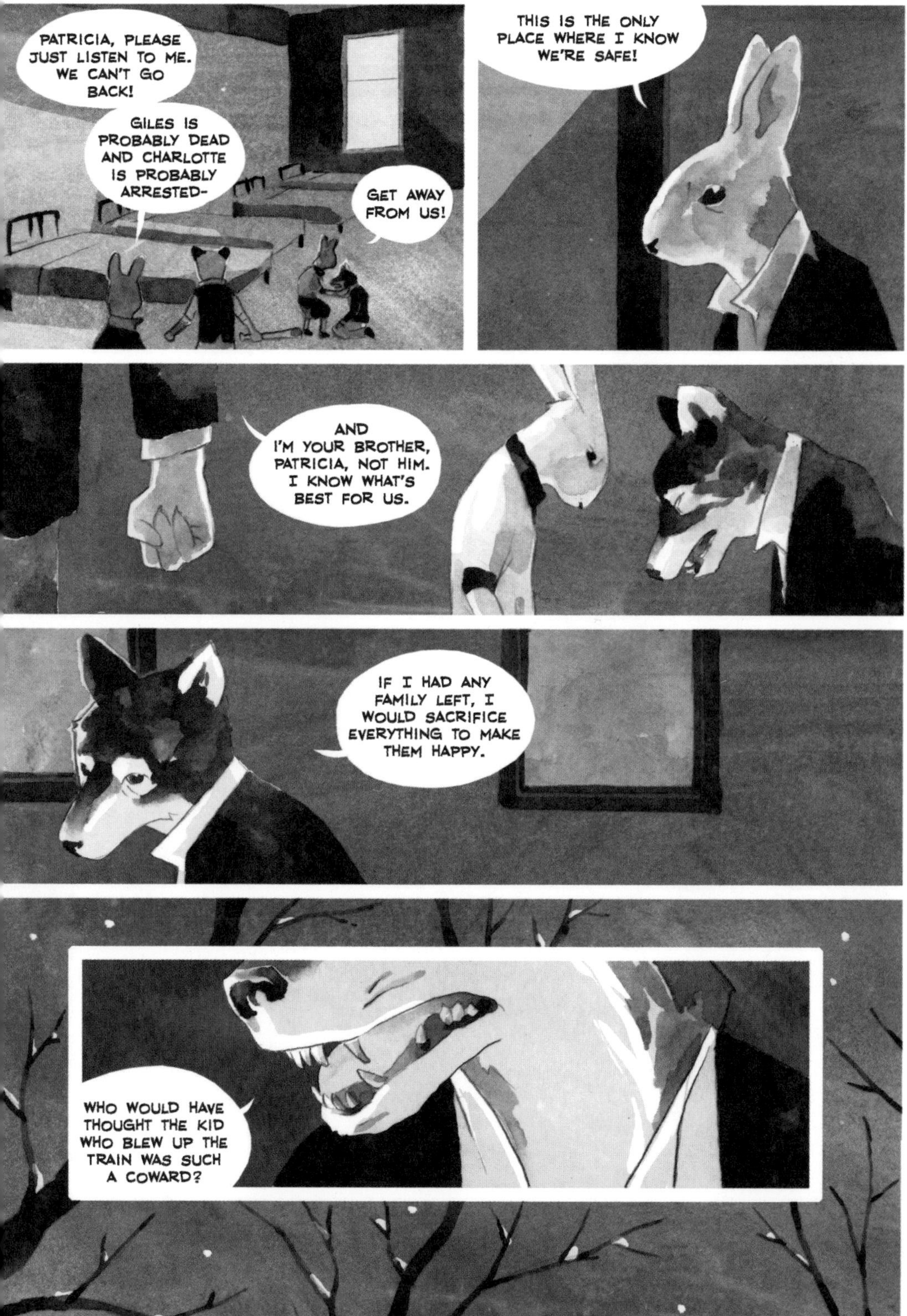
PATRICIA, PLEASE JUST LISTEN TO ME. WE CAN'T GO BACK!
GILES IS PROBABLY DEAD AND CHARLOTTE IS PROBABLY ARRESTED-
GET AWAY FROM US!
THIS IS THE ONLY PLACE WHERE I KNOW WE'RE SAFE!
AND I'M YOUR BROTHER, PATRICIA, NOT HIM. I KNOW WHAT'S BEST FOR US.
IF I HAD ANY FAMILY LEFT, I WOULD SACRIFICE EVERYTHING TO MAKE THEM HAPPY.
WHO WOULD HAVE THOUGHT THE KID WHO BLEW UP THE TRAIN WAS SUCH A COWARD?

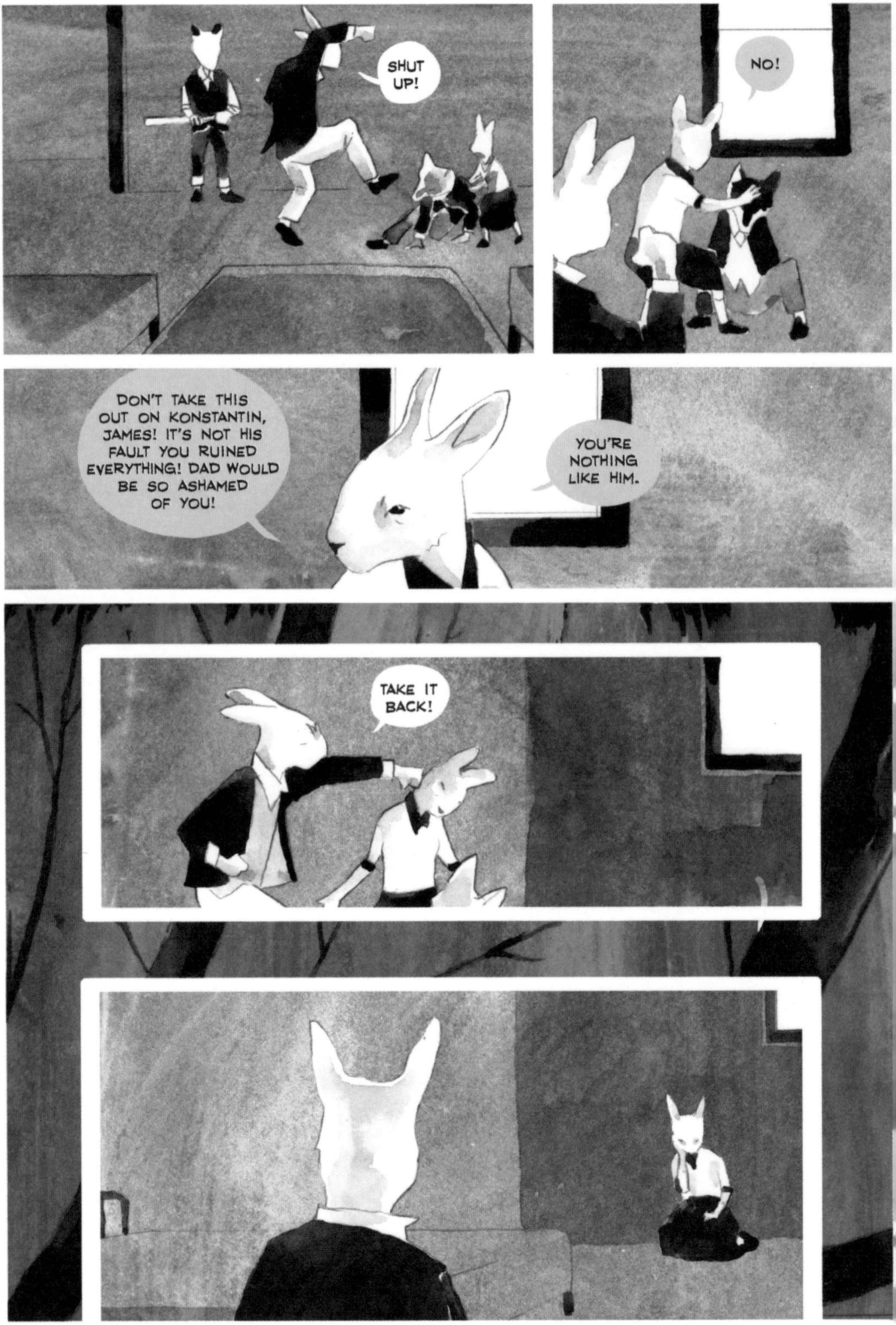
SHUT UP!
NO!
DON'T TAKE THIS OUT ON KONSTANTIN, JAMES! IT'S NOT HIS FAULT YOU RUINED EVERYTHING! DAD WOULD BE SO ASHAMED OF YOU!
YOU'RE NOTHING LIKE HIM.
TAKE IT BACK!

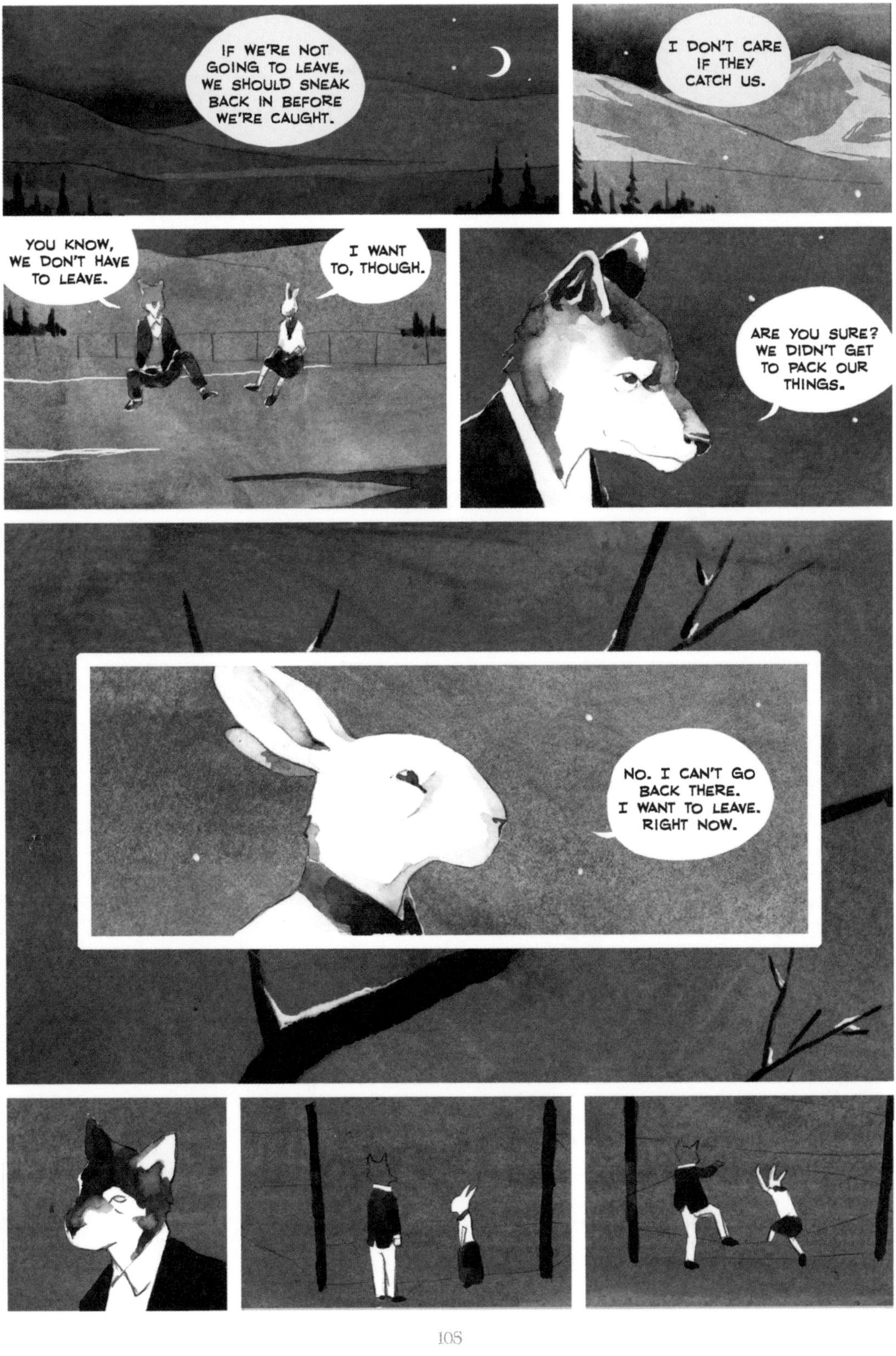
IF WE'RE NOT GOING TO LEAVE, WE SHOULD SNEAK BACK IN BEFORE WE'RE CAUGHT.
I DON'T CARE IF THEY CATCH US.
YOU KNOW, WE DON'T HAVE TO LEAVE.
I WANT TO, THOUGH.
ARE YOU SURE? WE DIDN'T GET TO PACK OUR THINGS.
NO. I CAN'T GO BACK THERE. I WANT TO LEAVE. RIGHT NOW.

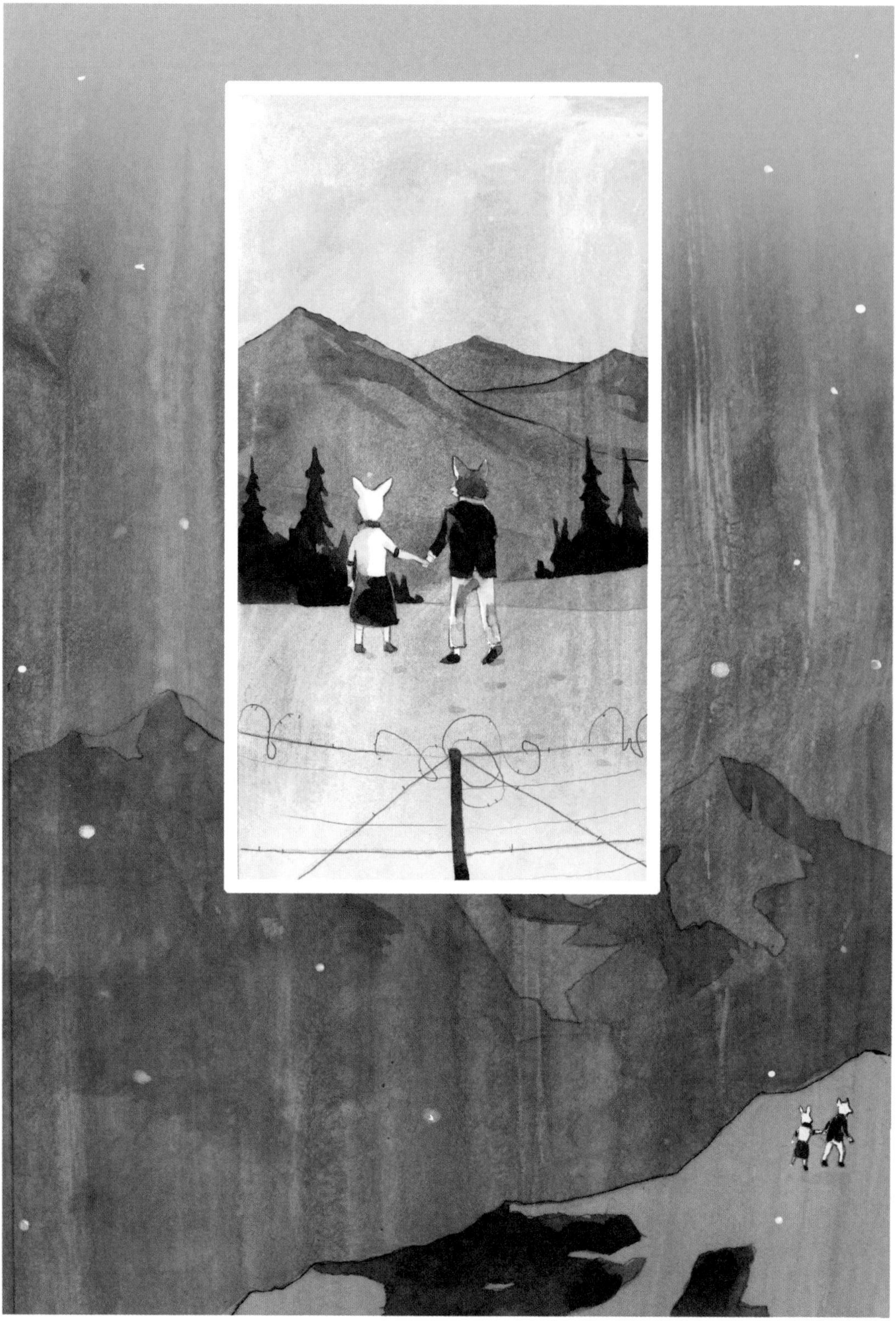

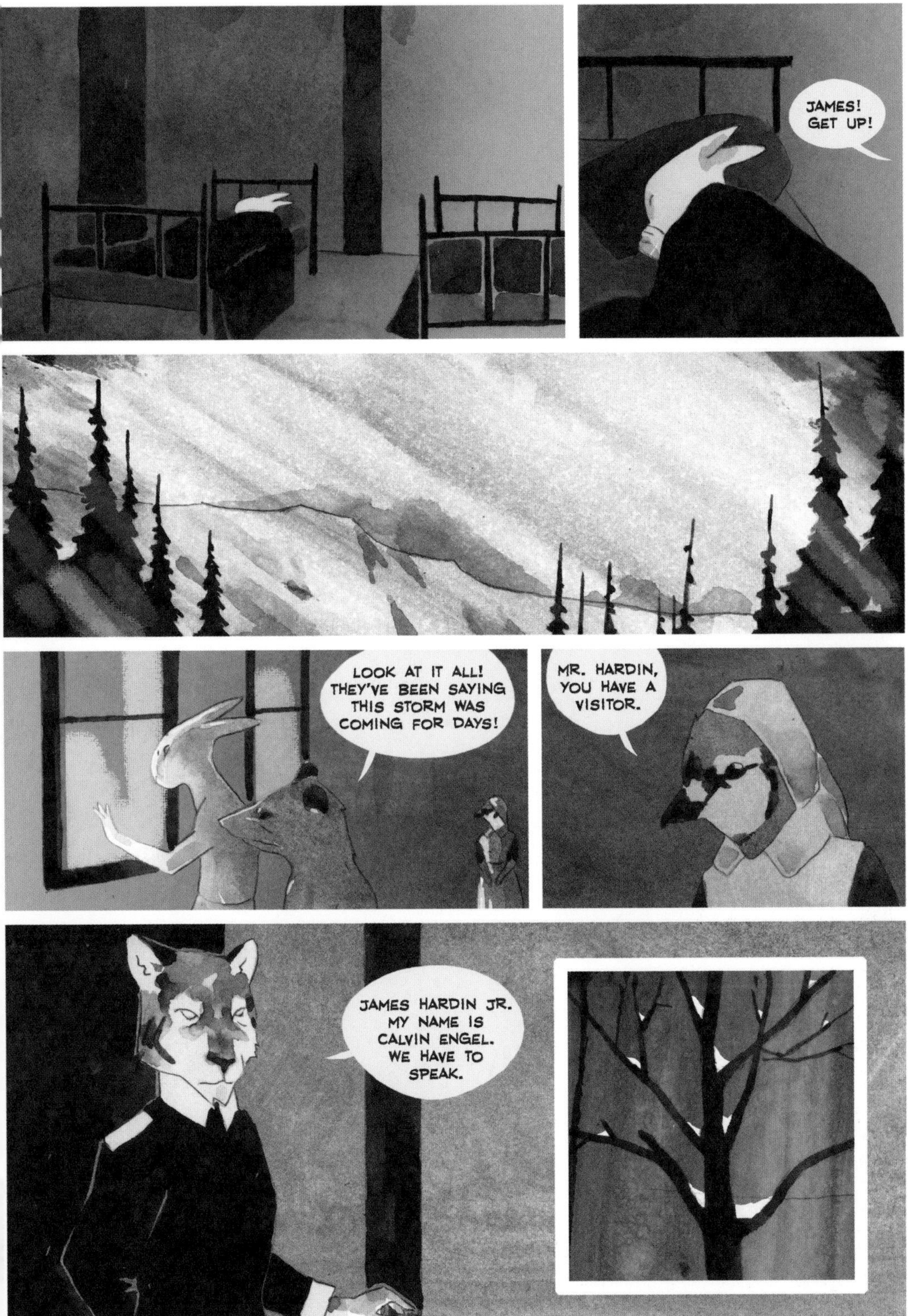
JAMES! GET UP!
LOOK AT IT ALL! THEY'VE BEEN SAYING THIS STORM WAS COMING FOR DAYS!
MR. HARDIN, YOU HAVE A VISITOR.
JAMES HARDIN JR. MY NAME IS CALVIN ENGEL. WE HAVE TO SPEAK.

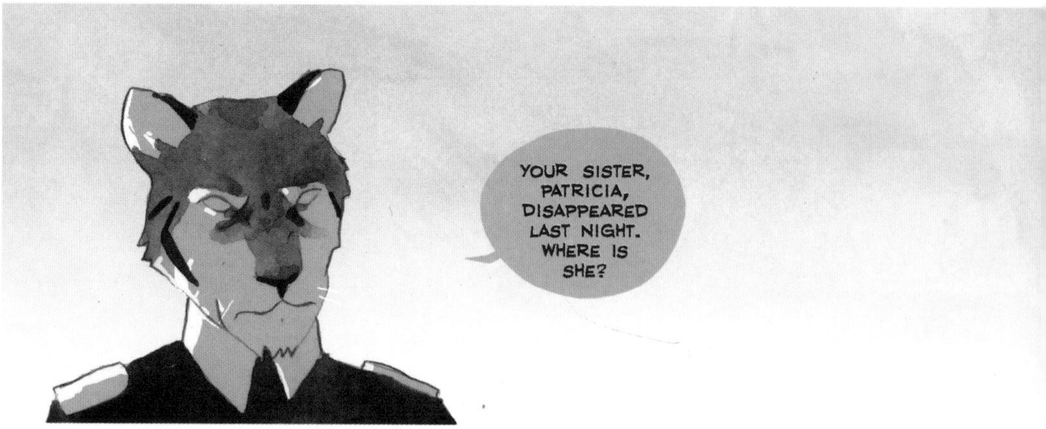
YOUR SISTER, PATRICIA, DISAPPEARED LAST NIGHT. WHERE IS SHE?

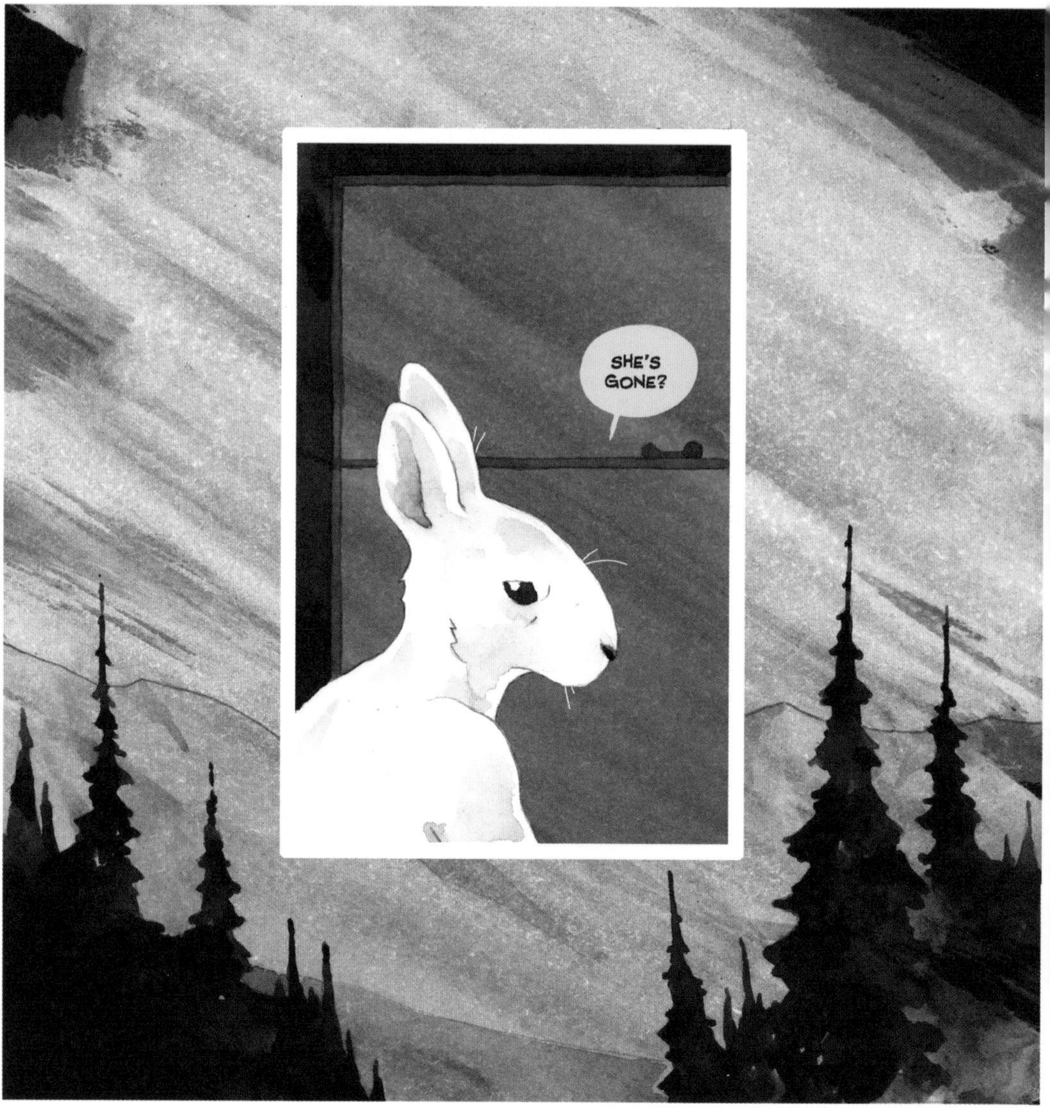
SHE'S GONE?

Daddy,

I hope you come home soon I miss you very much. Mom reads all of your letters and I am always so happy when you say my name. I say a prayer for you every night. Please come home soon!

xoxo

Patricia Kandin

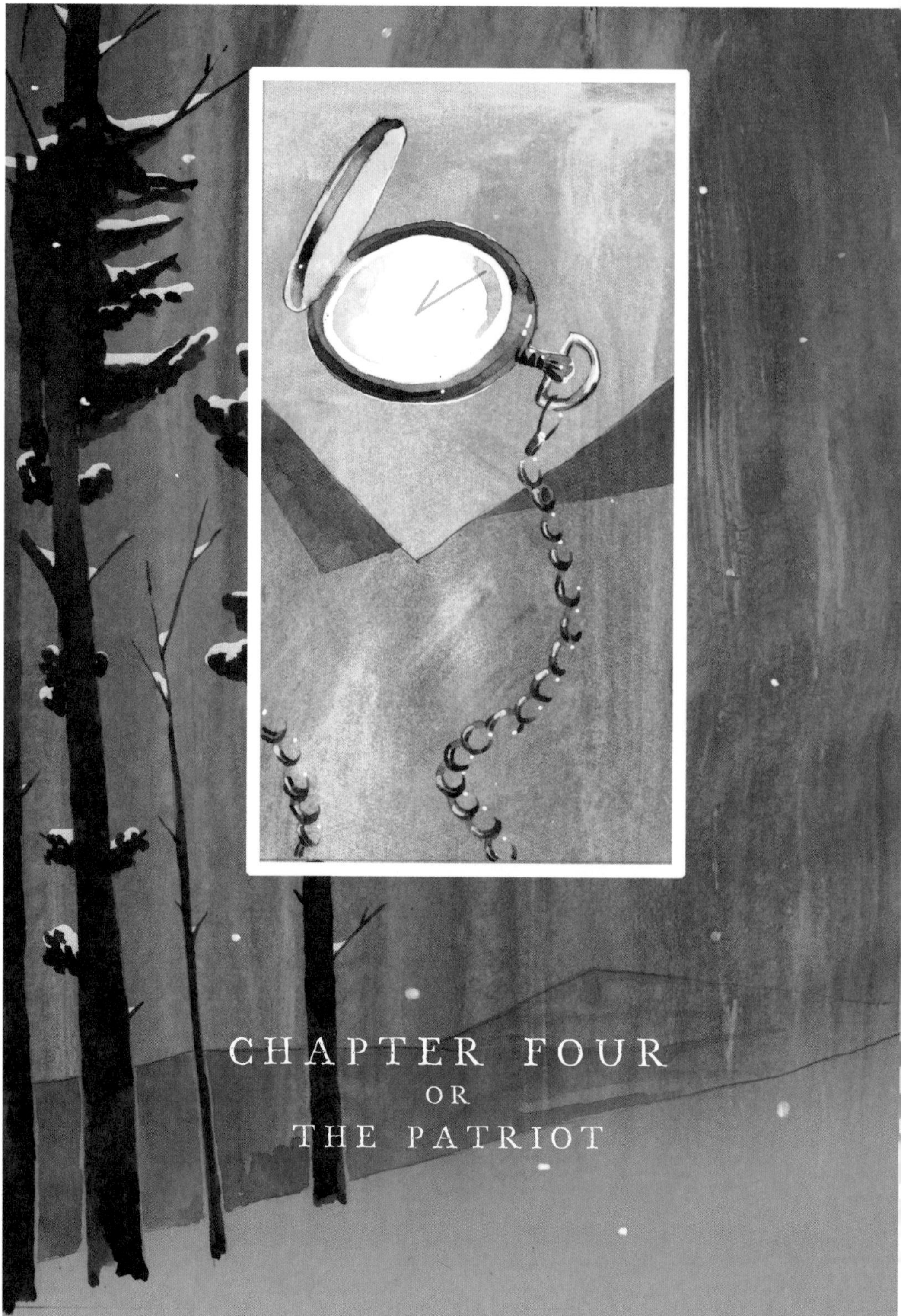

CHAPTER FOUR
OR
THE PATRIOT

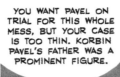

THEY ARE LOOKING AT US, ENGEL. THE TRAIN BOMBING HAS BEEN A HUGE EMBARRASSMENT.

GETTLEMAN WANTS HIS INVOLVEMENT MINIMIZED.

YOU WANT PAVEL ON TRIAL FOR THIS WHOLE MESS, BUT YOUR CASE IS TOO THIN. KORBIN PAVEL'S FATHER WAS A PROMINENT FIGURE.

YOUR WORD ALONE WON'T BE ENOUGH TO CONVINCE GETTLEMAN TO CHARGE HIM.

THIS WAS THE WORST ATTACK SINCE THE WAR ENDED. IT IS A SEVERE ACCUSATION.

BUT I PROMISE YOU, I WILL NOT SUFFER FOR PAVEL'S INCOMPETENCE. OR YOURS.

I KNOW I CAN DO THIS, SIR. I JUST NEED TIME.

YOU WEREN'T THERE, YOU DIDN'T SEE HOW PAVEL REACTED AT THE HOUSE. HE IS HIDING SOMETHING.

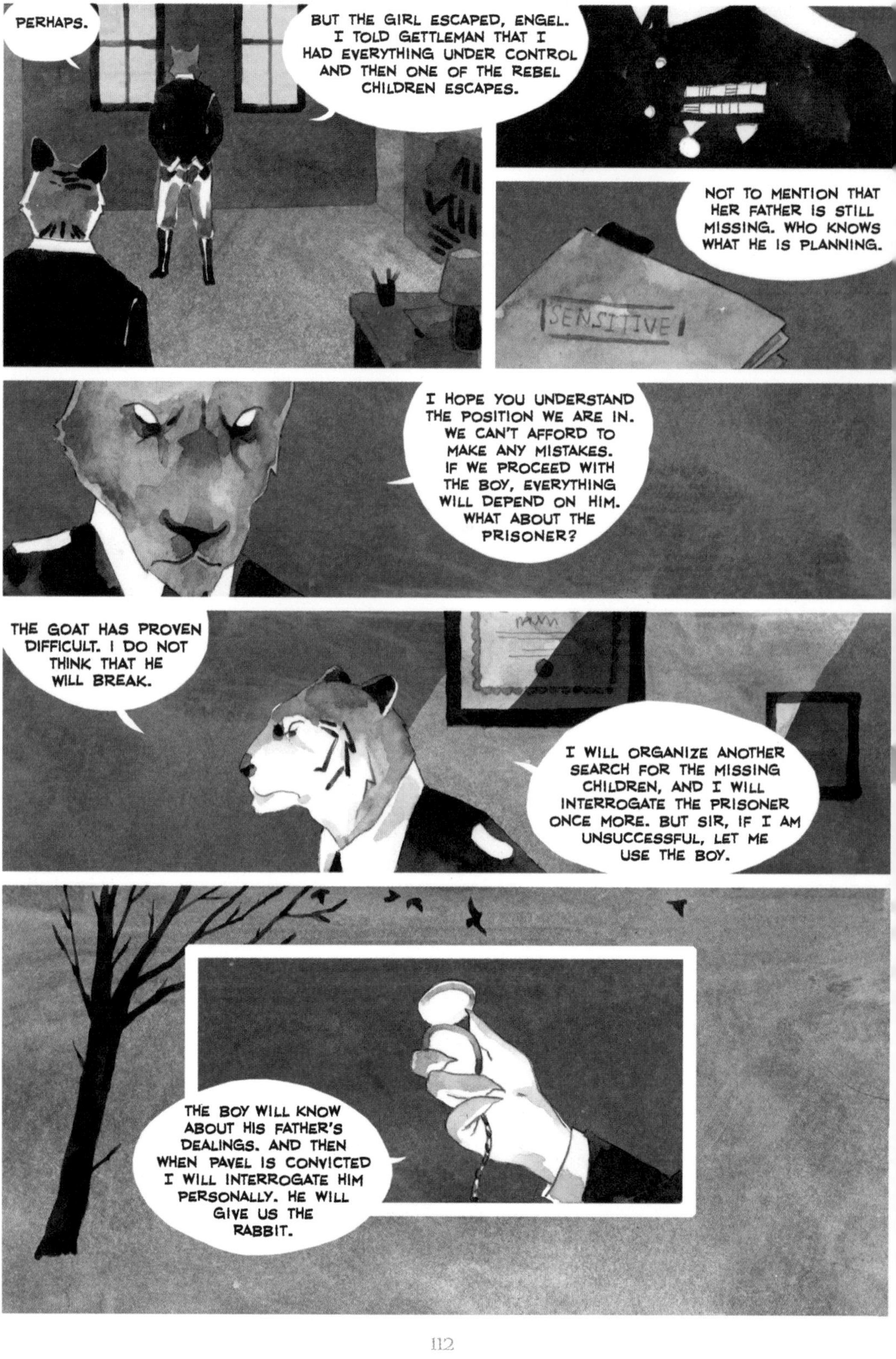
PERHAPS.
BUT THE GIRL ESCAPED, ENGEL. I TOLD GETTLEMAN THAT I HAD EVERYTHING UNDER CONTROL AND THEN ONE OF THE REBEL CHILDREN ESCAPES.
NOT TO MENTION THAT HER FATHER IS STILL MISSING. WHO KNOWS WHAT HE IS PLANNING.
SENSITIVE
I HOPE YOU UNDERSTAND THE POSITION WE ARE IN. WE CAN'T AFFORD TO MAKE ANY MISTAKES. IF WE PROCEED WITH THE BOY, EVERYTHING WILL DEPEND ON HIM. WHAT ABOUT THE PRISONER?
THE GOAT HAS PROVEN DIFFICULT. I DO NOT THINK THAT HE WILL BREAK.
I WILL ORGANIZE ANOTHER SEARCH FOR THE MISSING CHILDREN, AND I WILL INTERROGATE THE PRISONER ONCE MORE. BUT SIR, IF I AM UNSUCCESSFUL, LET ME USE THE BOY.
THE BOY WILL KNOW ABOUT HIS FATHER'S DEALINGS. AND THEN WHEN PAVEL IS CONVICTED I WILL INTERROGATE HIM PERSONALLY. HE WILL GIVE US THE RABBIT.

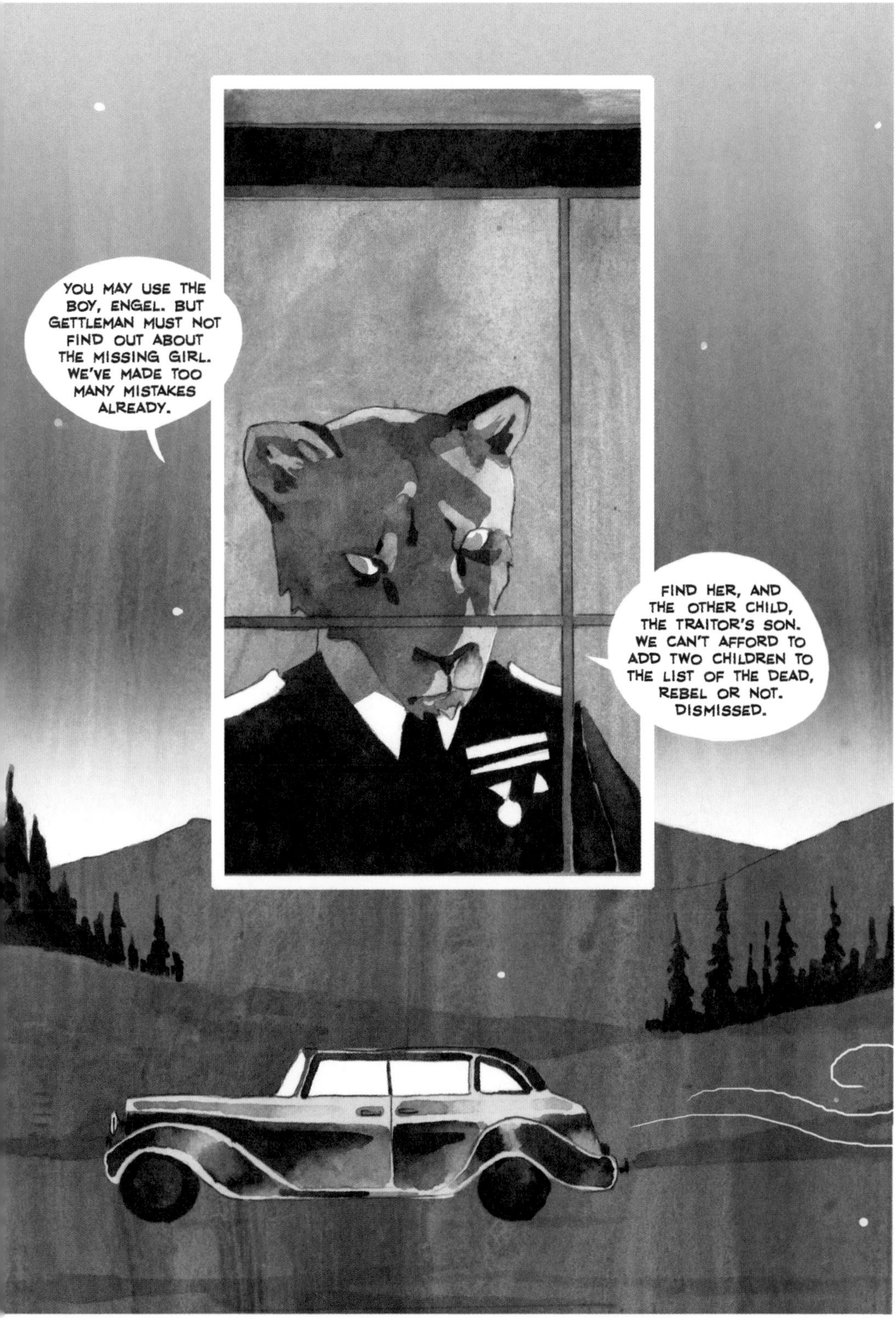
YOU MAY USE THE BOY, ENGEL. BUT GETTLEMAN MUST NOT FIND OUT ABOUT THE MISSING GIRL. WE'VE MADE TOO MANY MISTAKES ALREADY.
FIND HER, AND THE OTHER CHILD, THE TRAITOR'S SON. WE CAN'T AFFORD TO ADD TWO CHILDREN TO THE LIST OF THE DEAD, REBEL OR NOT. DISMISSED.

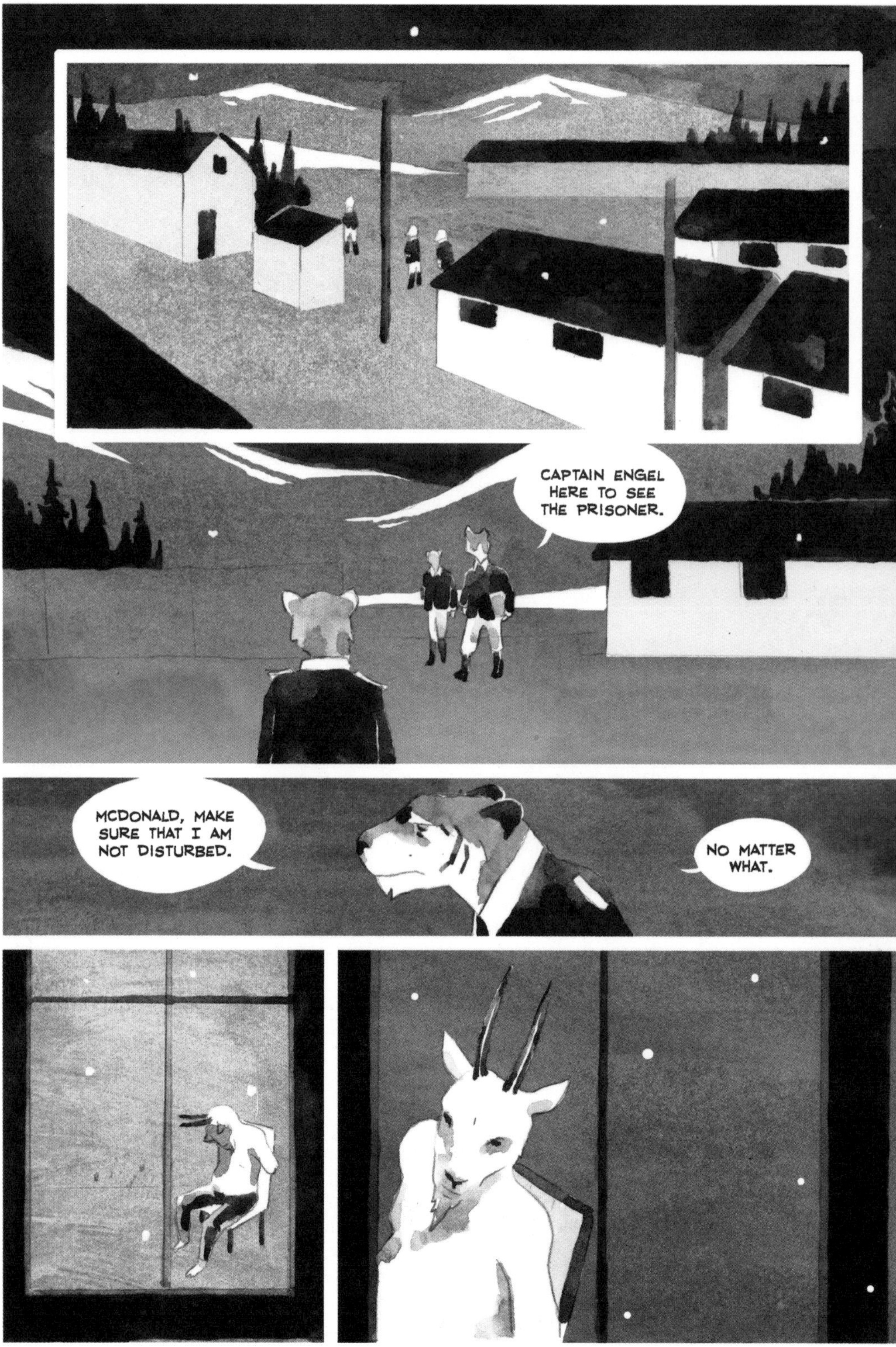
CAPTAIN ENGEL HERE TO SEE THE PRISONER.
MCDONALD, MAKE SURE THAT I AM NOT DISTURBED.
NO MATTER WHAT.

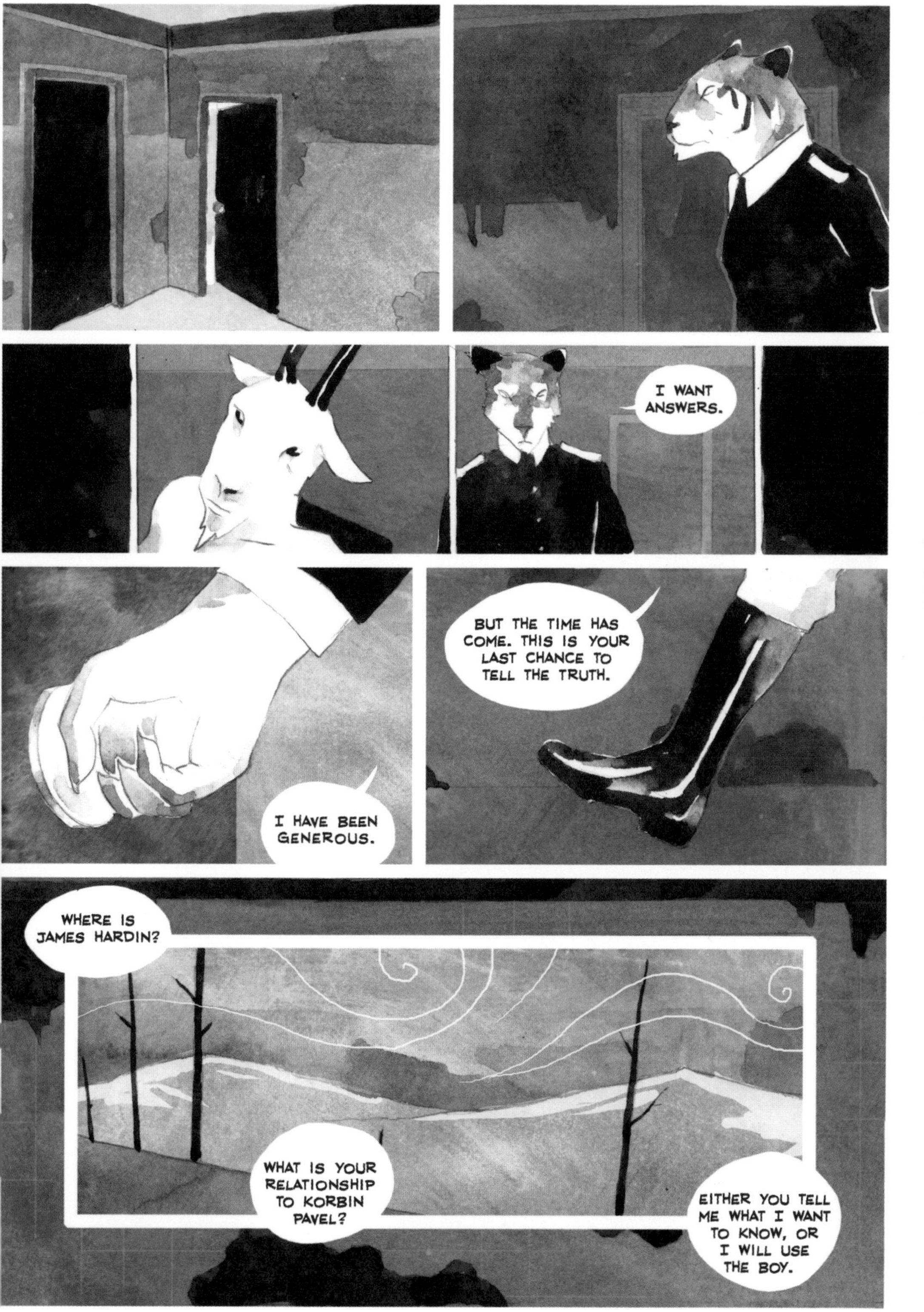
I WANT ANSWERS.
I HAVE BEEN GENEROUS.
BUT THE TIME HAS COME. THIS IS YOUR LAST CHANCE TO TELL THE TRUTH.
WHERE IS JAMES HARDIN?
WHAT IS YOUR RELATIONSHIP TO KORBIN PAVEL?
EITHER YOU TELL ME WHAT I WANT TO KNOW, OR I WILL USE THE BOY.

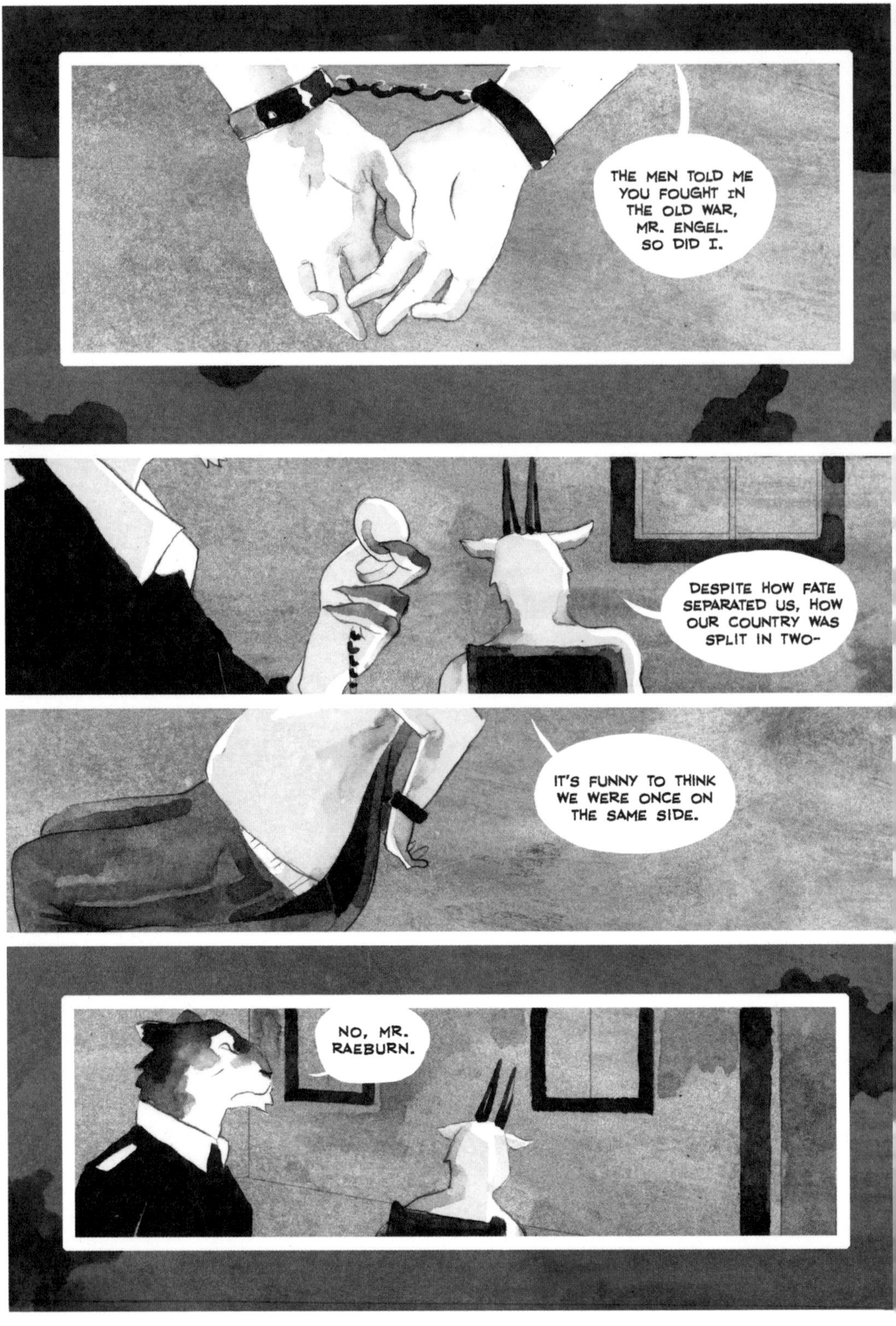
THE MEN TOLD ME YOU FOUGHT IN THE OLD WAR, MR. ENGEL. SO DID I.
DESPITE HOW FATE SEPARATED US, HOW OUR COUNTRY WAS SPLIT IN TWO-
IT'S FUNNY TO THINK WE WERE ONCE ON THE SAME SIDE.
NO, MR. RAEBURN.

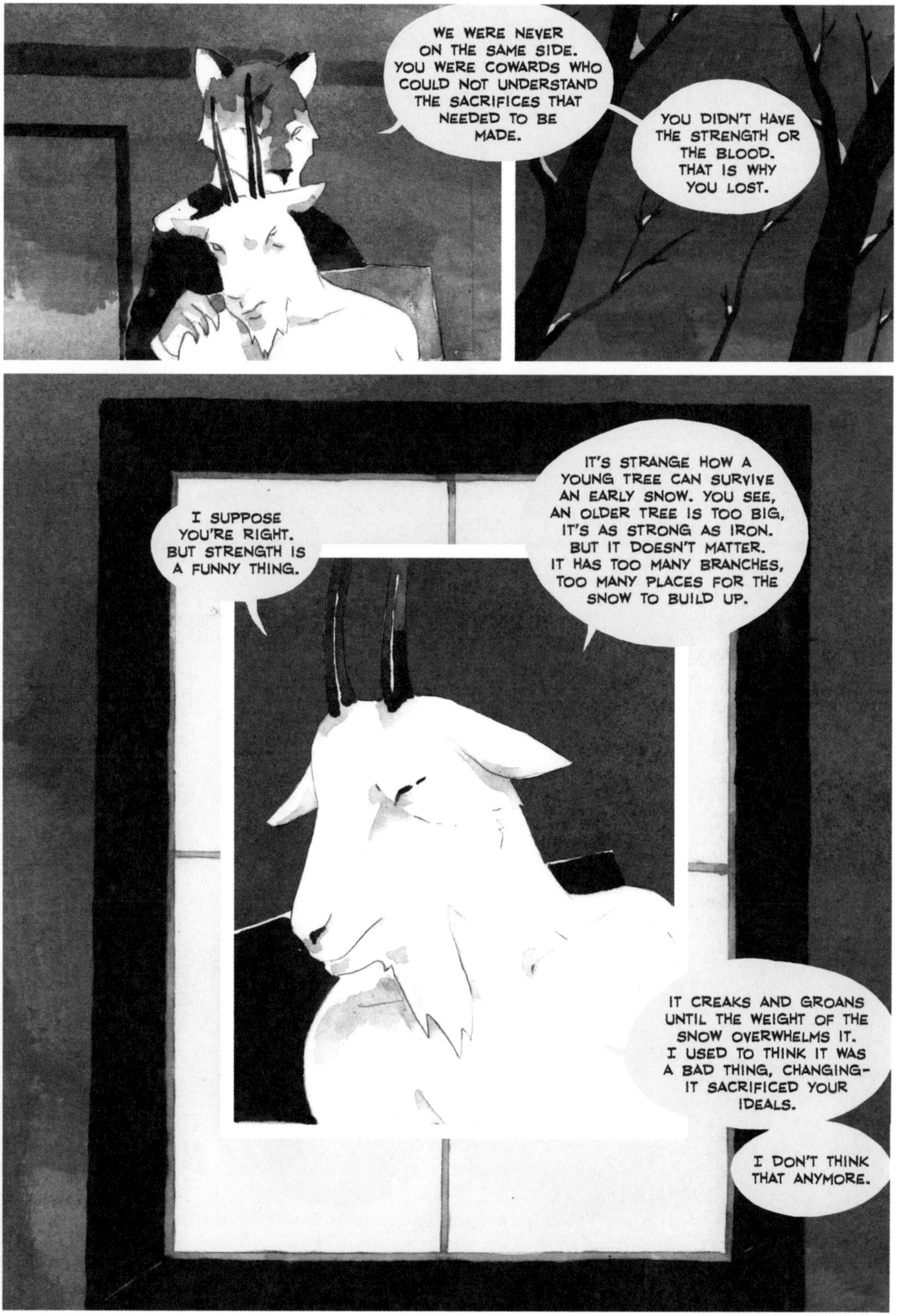
WE WERE NEVER ON THE SAME SIDE. YOU WERE COWARDS WHO COULD NOT UNDERSTAND THE SACRIFICES THAT NEEDED TO BE MADE.
YOU DIDN'T HAVE THE STRENGTH OR THE BLOOD. THAT IS WHY YOU LOST.
I SUPPOSE YOU'RE RIGHT. BUT STRENGTH IS A FUNNY THING.
IT'S STRANGE HOW A YOUNG TREE CAN SURVIVE AN EARLY SNOW. YOU SEE, AN OLDER TREE IS TOO BIG, IT'S AS STRONG AS IRON. BUT IT DOESN'T MATTER. IT HAS TOO MANY BRANCHES, TOO MANY PLACES FOR THE SNOW TO BUILD UP.
IT CREAKS AND GROANS UNTIL THE WEIGHT OF THE SNOW OVERWHELMS IT. I USED TO THINK IT WAS A BAD THING, CHANGING- IT SACRIFICED YOUR IDEALS.
I DON'T THINK THAT ANYMORE.

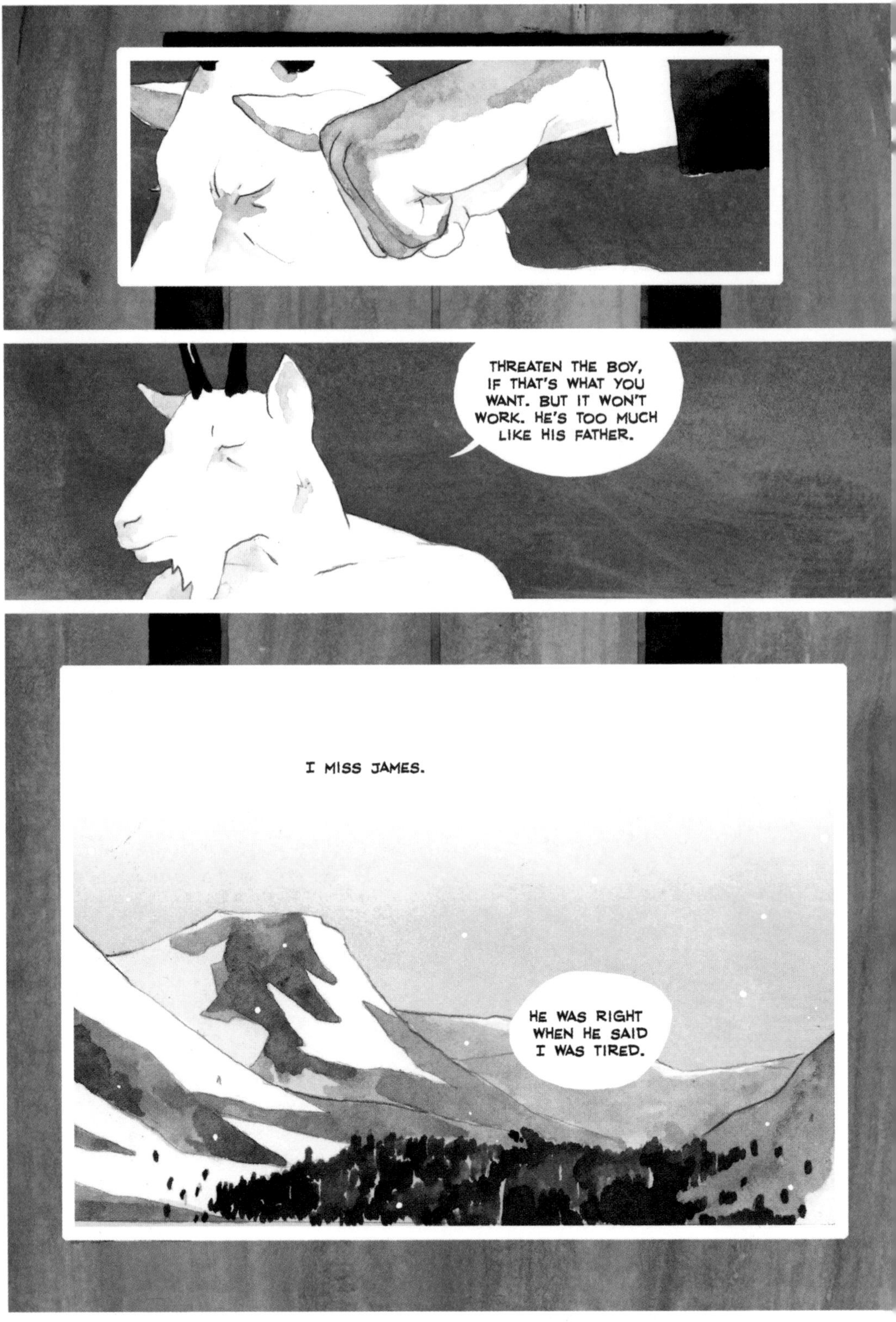
THREATEN THE BOY, IF THAT'S WHAT YOU WANT. BUT IT WON'T WORK. HE'S TOO MUCH LIKE HIS FATHER.
I MISS JAMES.
HE WAS RIGHT WHEN HE SAID I WAS TIRED.

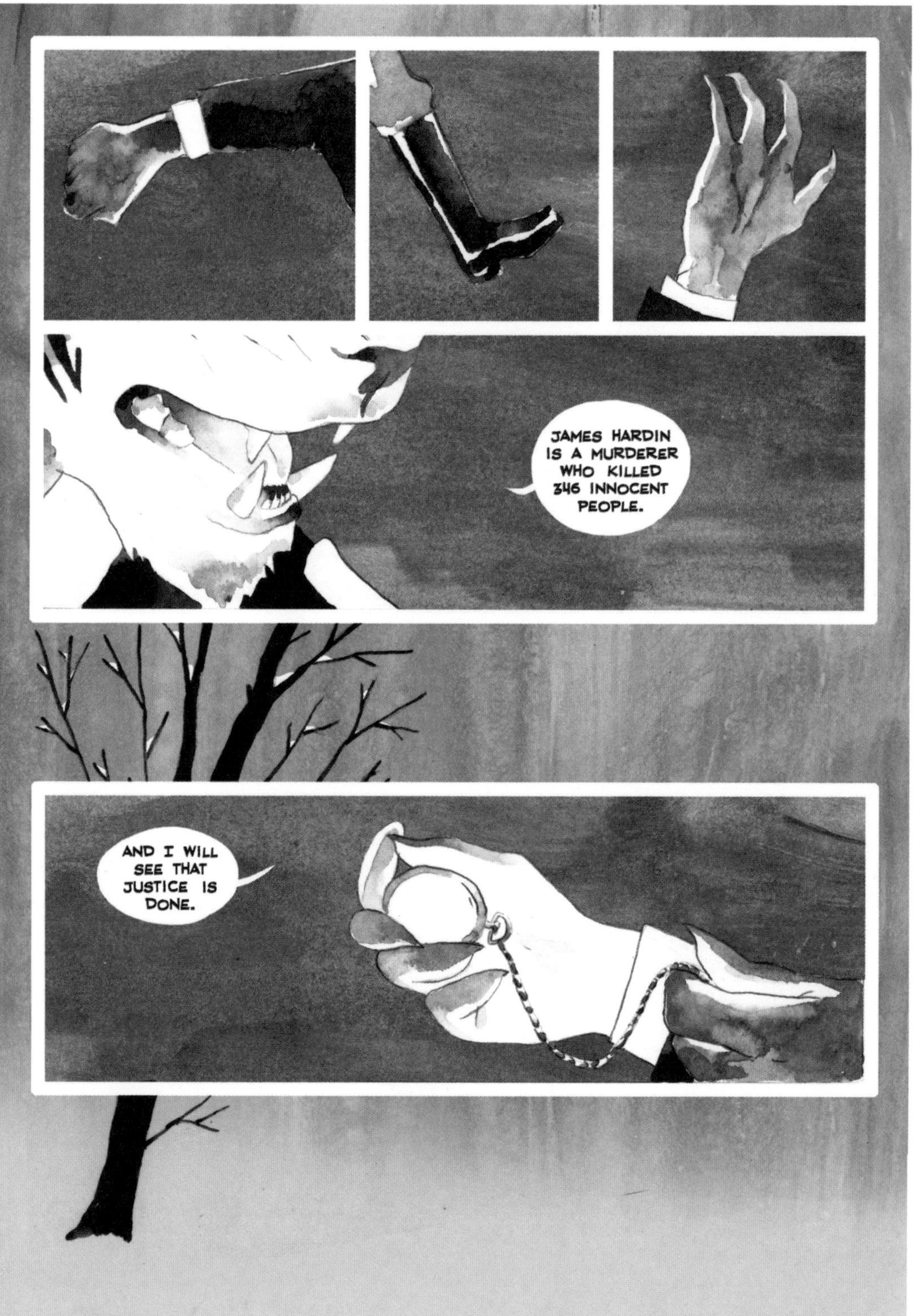
JAMES HARDIN IS A MURDERER WHO KILLED 346 INNOCENT PEOPLE.
AND I WILL SEE THAT JUSTICE IS DONE.

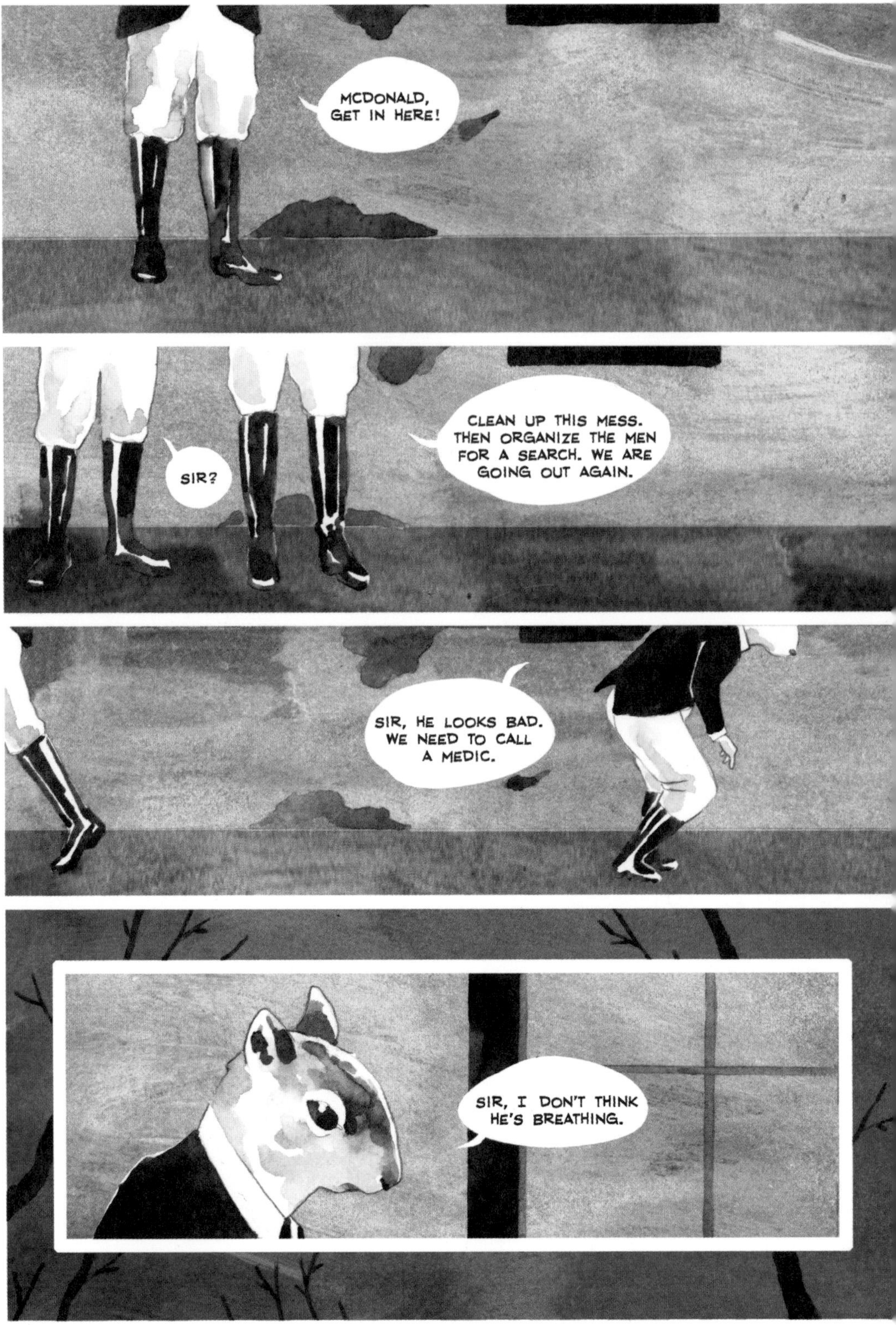
MCDONALD, GET IN HERE!
SIR?
CLEAN UP THIS MESS. THEN ORGANIZE THE MEN FOR A SEARCH. WE ARE GOING OUT AGAIN.
SIR, HE LOOKS BAD. WE NEED TO CALL A MEDIC.
SIR, I DON'T THINK HE'S BREATHING.

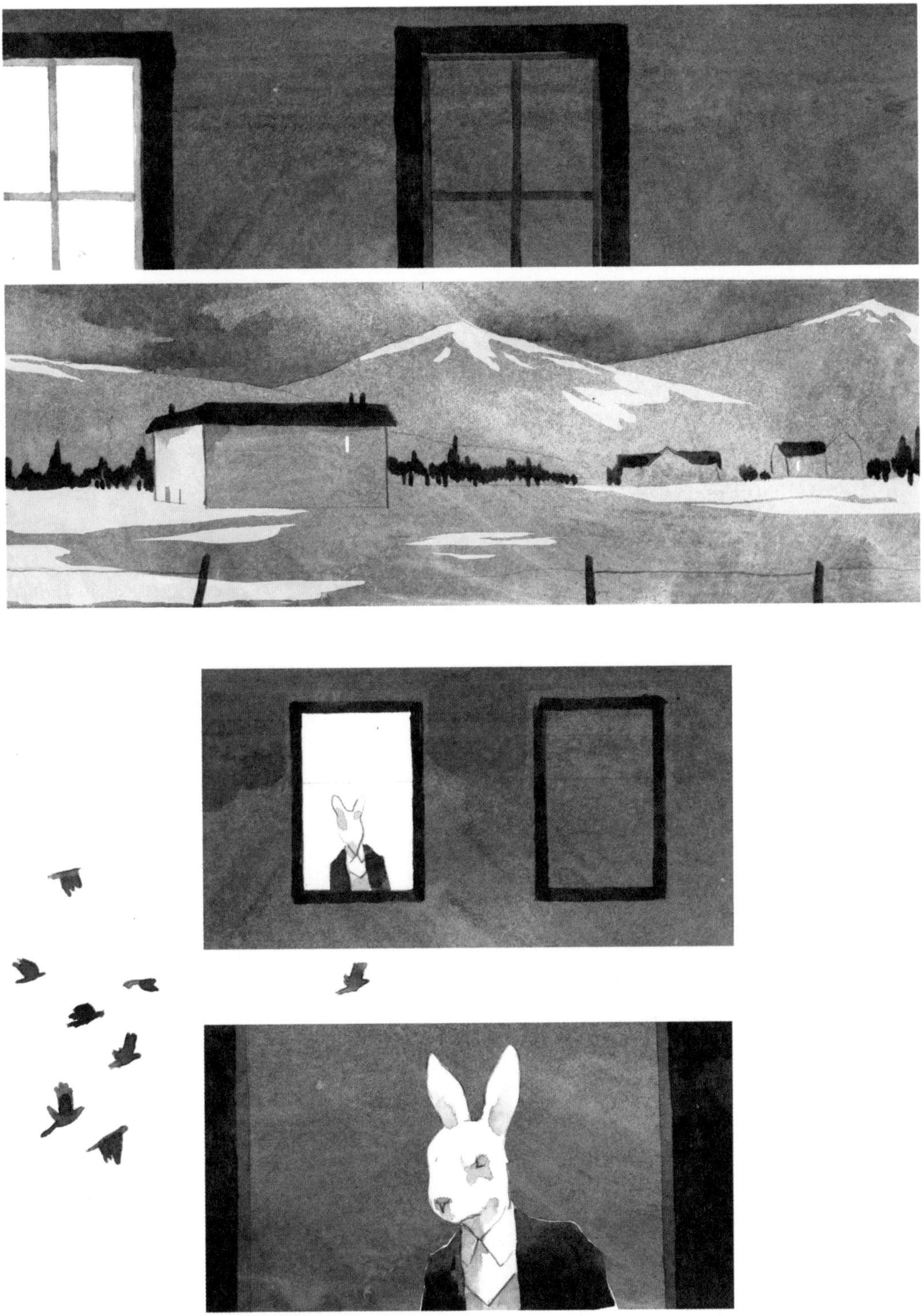

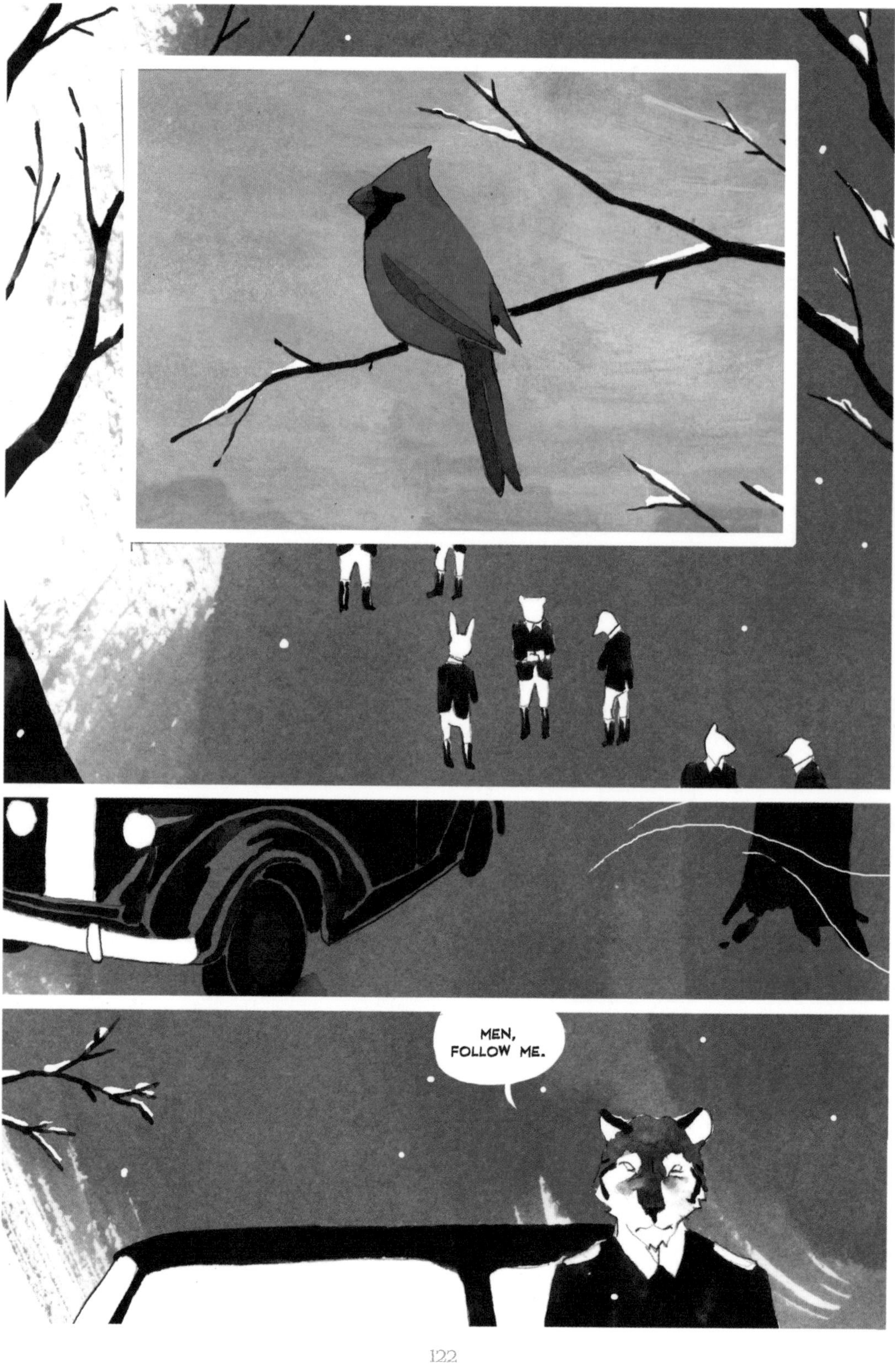
MEN,
FOLLOW ME.

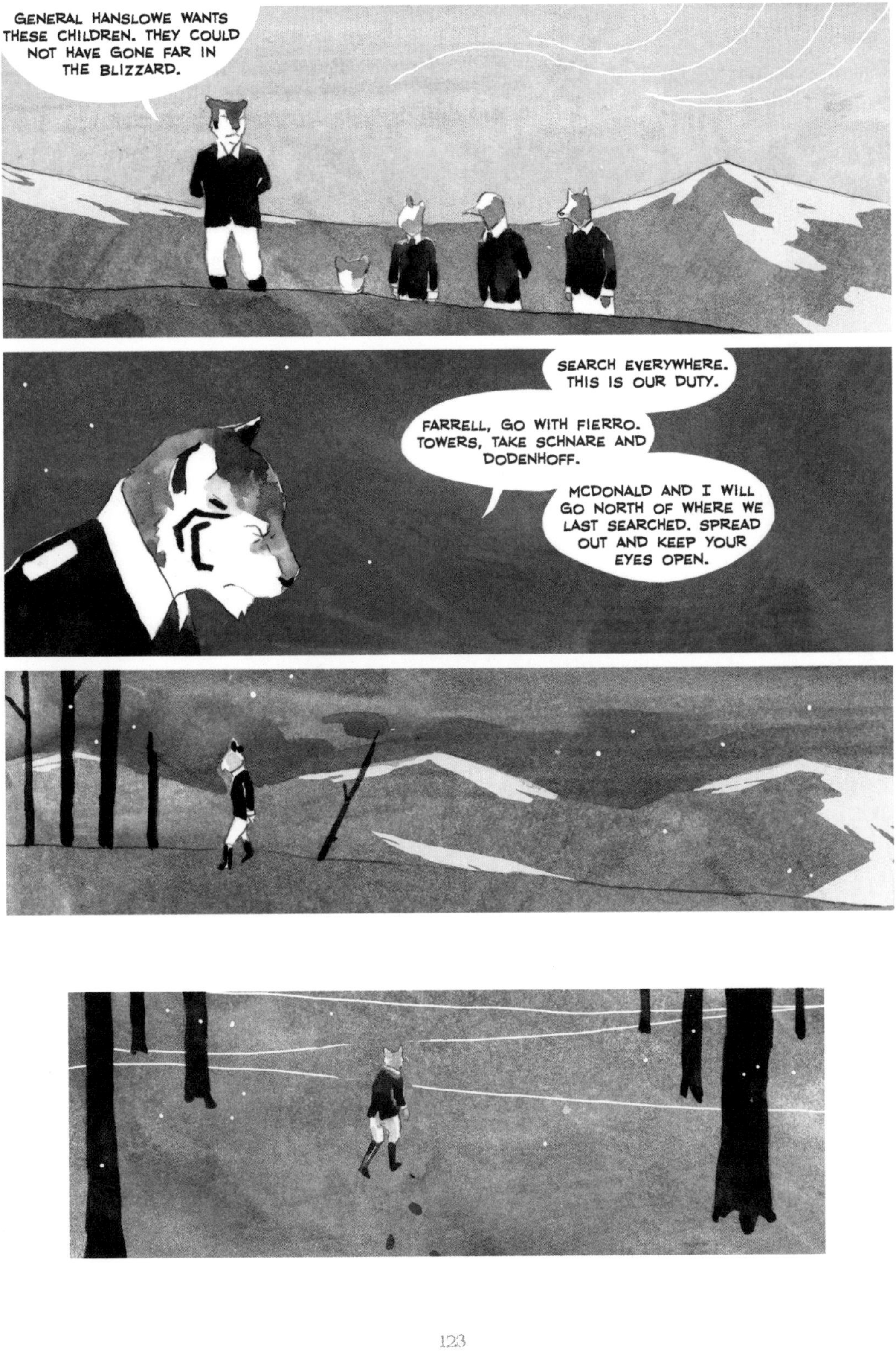
GENERAL HANSLOWE WANTS THESE CHILDREN. THEY COULD NOT HAVE GONE FAR IN THE BLIZZARD.
SEARCH EVERYWHERE. THIS IS OUR DUTY.
FARRELL, GO WITH FIERRO. TOWERS, TAKE SCHNARE AND DODENHOFF.
MCDONALD AND I WILL GO NORTH OF WHERE WE LAST SEARCHED. SPREAD OUT AND KEEP YOUR EYES OPEN.

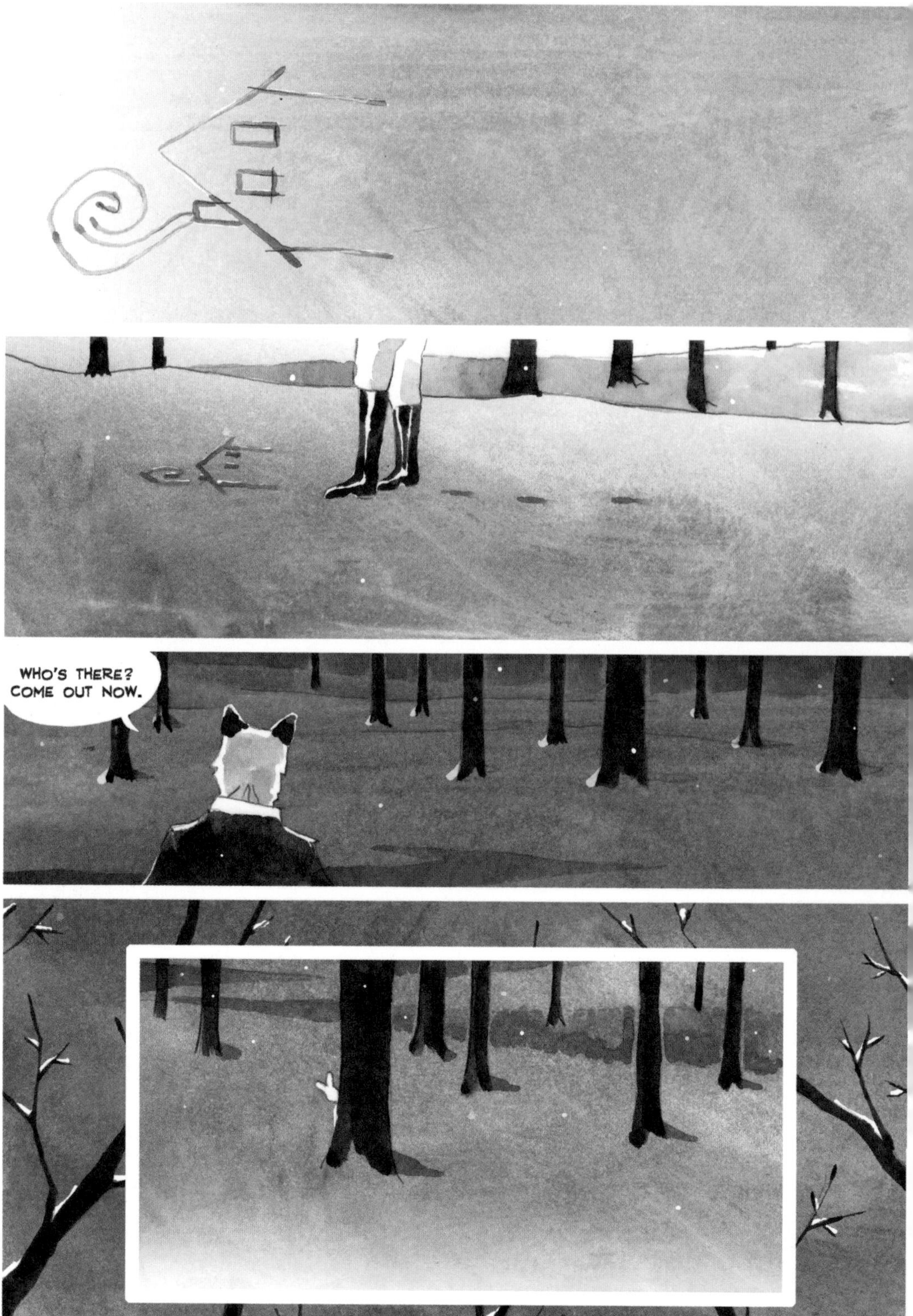
WHO'S THERE? COME OUT NOW.

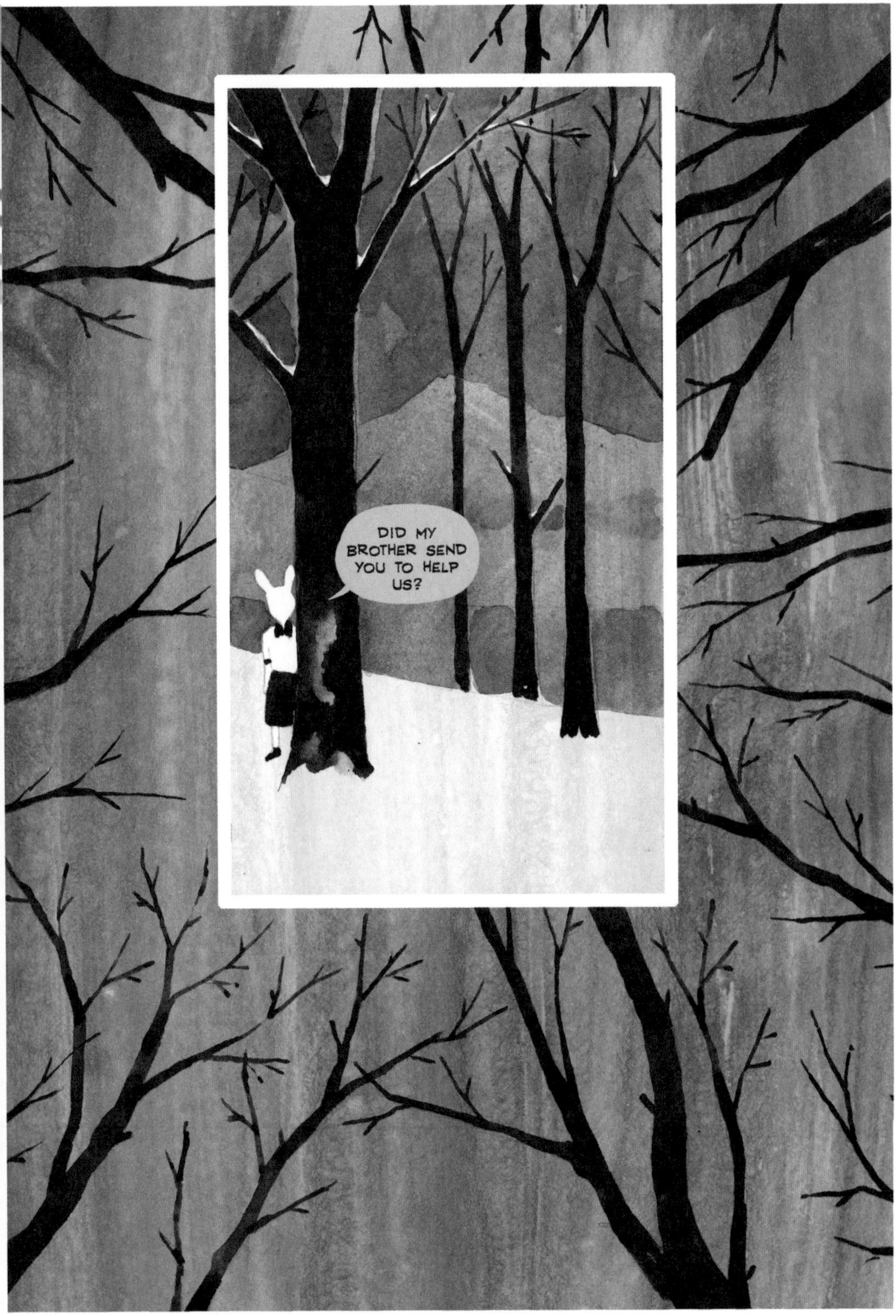
DID MY BROTHER SEND YOU TO HELP US?

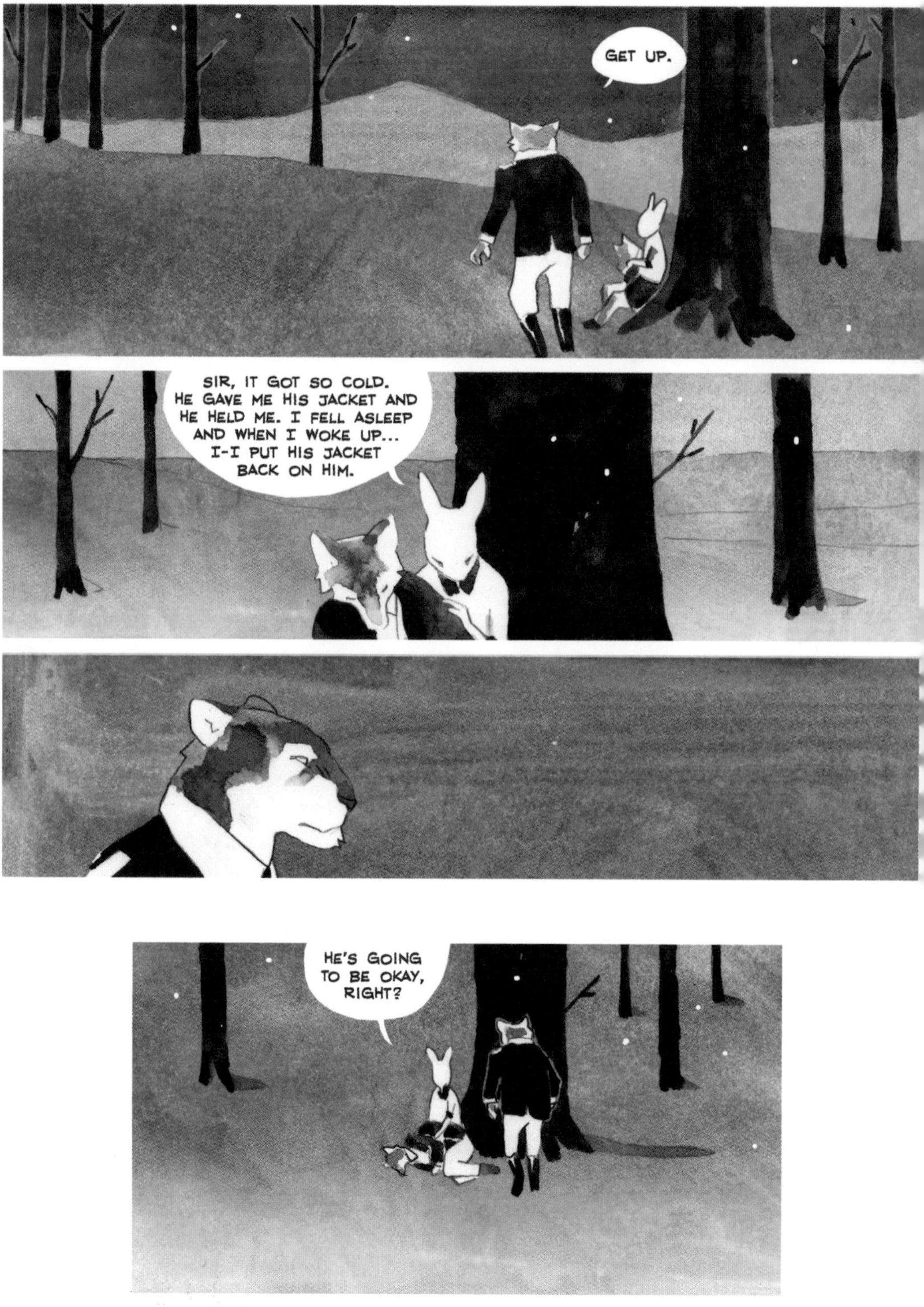
GET UP.
SIR, IT GOT SO COLD. HE GAVE ME HIS JACKET AND HE HELD ME. I FELL ASLEEP AND WHEN I WOKE UP... I-I PUT HIS JACKET BACK ON HIM.
HE'S GOING TO BE OKAY, RIGHT?

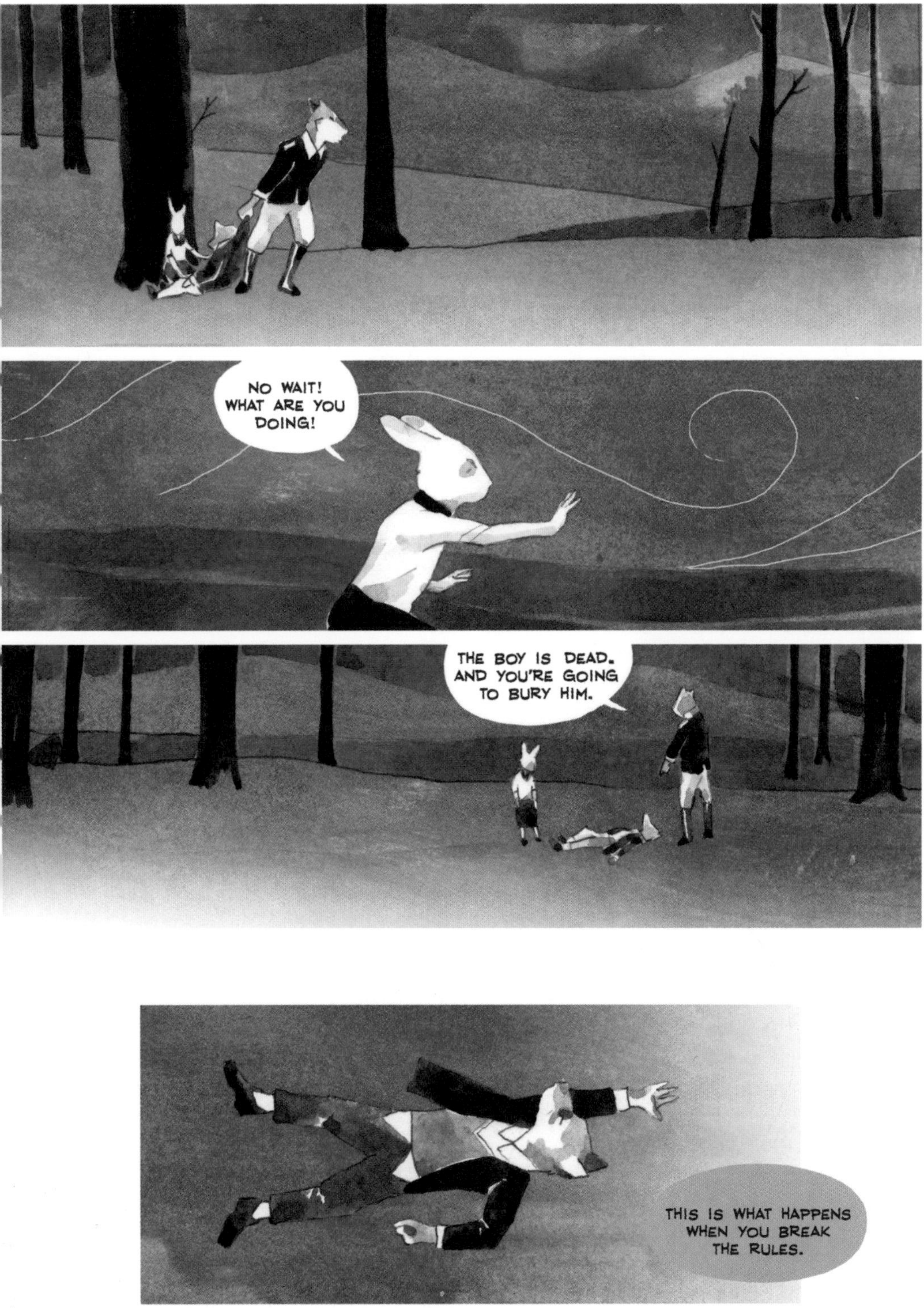
NO WAIT! WHAT ARE YOU DOING!
THE BOY IS DEAD. AND YOU'RE GOING TO BURY HIM.
THIS IS WHAT HAPPENS WHEN YOU BREAK THE RULES.

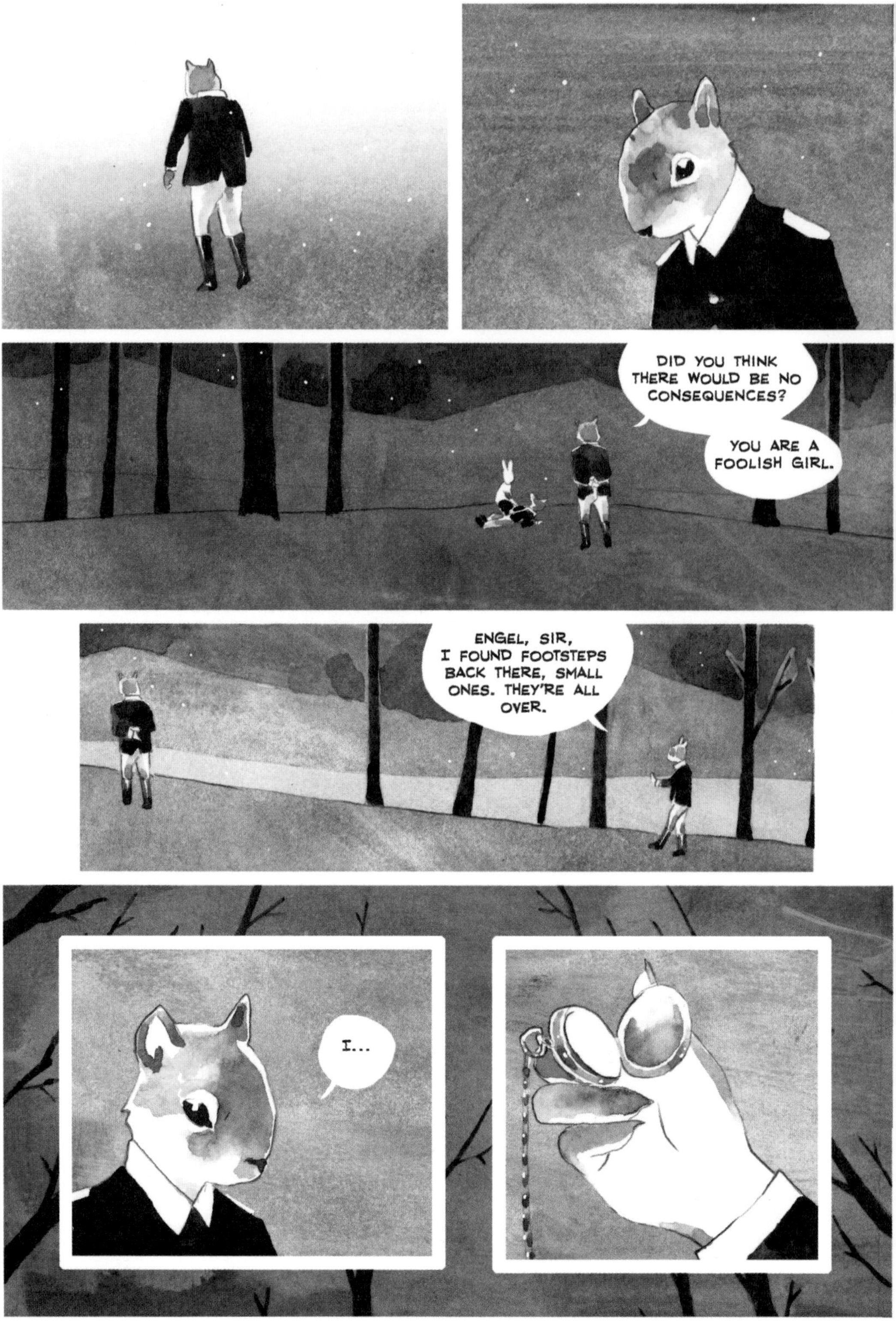
DID YOU THINK THERE WOULD BE NO CONSEQUENCES?
YOU ARE A FOOLISH GIRL.
ENGEL, SIR, I FOUND FOOTSTEPS BACK THERE, SMALL ONES. THEY'RE ALL OVER.
I...

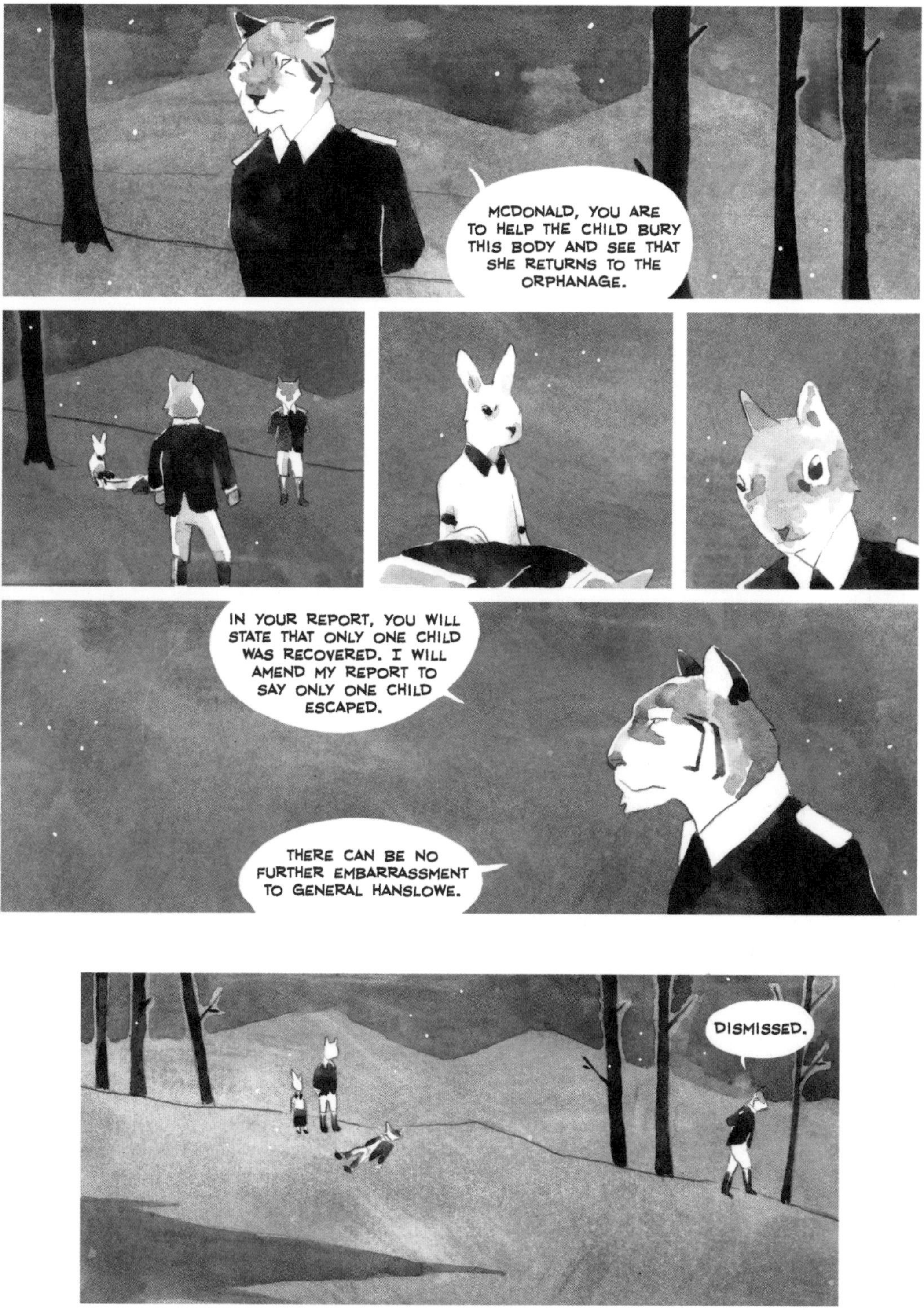
MCDONALD, YOU ARE TO HELP THE CHILD BURY THIS BODY AND SEE THAT SHE RETURNS TO THE ORPHANAGE.
IN YOUR REPORT, YOU WILL STATE THAT ONLY ONE CHILD WAS RECOVERED. I WILL AMEND MY REPORT TO SAY ONLY ONE CHILD ESCAPED.
THERE CAN BE NO FURTHER EMBARRASSMENT TO GENERAL HANSLOWE.
DISMISSED.

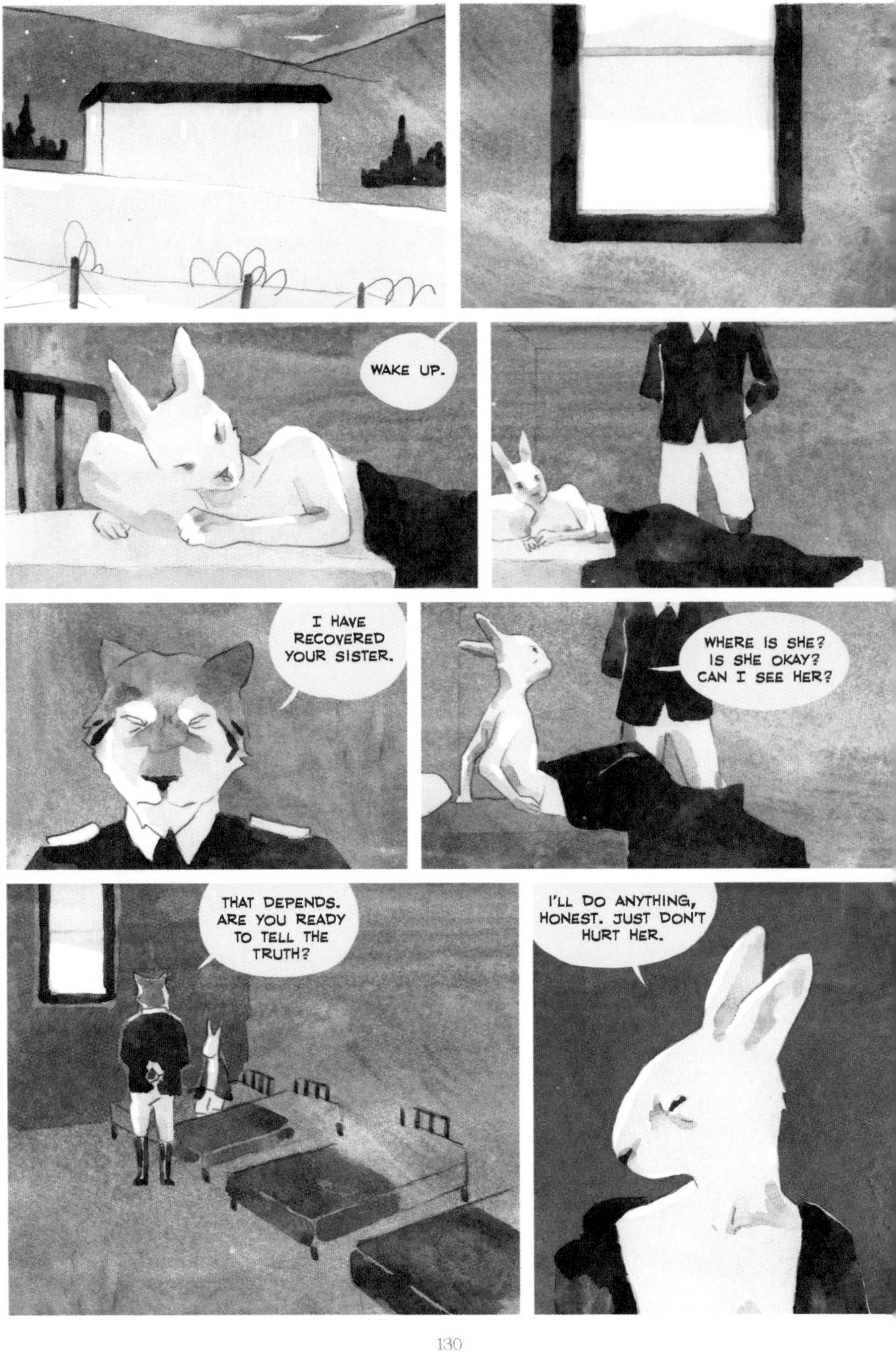
WAKE UP.
I HAVE RECOVERED YOUR SISTER.
WHERE IS SHE? IS SHE OKAY? CAN I SEE HER?
THAT DEPENDS. ARE YOU READY TO TELL THE TRUTH?
I'LL DO ANYTHING, HONEST. JUST DON'T HURT HER.

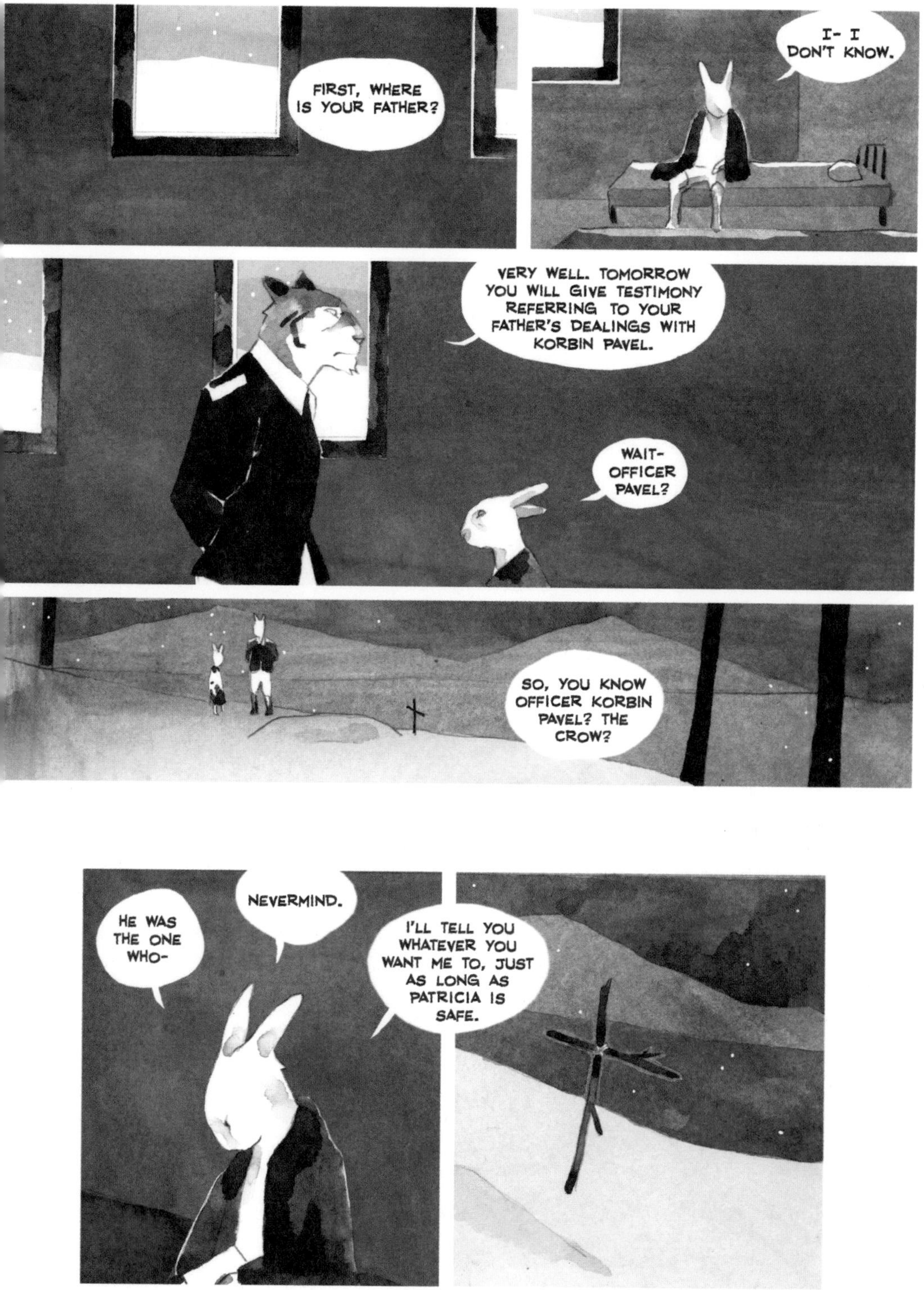
FIRST, WHERE IS YOUR FATHER?
I- I DON'T KNOW.
VERY WELL. TOMORROW YOU WILL GIVE TESTIMONY REFERRING TO YOUR FATHER'S DEALINGS WITH KORBIN PAVEL.
WAIT- OFFICER PAVEL?
SO, YOU KNOW OFFICER KORBIN PAVEL? THE CROW?
HE WAS THE ONE WHO-
NEVERMIND.
I'LL TELL YOU WHATEVER YOU WANT ME TO, JUST AS LONG AS PATRICIA IS SAFE.

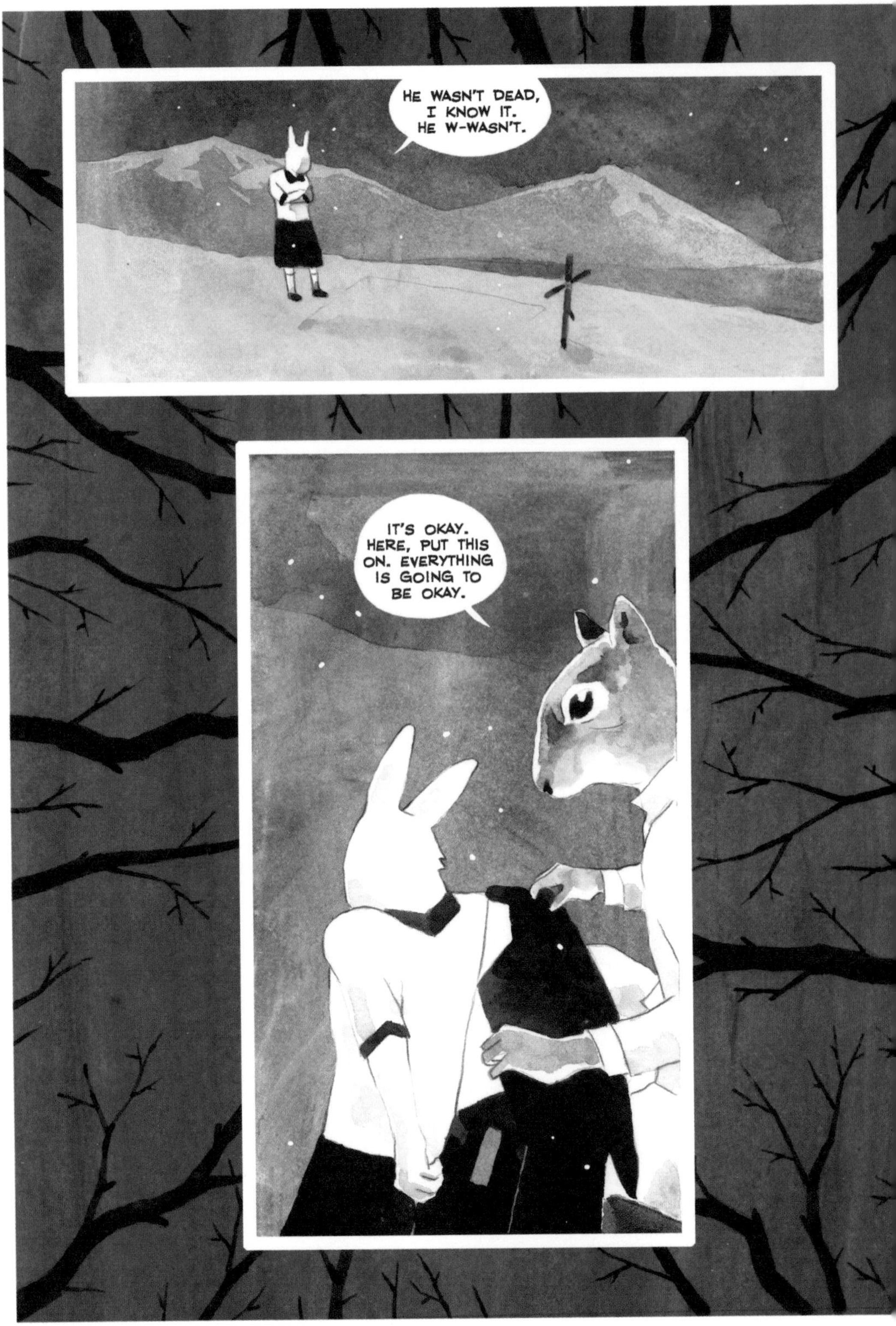
HE WASN'T DEAD,
I KNOW IT.
HE W-WASN'T.
IT'S OKAY.
HERE, PUT THIS
ON. EVERYTHING
IS GOING TO
BE OKAY.

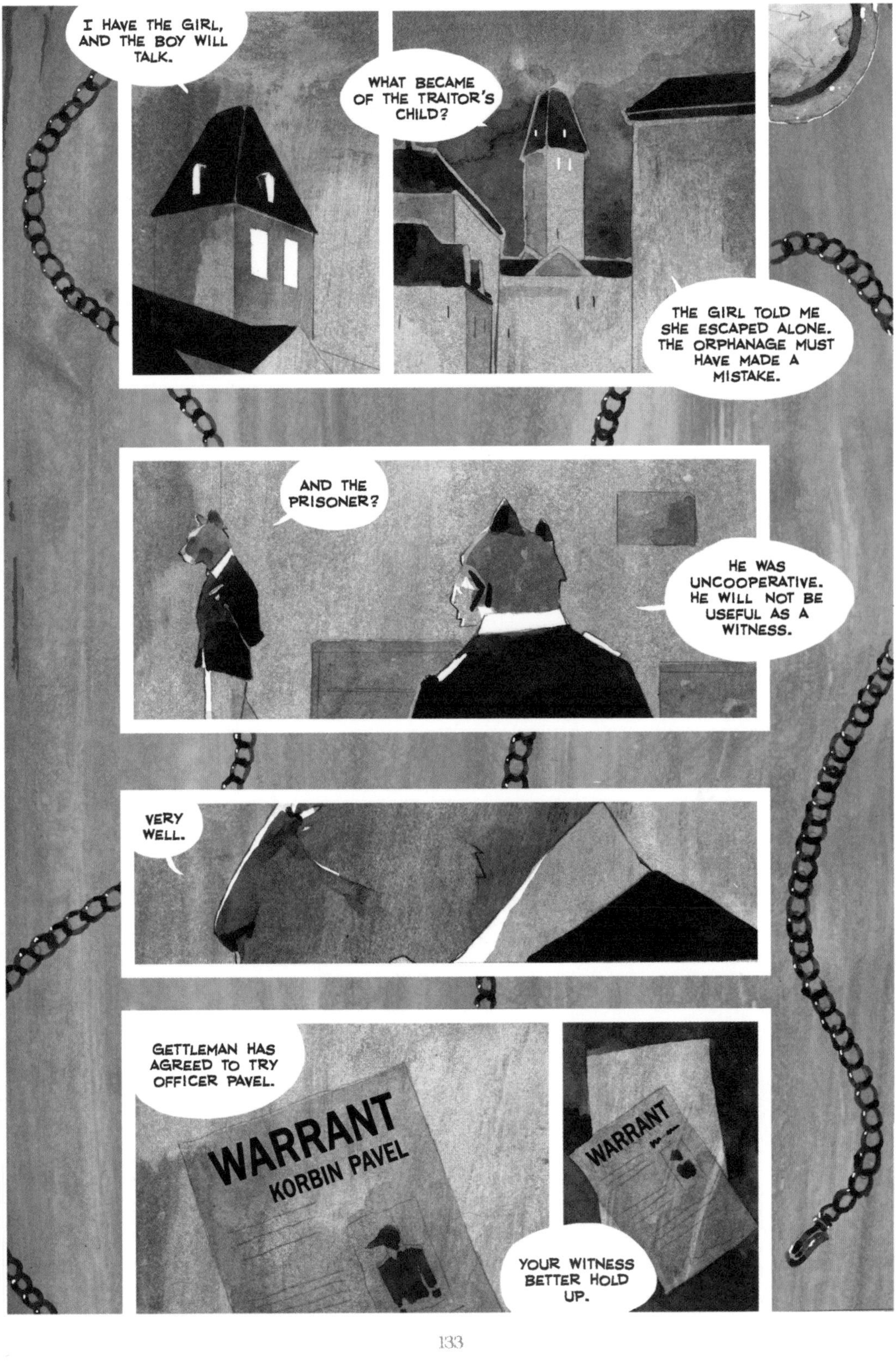
I HAVE THE GIRL, AND THE BOY WILL TALK.
WHAT BECAME OF THE TRAITOR'S CHILD?
THE GIRL TOLD ME SHE ESCAPED ALONE. THE ORPHANAGE MUST HAVE MADE A MISTAKE.
AND THE PRISONER?
HE WAS UNCOOPERATIVE. HE WILL NOT BE USEFUL AS A WITNESS.
VERY WELL.
GETTLEMAN HAS AGREED TO TRY OFFICER PAVEL.
WARRANT
KORBIN PAVEL
WARRANT
YOUR WITNESS BETTER HOLD UP.

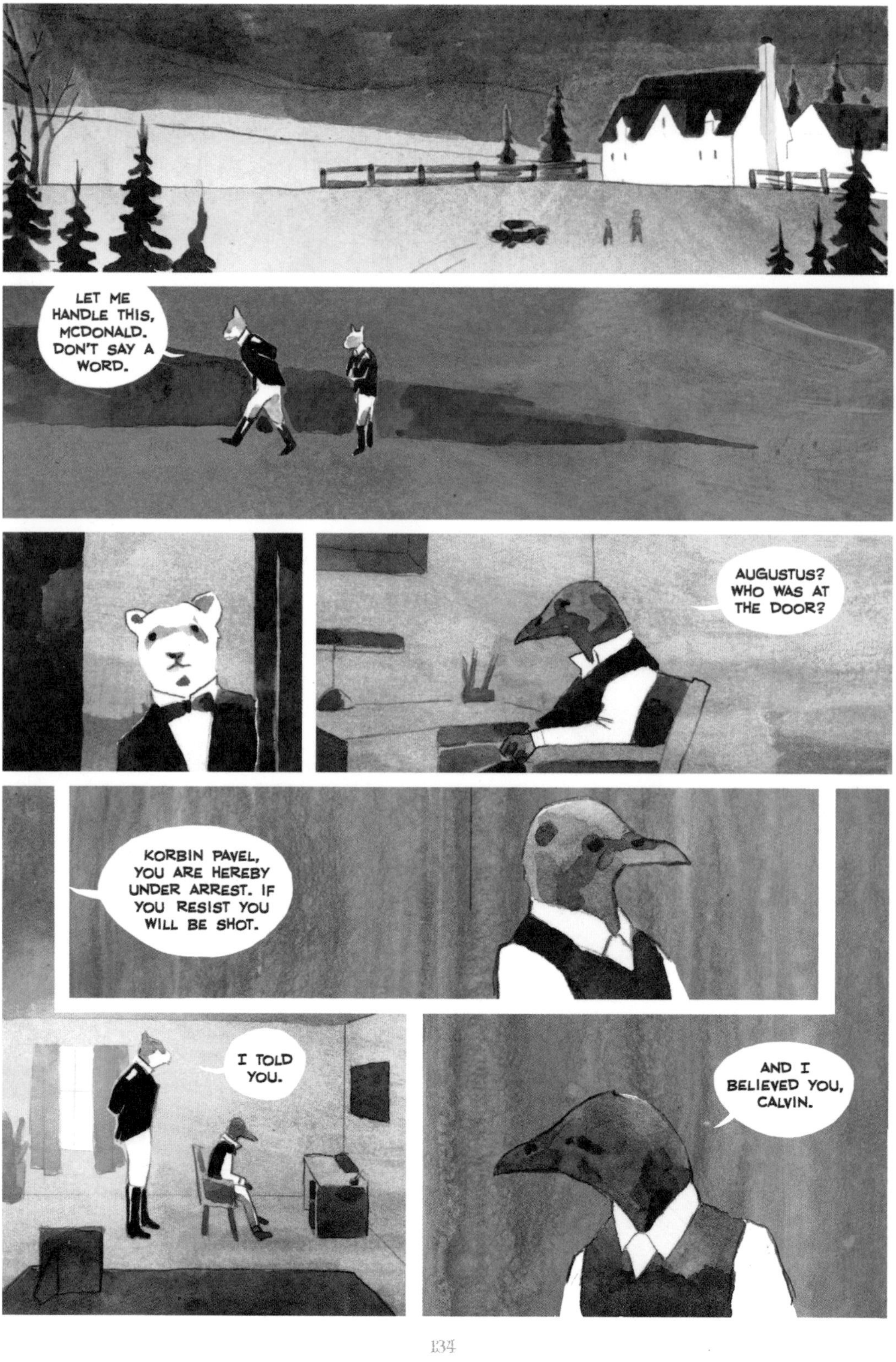
LET ME HANDLE THIS, MCDONALD. DON'T SAY A WORD.
AUGUSTUS? WHO WAS AT THE DOOR?
KORBIN PAVEL, YOU ARE HEREBY UNDER ARREST. IF YOU RESIST YOU WILL BE SHOT.
I TOLD YOU.
AND I BELIEVED YOU, CALVIN.

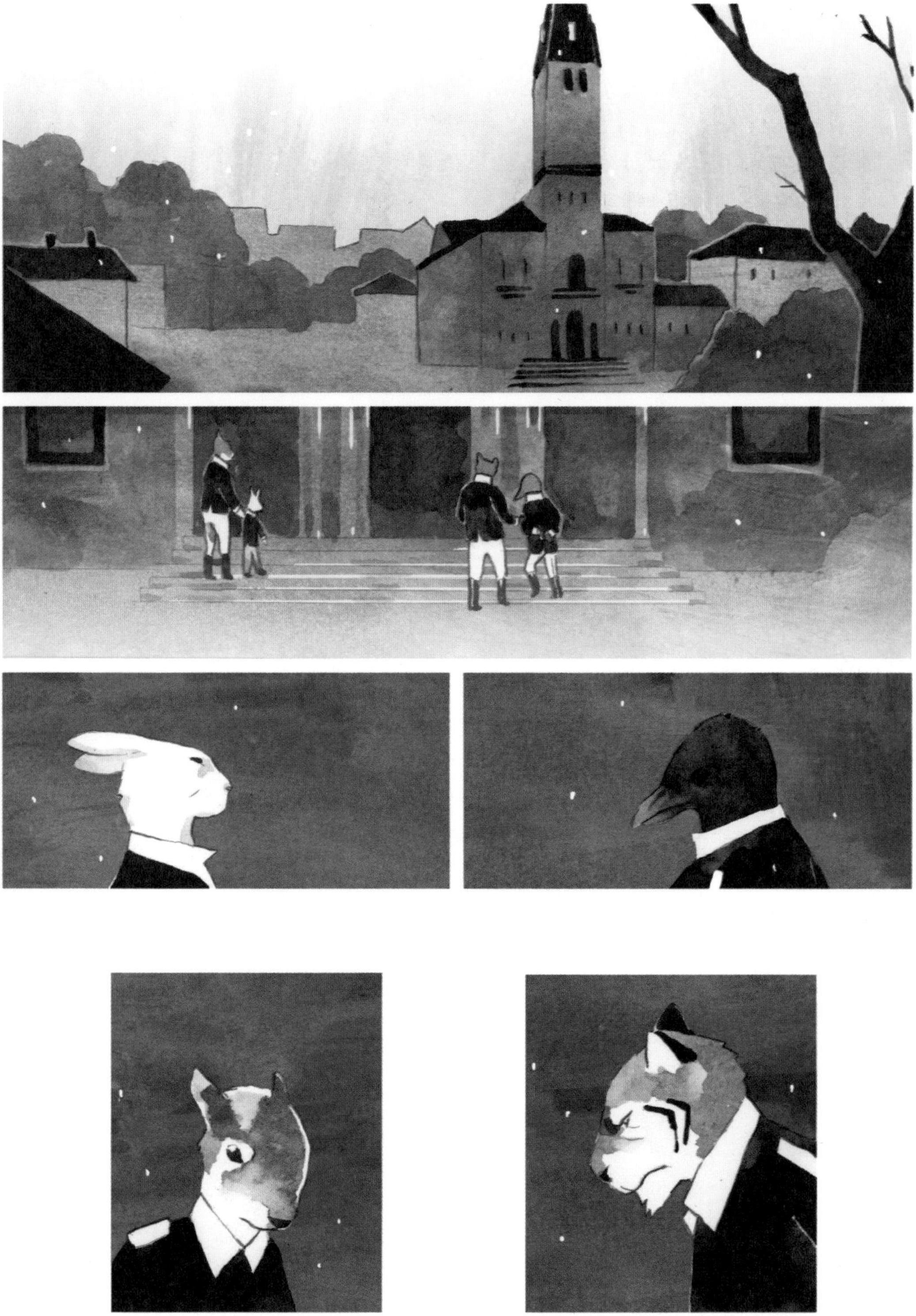

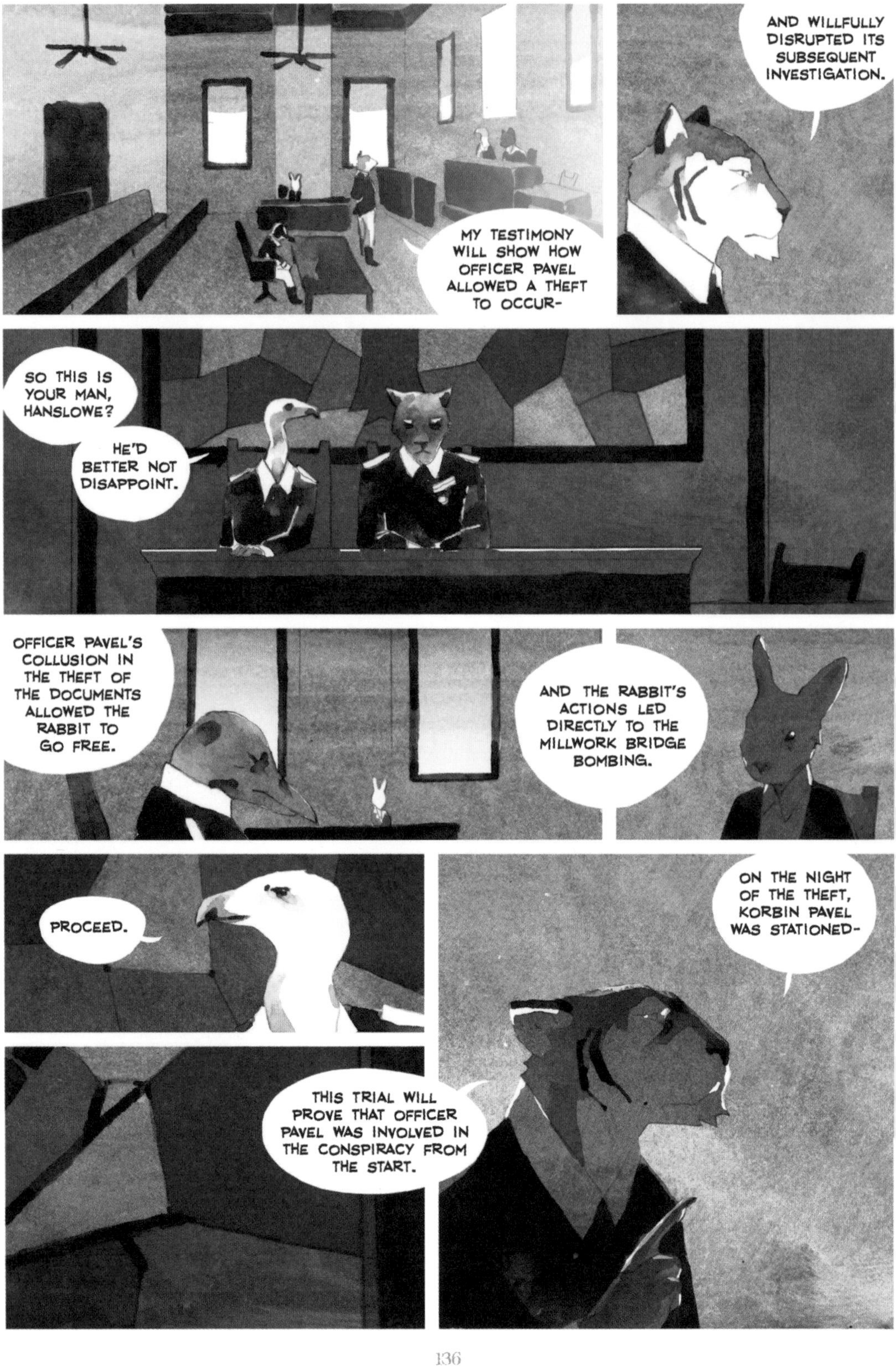
MY TESTIMONY WILL SHOW HOW OFFICER PAVEL ALLOWED A THEFT TO OCCUR-
AND WILLFULLY DISRUPTED ITS SUBSEQUENT INVESTIGATION.
SO THIS IS YOUR MAN, HANSLOWE?
HE'D BETTER NOT DISAPPOINT.
OFFICER PAVEL'S COLLUSION IN THE THEFT OF THE DOCUMENTS ALLOWED THE RABBIT TO GO FREE.
AND THE RABBIT'S ACTIONS LED DIRECTLY TO THE MILLWORK BRIDGE BOMBING.
PROCEED.
ON THE NIGHT OF THE THEFT, KORBIN PAVEL WAS STATIONED-
THIS TRIAL WILL PROVE THAT OFFICER PAVEL WAS INVOLVED IN THE CONSPIRACY FROM THE START.

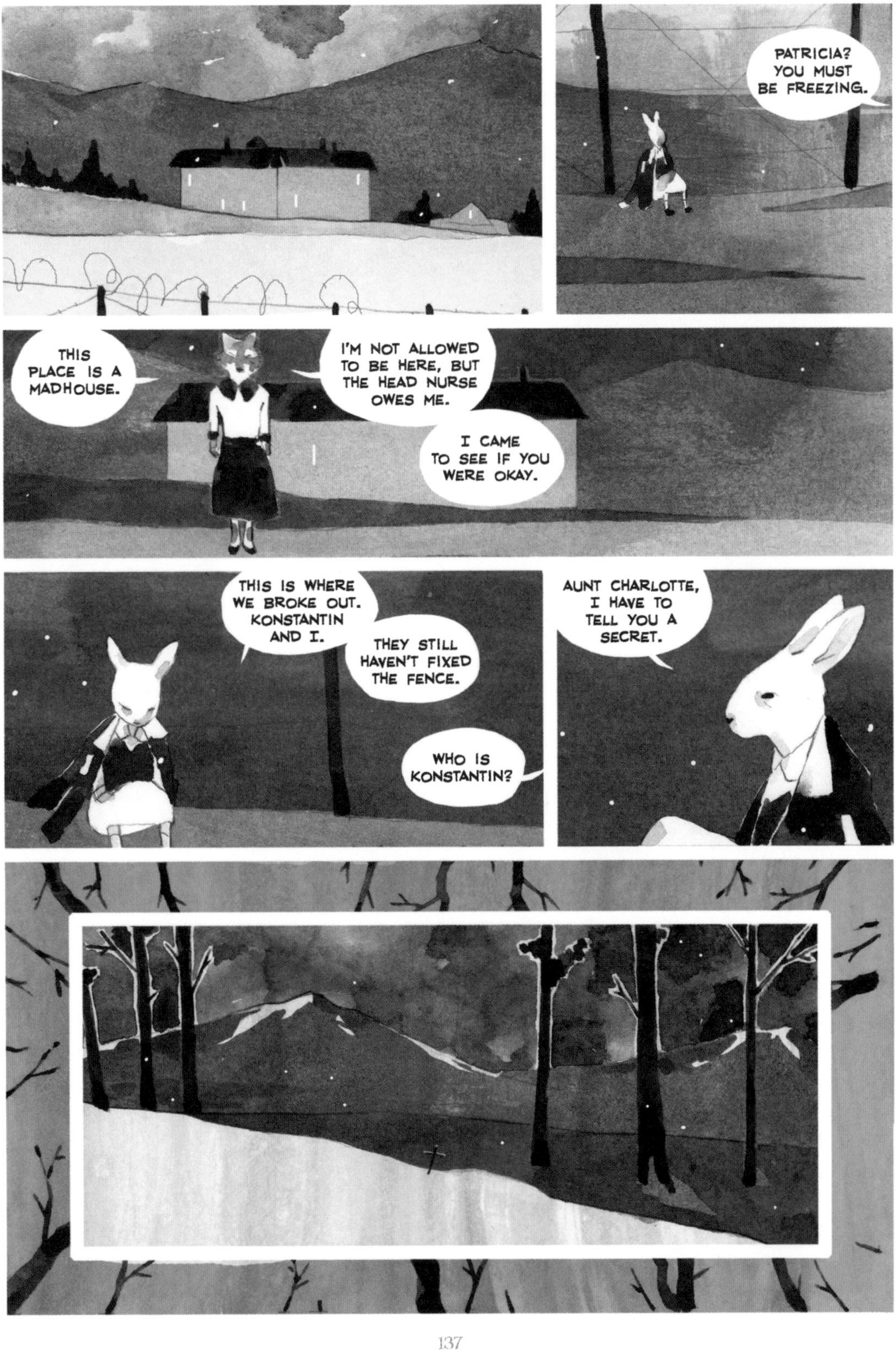
PATRICIA? YOU MUST BE FREEZING.
THIS PLACE IS A MADHOUSE.
I'M NOT ALLOWED TO BE HERE, BUT THE HEAD NURSE OWES ME.
I CAME TO SEE IF YOU WERE OKAY.
THIS IS WHERE WE BROKE OUT. KONSTANTIN AND I.
THEY STILL HAVEN'T FIXED THE FENCE.
WHO IS KONSTANTIN?
AUNT CHARLOTTE, I HAVE TO TELL YOU A SECRET.

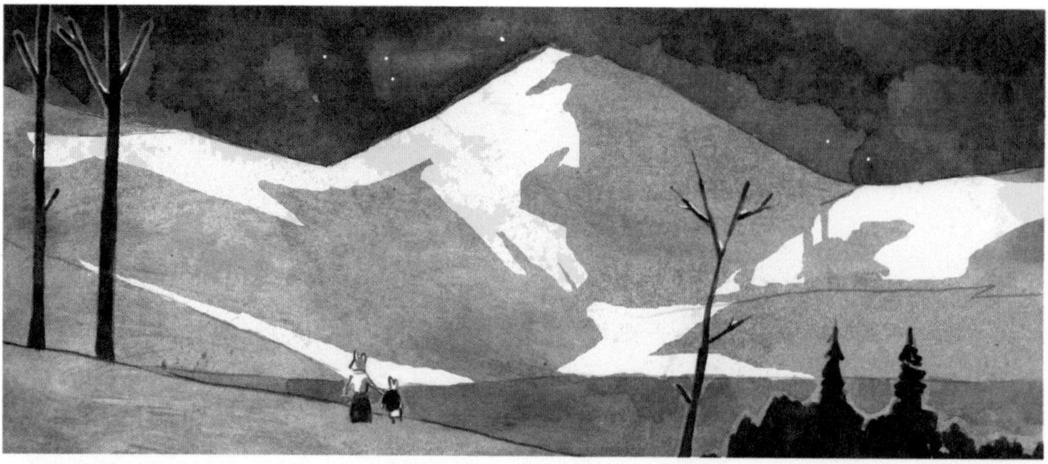

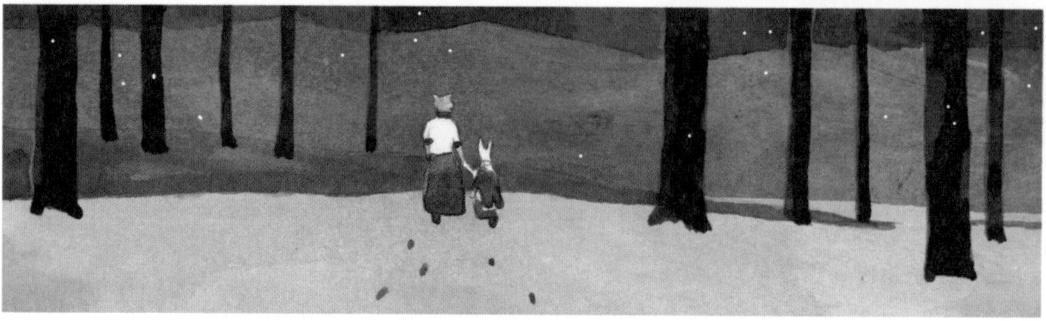

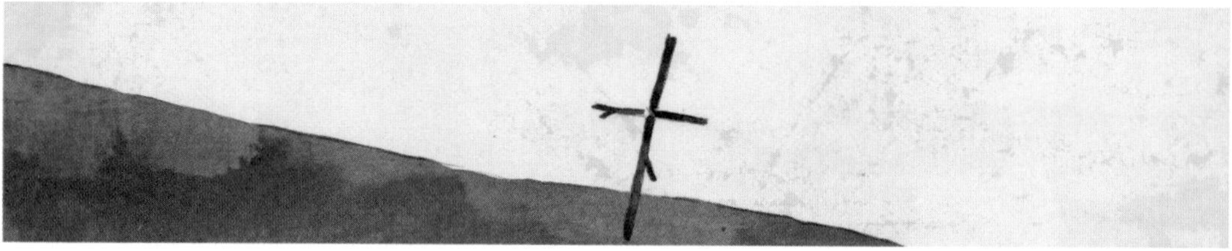

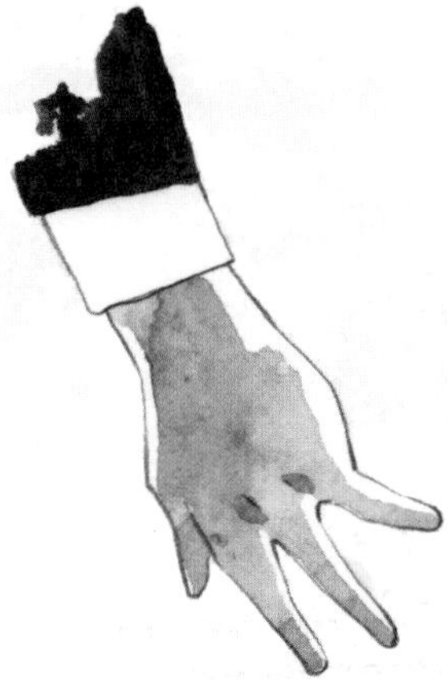

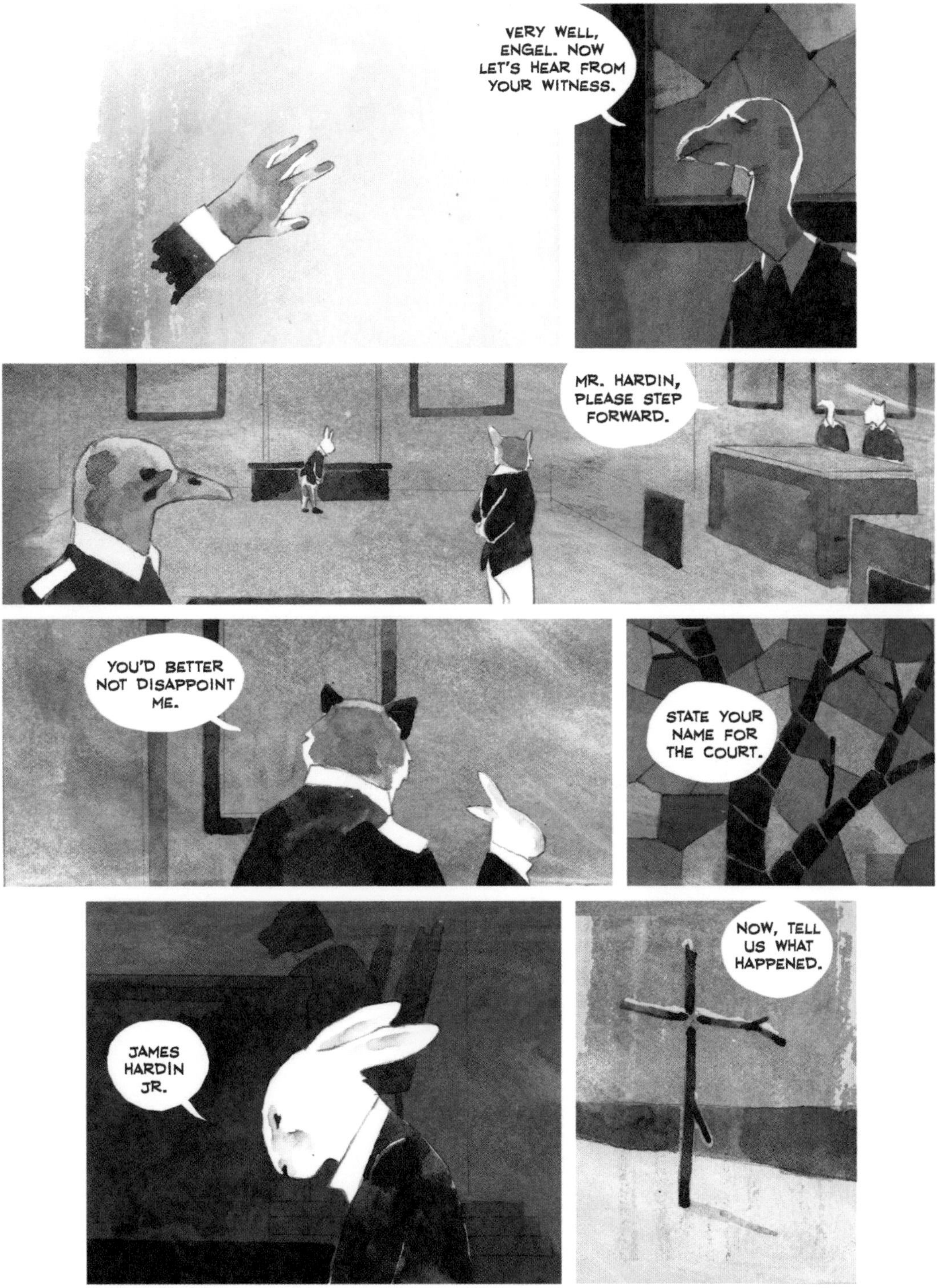
VERY WELL, ENGEL. NOW LET'S HEAR FROM YOUR WITNESS.
MR. HARDIN, PLEASE STEP FORWARD.
YOU'D BETTER NOT DISAPPOINT ME.
STATE YOUR NAME FOR THE COURT.
JAMES HARDIN JR.
NOW, TELL US WHAT HAPPENED.

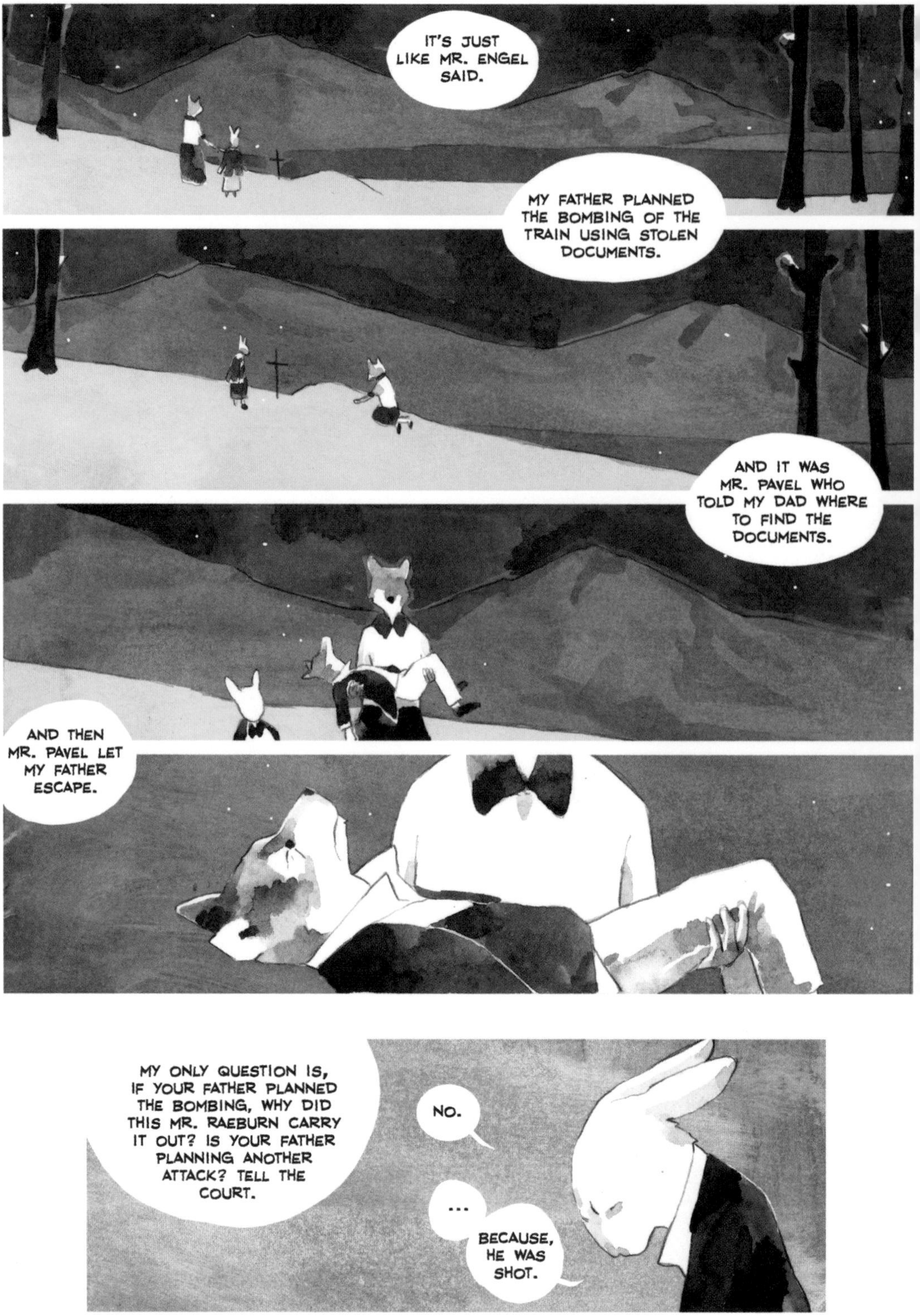
IT'S JUST LIKE MR. ENGEL SAID.
MY FATHER PLANNED THE BOMBING OF THE TRAIN USING STOLEN DOCUMENTS.
AND IT WAS MR. PAVEL WHO TOLD MY DAD WHERE TO FIND THE DOCUMENTS.
AND THEN MR. PAVEL LET MY FATHER ESCAPE.
MY ONLY QUESTION IS, IF YOUR FATHER PLANNED THE BOMBING, WHY DID THIS MR. RAEBURN CARRY IT OUT? IS YOUR FATHER PLANNING ANOTHER ATTACK? TELL THE COURT.
NO.
...
BECAUSE, HE WAS SHOT.

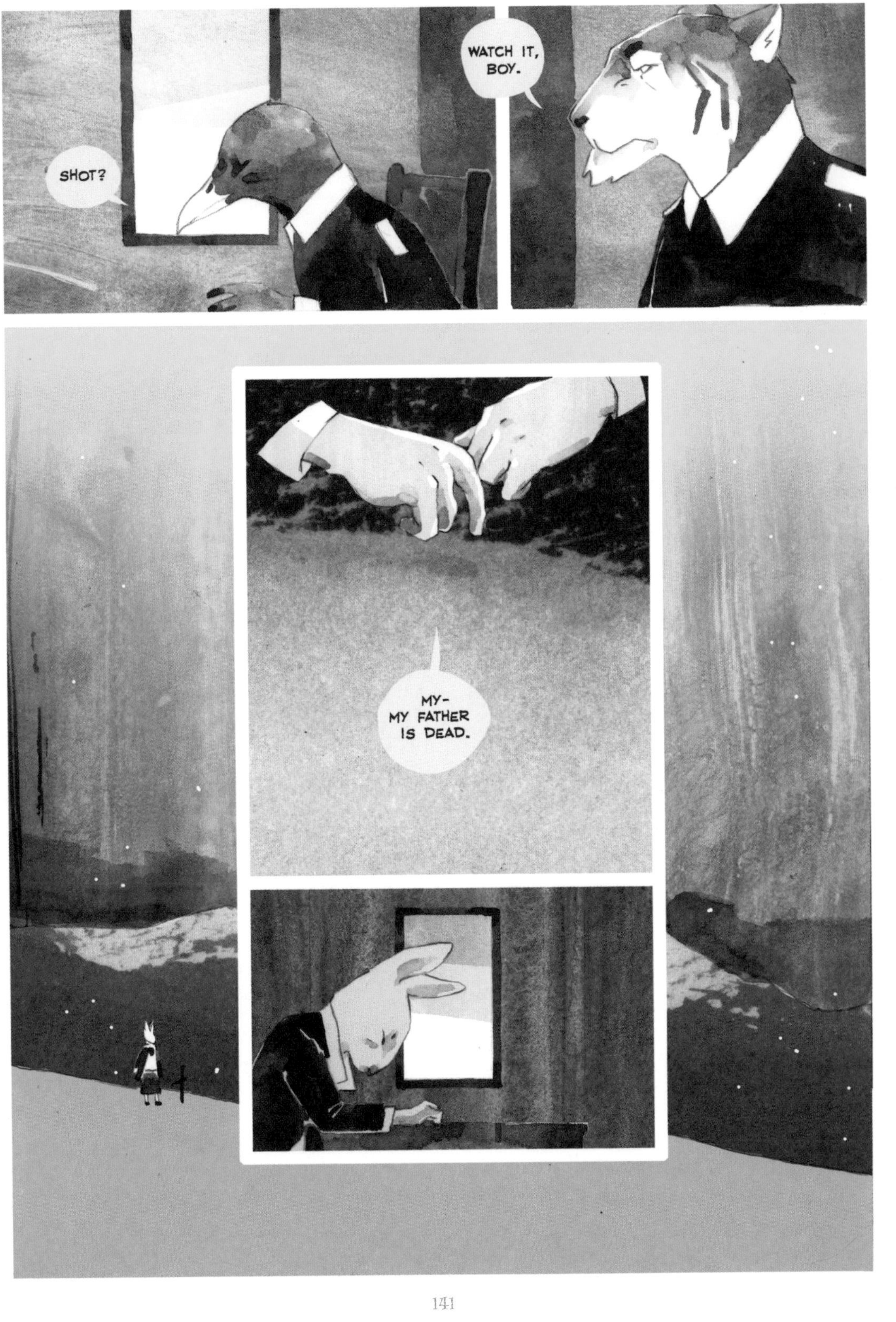
SHOT?
WATCH IT, BOY.
MY- MY FATHER IS DEAD.

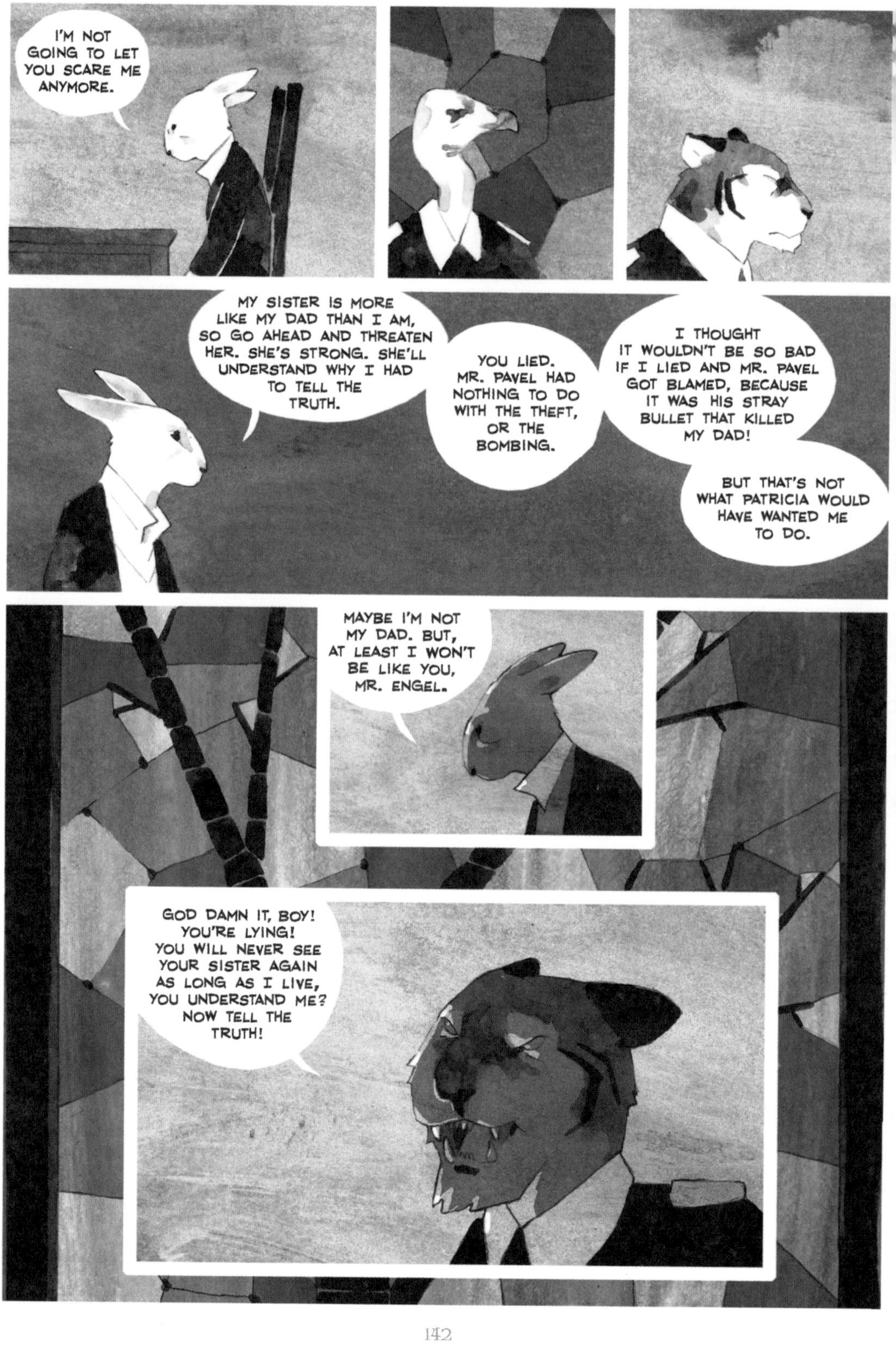
I'M NOT GOING TO LET YOU SCARE ME ANYMORE.
MY SISTER IS MORE LIKE MY DAD THAN I AM, SO GO AHEAD AND THREATEN HER. SHE'S STRONG. SHE'LL UNDERSTAND WHY I HAD TO TELL THE TRUTH.
YOU LIED. MR. PAVEL HAD NOTHING TO DO WITH THE THEFT, OR THE BOMBING.
I THOUGHT IT WOULDN'T BE SO BAD IF I LIED AND MR. PAVEL GOT BLAMED, BECAUSE IT WAS HIS STRAY BULLET THAT KILLED MY DAD!
BUT THAT'S NOT WHAT PATRICIA WOULD HAVE WANTED ME TO DO.
MAYBE I'M NOT MY DAD. BUT, AT LEAST I WON'T BE LIKE YOU, MR. ENGEL.
GOD DAMN IT, BOY! YOU'RE LYING! YOU WILL NEVER SEE YOUR SISTER AGAIN AS LONG AS I LIVE, YOU UNDERSTAND ME? NOW TELL THE TRUTH!

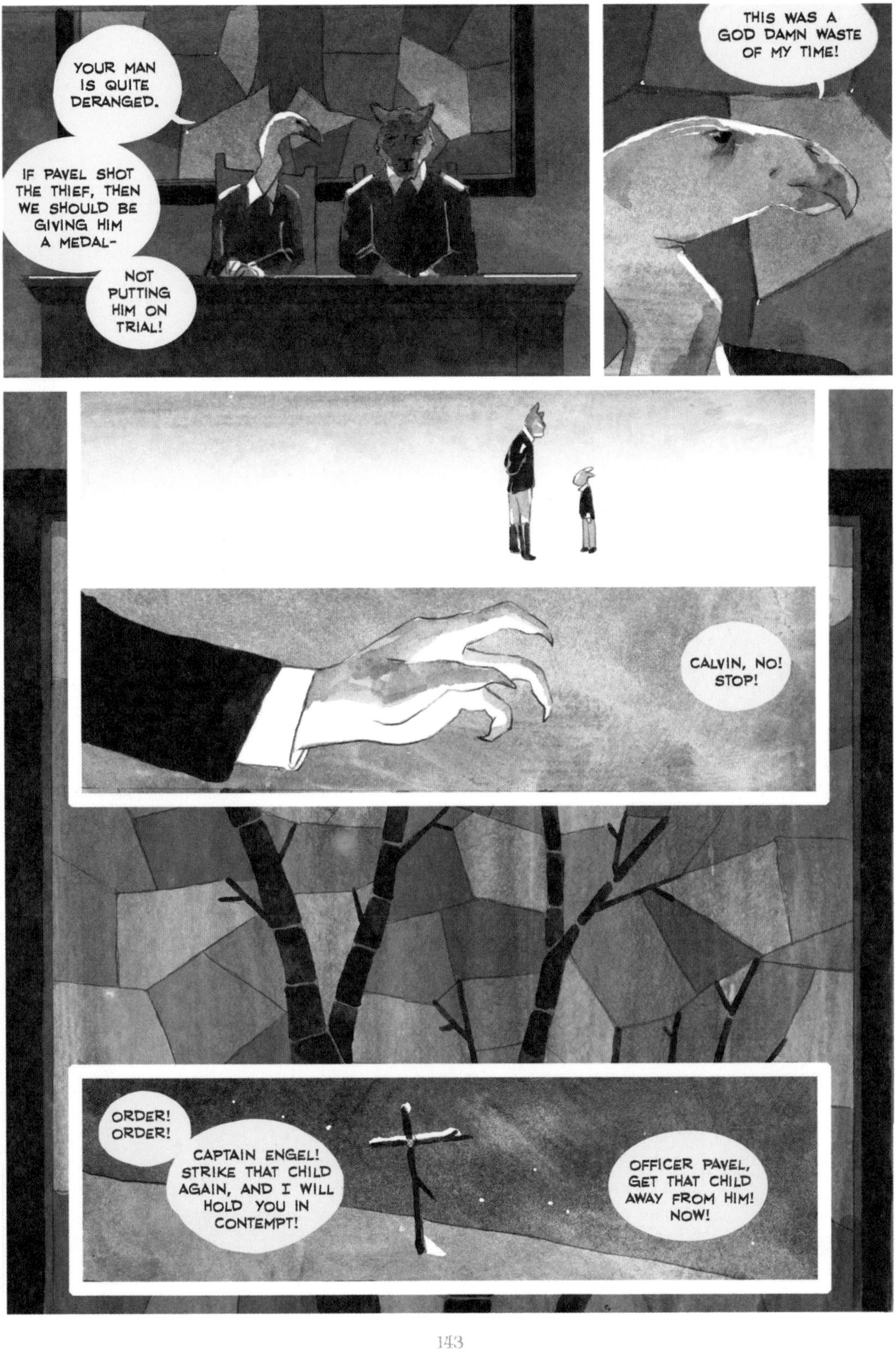
YOUR MAN IS QUITE DERANGED.
IF PAVEL SHOT THE THIEF, THEN WE SHOULD BE GIVING HIM A MEDAL-
NOT PUTTING HIM ON TRIAL!
THIS WAS A GOD DAMN WASTE OF MY TIME!
CALVIN, NO! STOP!
ORDER! ORDER!
CAPTAIN ENGEL! STRIKE THAT CHILD AGAIN, AND I WILL HOLD YOU IN CONTEMPT!
OFFICER PAVEL, GET THAT CHILD AWAY FROM HIM! NOW!

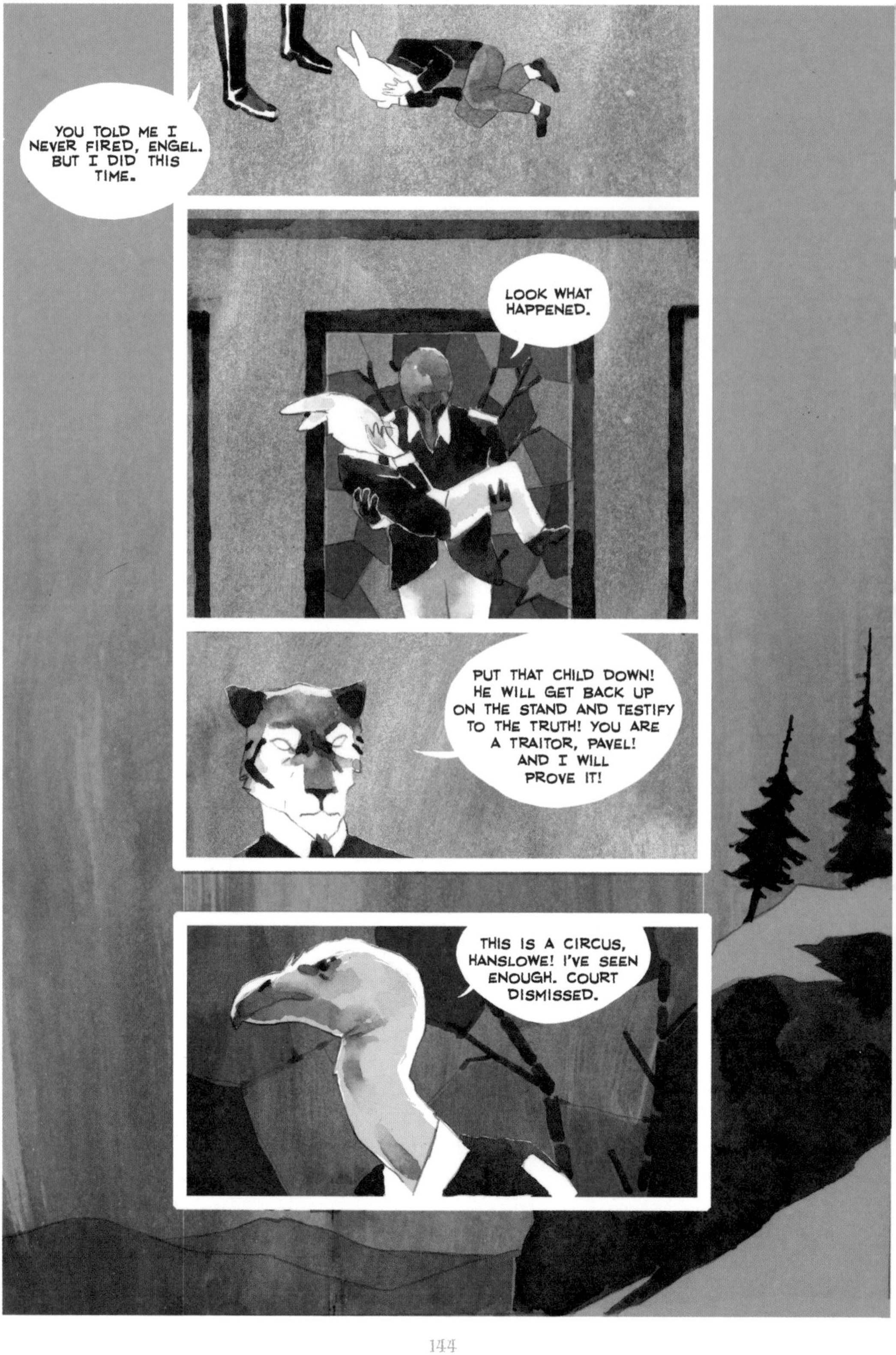
YOU TOLD ME I NEVER FIRED, ENGEL. BUT I DID THIS TIME.
LOOK WHAT HAPPENED.
PUT THAT CHILD DOWN! HE WILL GET BACK UP ON THE STAND AND TESTIFY TO THE TRUTH! YOU ARE A TRAITOR, PAVEL! AND I WILL PROVE IT!
THIS IS A CIRCUS, HANSLOWE! I'VE SEEN ENOUGH. COURT DISMISSED.

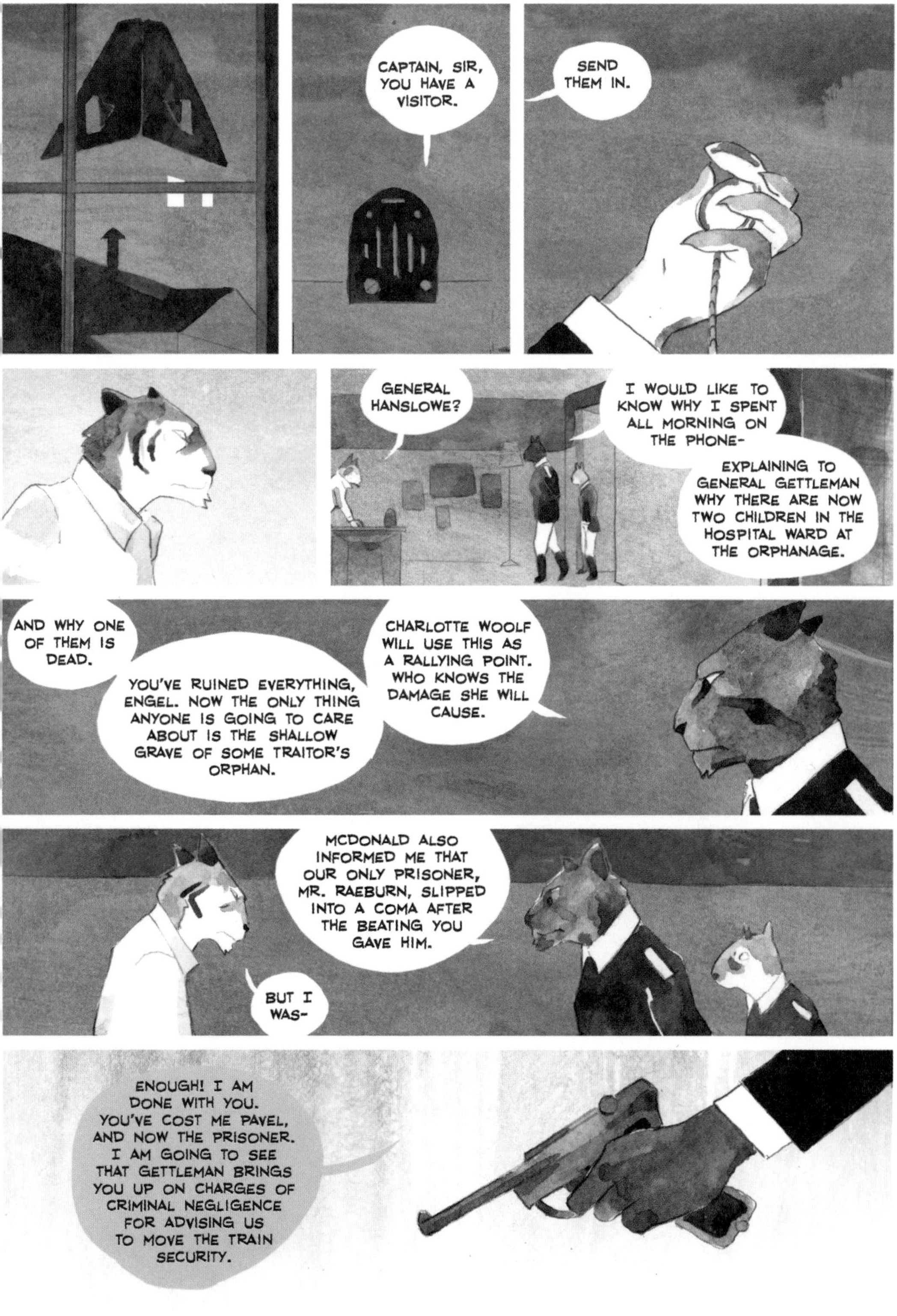
CAPTAIN, SIR, YOU HAVE A VISITOR.
SEND THEM IN.
GENERAL HANSLOWE?
I WOULD LIKE TO KNOW WHY I SPENT ALL MORNING ON THE PHONE-
EXPLAINING TO GENERAL GETTLEMAN WHY THERE ARE NOW TWO CHILDREN IN THE HOSPITAL WARD AT THE ORPHANAGE.
AND WHY ONE OF THEM IS DEAD.
YOU'VE RUINED EVERYTHING, ENGEL. NOW THE ONLY THING ANYONE IS GOING TO CARE ABOUT IS THE SHALLOW GRAVE OF SOME TRAITOR'S ORPHAN.
CHARLOTTE WOOLF WILL USE THIS AS A RALLYING POINT. WHO KNOWS THE DAMAGE SHE WILL CAUSE.
MCDONALD ALSO INFORMED ME THAT OUR ONLY PRISONER, MR. RAEBURN, SLIPPED INTO A COMA AFTER THE BEATING YOU GAVE HIM.
BUT I WAS-
ENOUGH! I AM DONE WITH YOU. YOU'VE COST ME PAVEL, AND NOW THE PRISONER. I AM GOING TO SEE THAT GETTLEMAN BRINGS YOU UP ON CHARGES OF CRIMINAL NEGLIGENCE FOR ADVISING US TO MOVE THE TRAIN SECURITY.

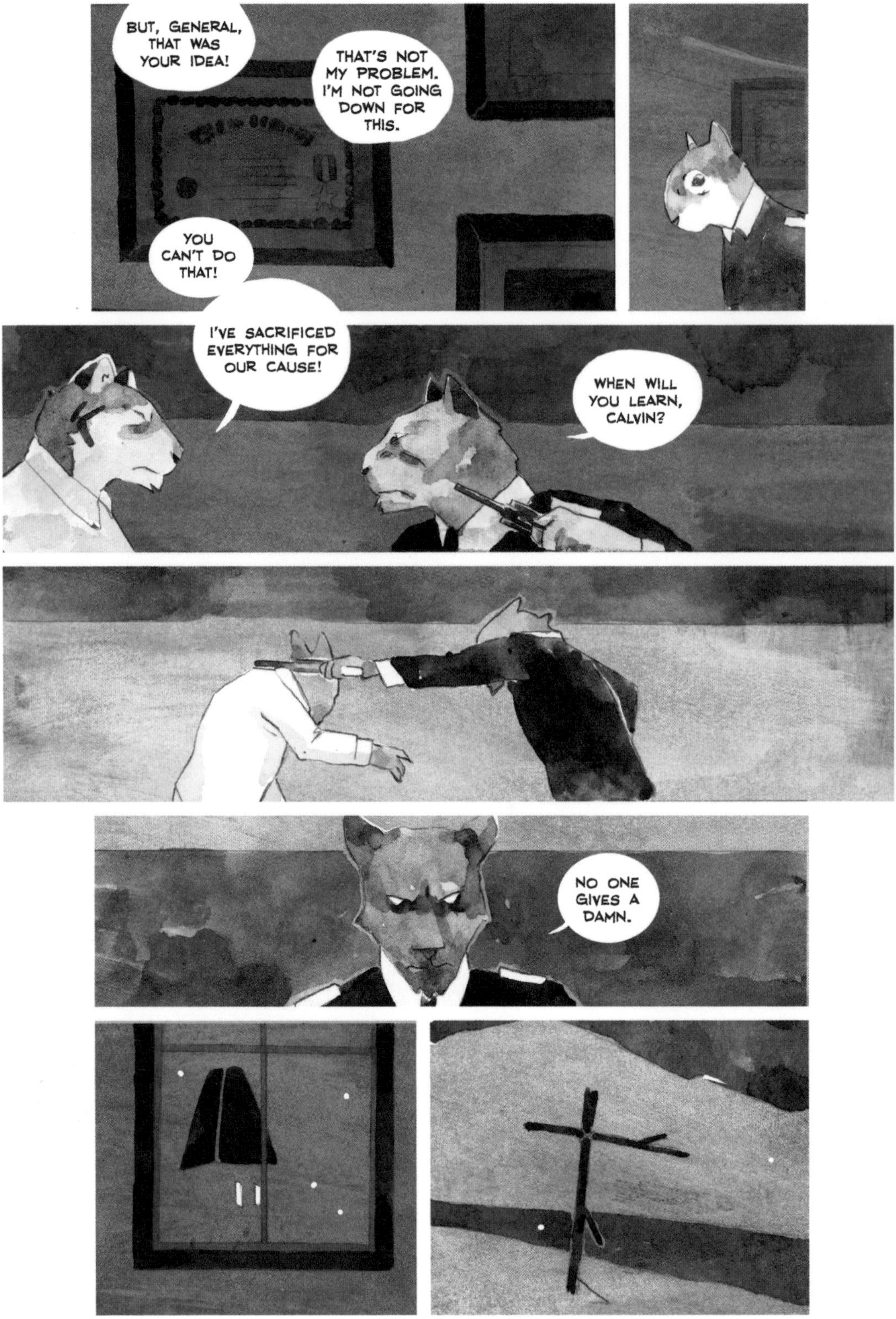
BUT, GENERAL, THAT WAS YOUR IDEA!
THAT'S NOT MY PROBLEM. I'M NOT GOING DOWN FOR THIS.
YOU CAN'T DO THAT!
I'VE SACRIFICED EVERYTHING FOR OUR CAUSE!
WHEN WILL YOU LEARN, CALVIN?
NO ONE GIVES A DAMN.

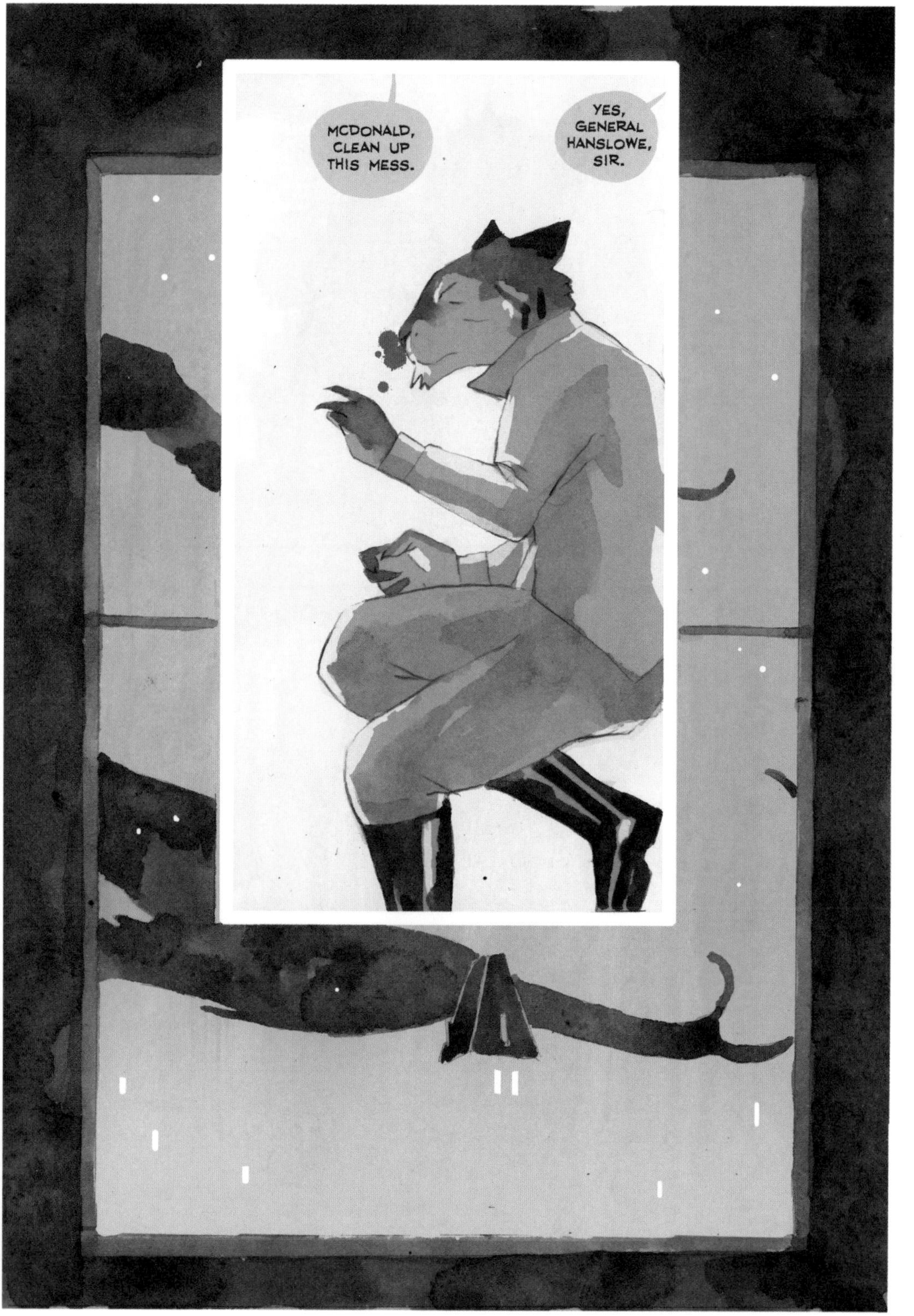
MCDONALD, CLEAN UP THIS MESS.
YES, GENERAL HANSLOWE, SIR.

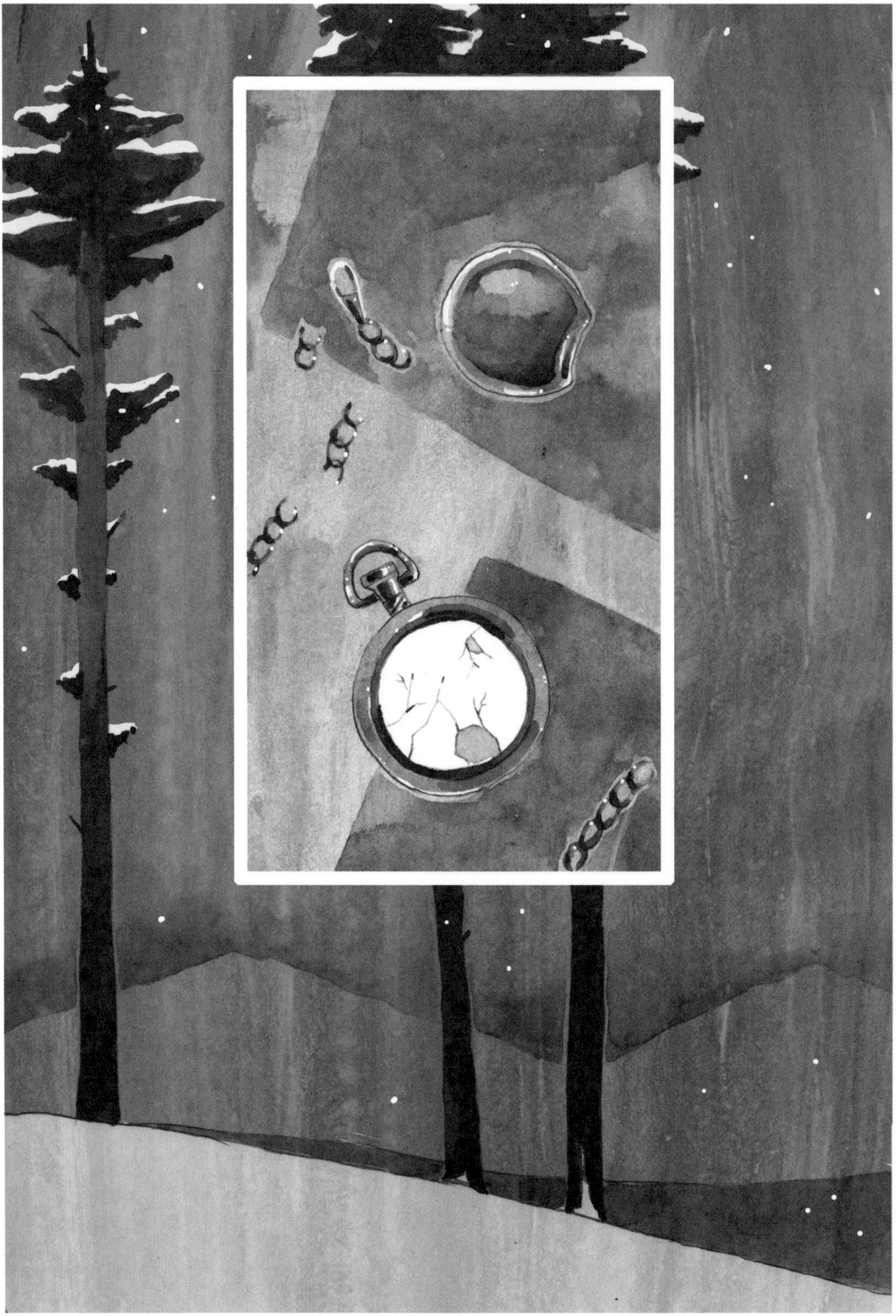

DEPARTMENT OF MILITARY INTELLIGENCE
EPPWOOD

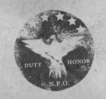

Gen. Tasker H. Engel
Office of the Quartermaster General
The National People's Organization
Eppwood

Father,

I have news that I hope will please you. I have been promoted and I have been awarded a bronze star for valor. I was given this commendation because of my involvement in an exceptionally successful mission. Acting on information I had obtained, Officer Pavel and I located a particularly well-hidden enemy base. Once we returned with the coordinates, we were able to utilise our formidable artillery. The artillery Captain thanked me personally for my initiative.

I understand you knew Officer Pavel's father. I do not dislike Officer Pavel, and he was very helpful in this situation, but I think he lacks the iron will one needs to be successful in this conflict. It is like you taught me. We must never sacrifice our ideals, for they are what give us strength. Our bodies are weak and easily broken. I am reminded of this every day. But we stand on the precipice of victory, not because we are mightier, but because our ideals have not been compromised.

We will finally obtain the dream of peace we have fought our entire lives to realize. They have lost, Father. There will be no other war after this.

Your son,

Calvin

Cpt. Calvin H. Engel
301st Military Intelligence Division, NPO
Southmark

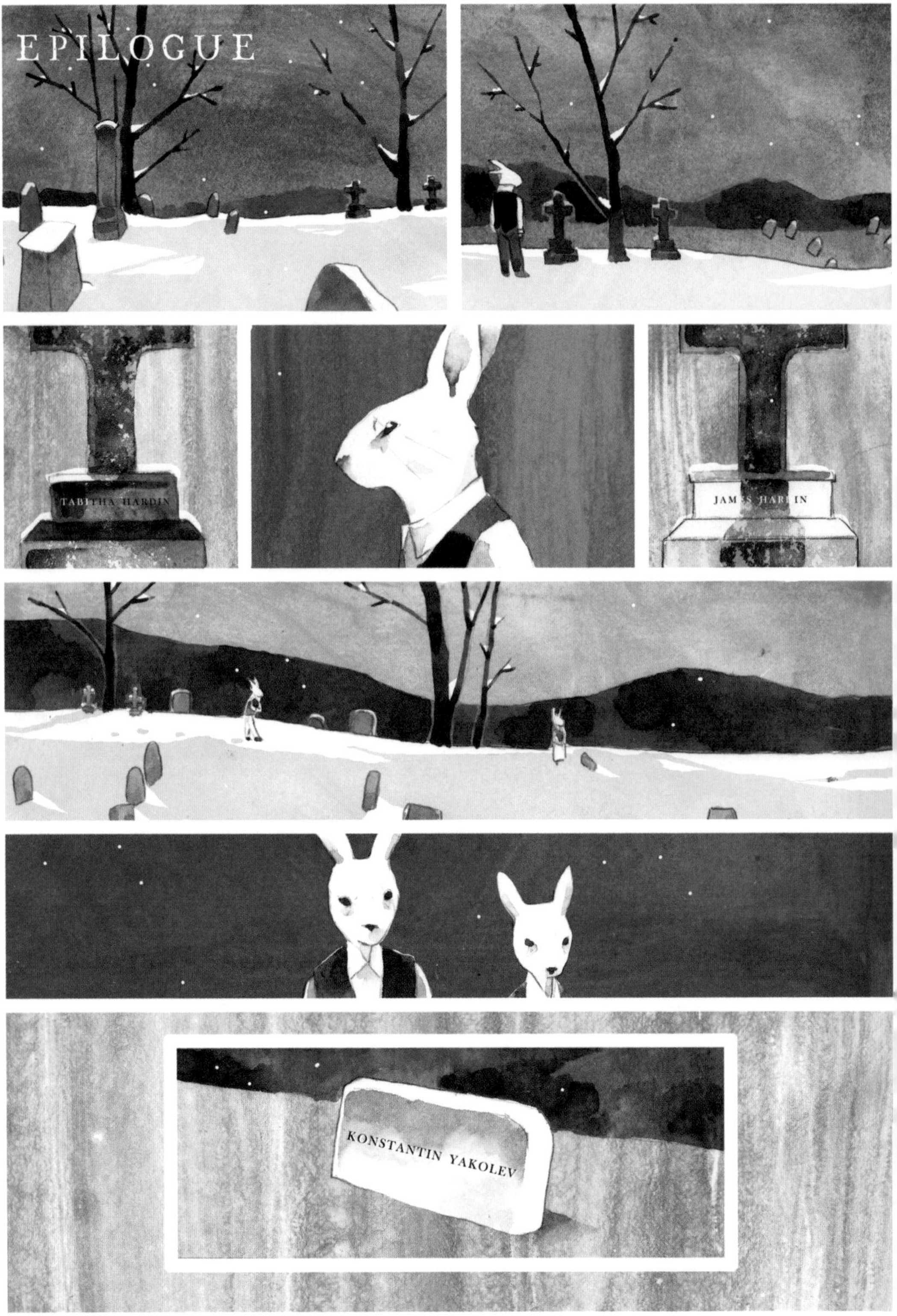
EPILOGUE
TABITHA HARDIN
KONSTANTIN YAKOLEV

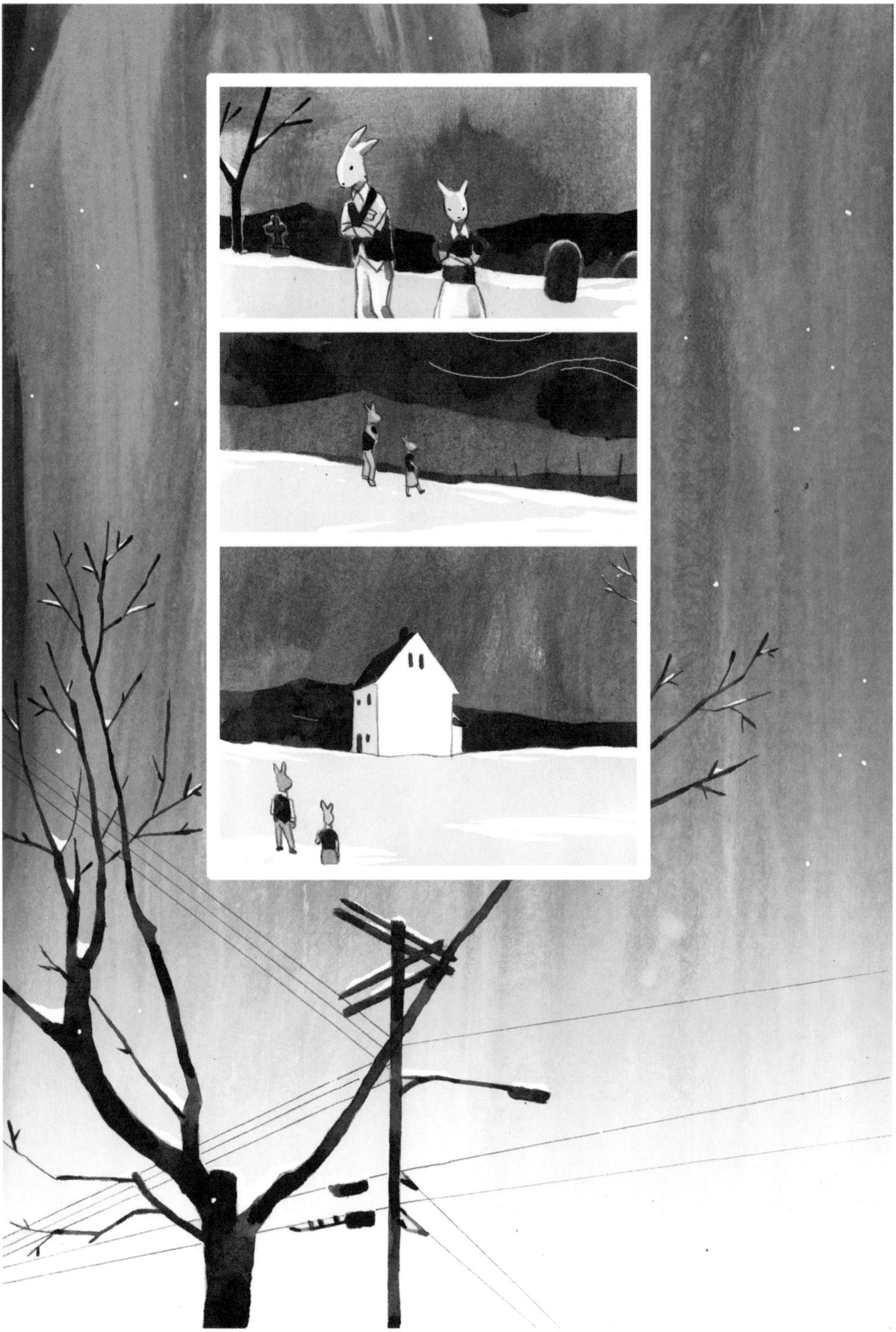

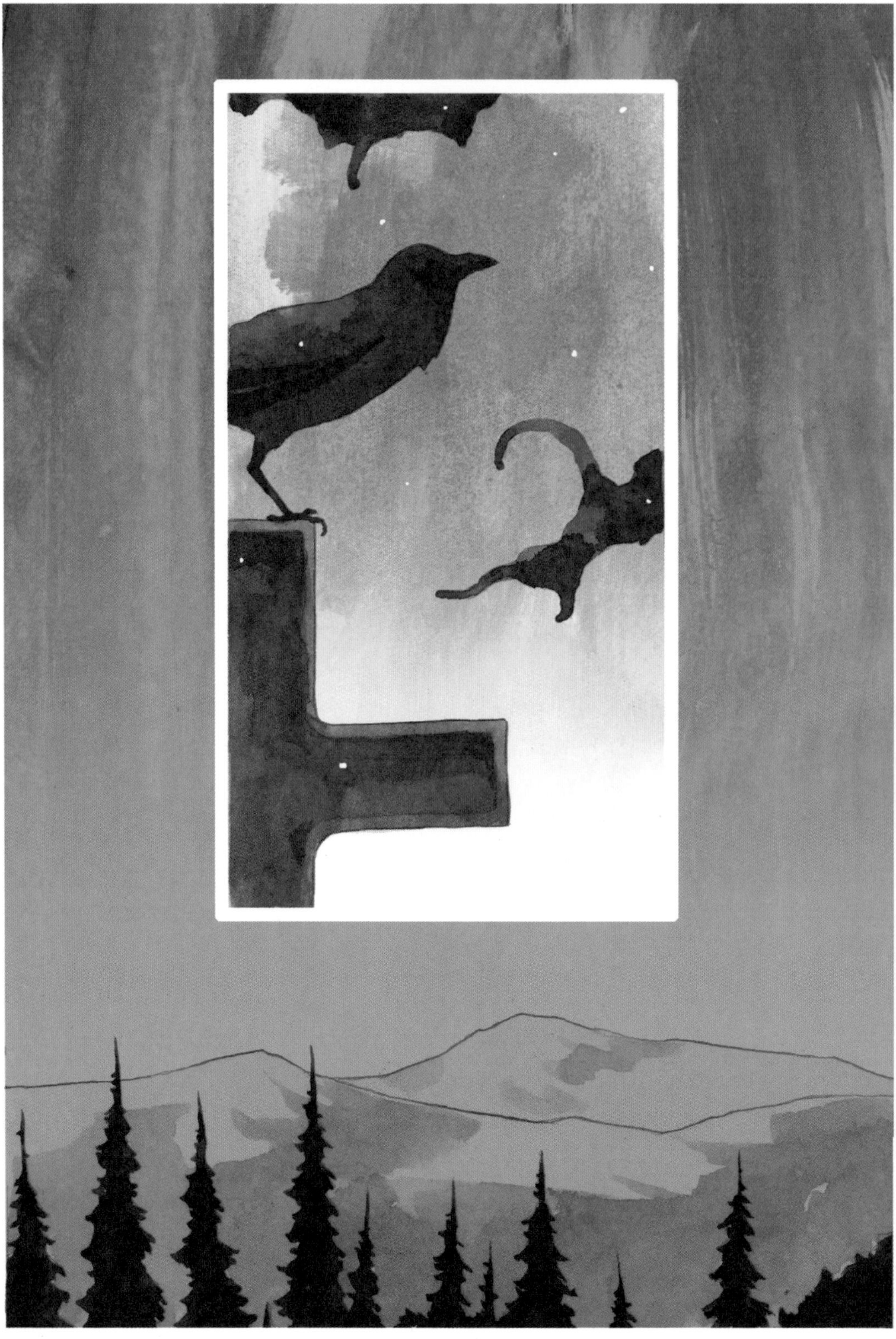

THE END

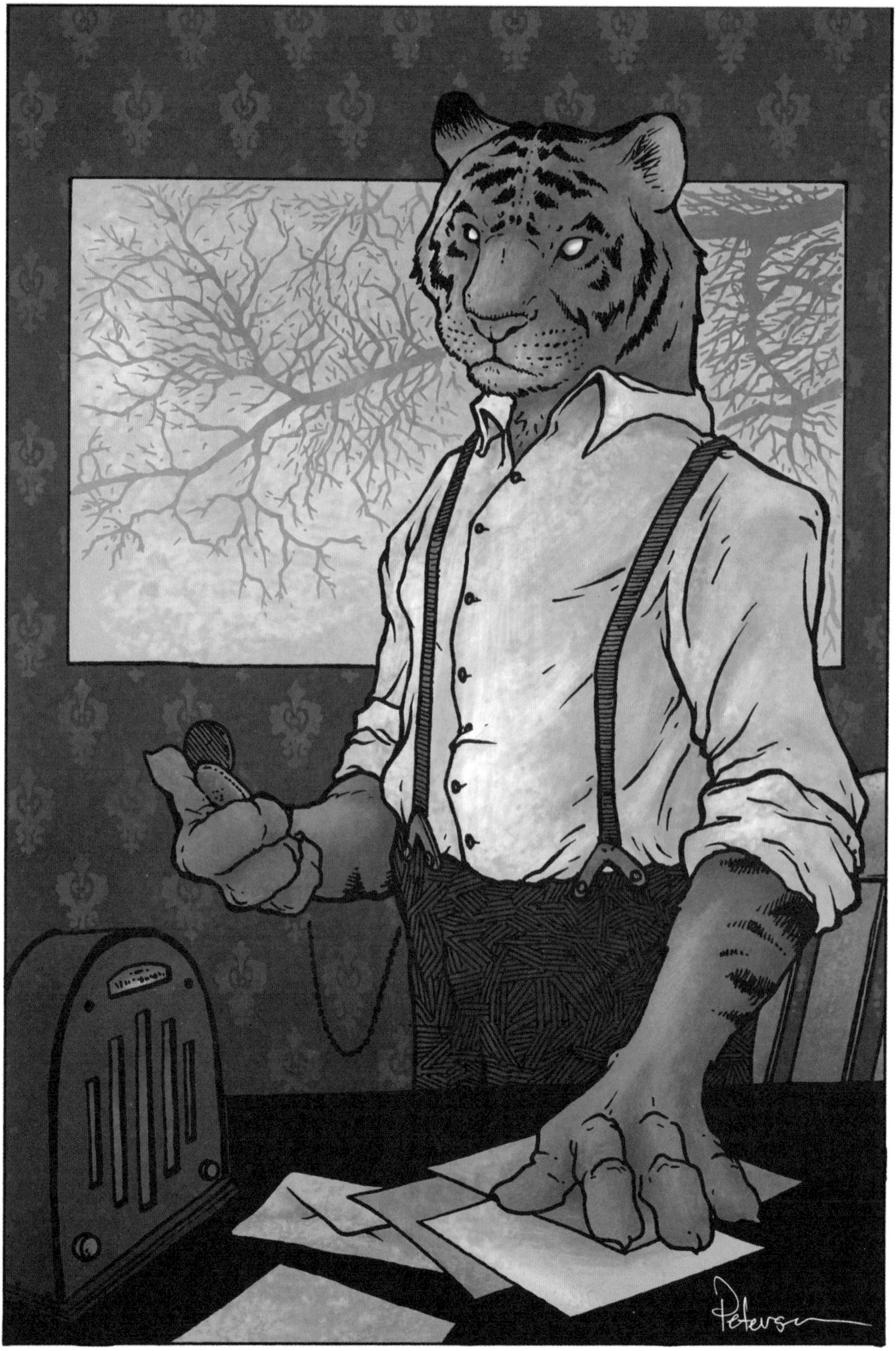
Petersen

DAVID PETERSEN, Author of *Mouse Guard*

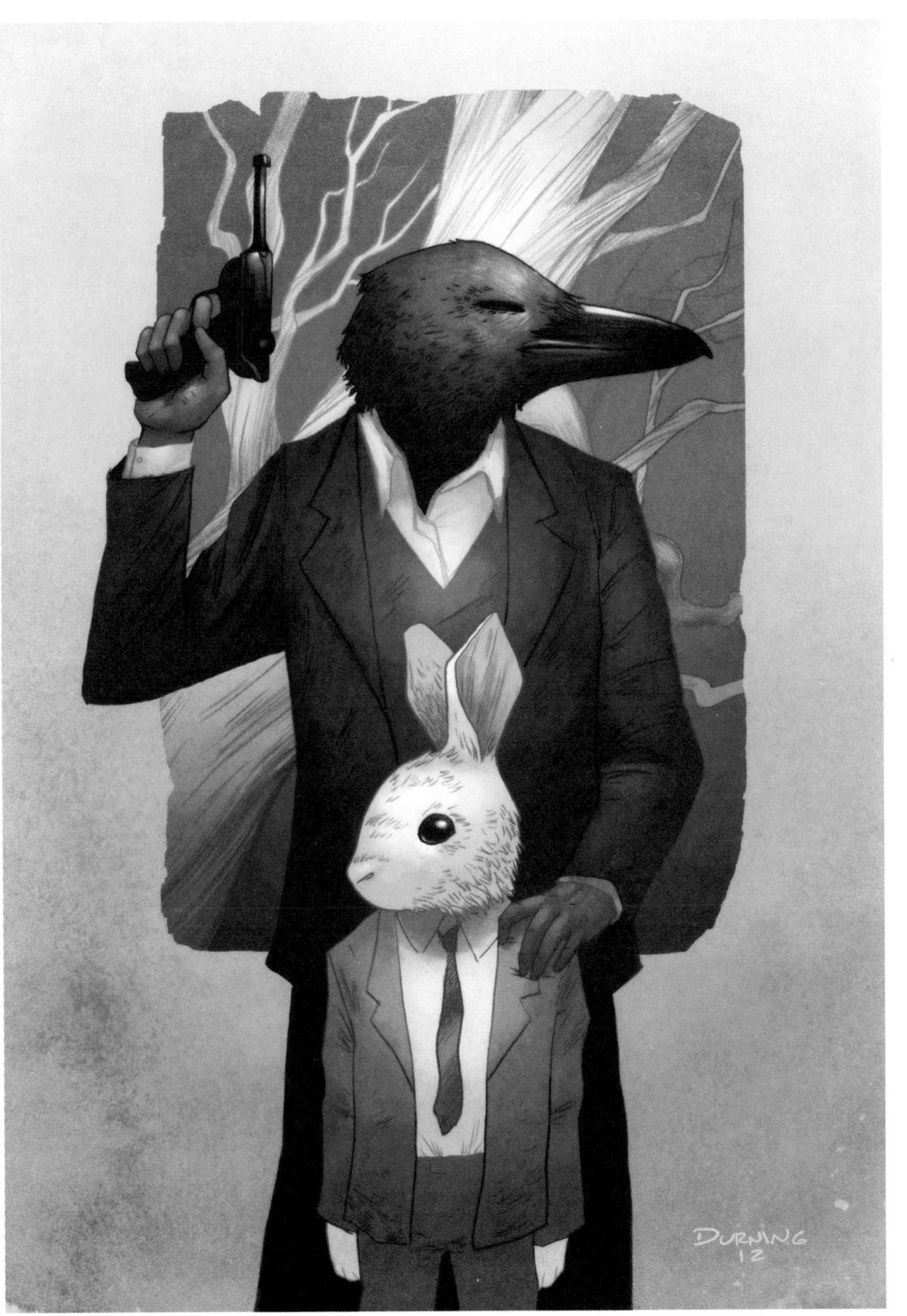
DURNING
12

TIM DURNING

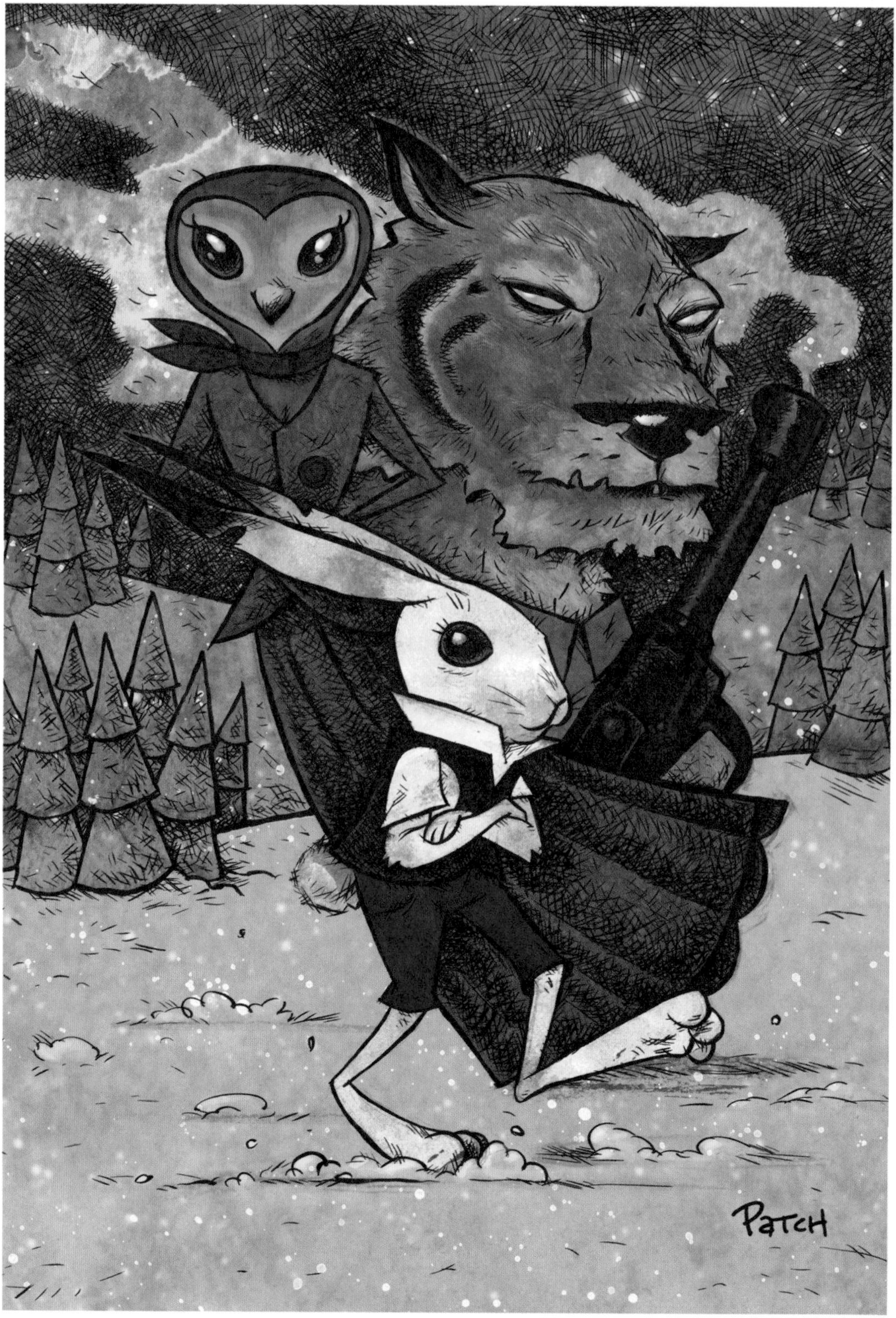
PATCH

CHRISTIAN 'PATCH' PATCHELL

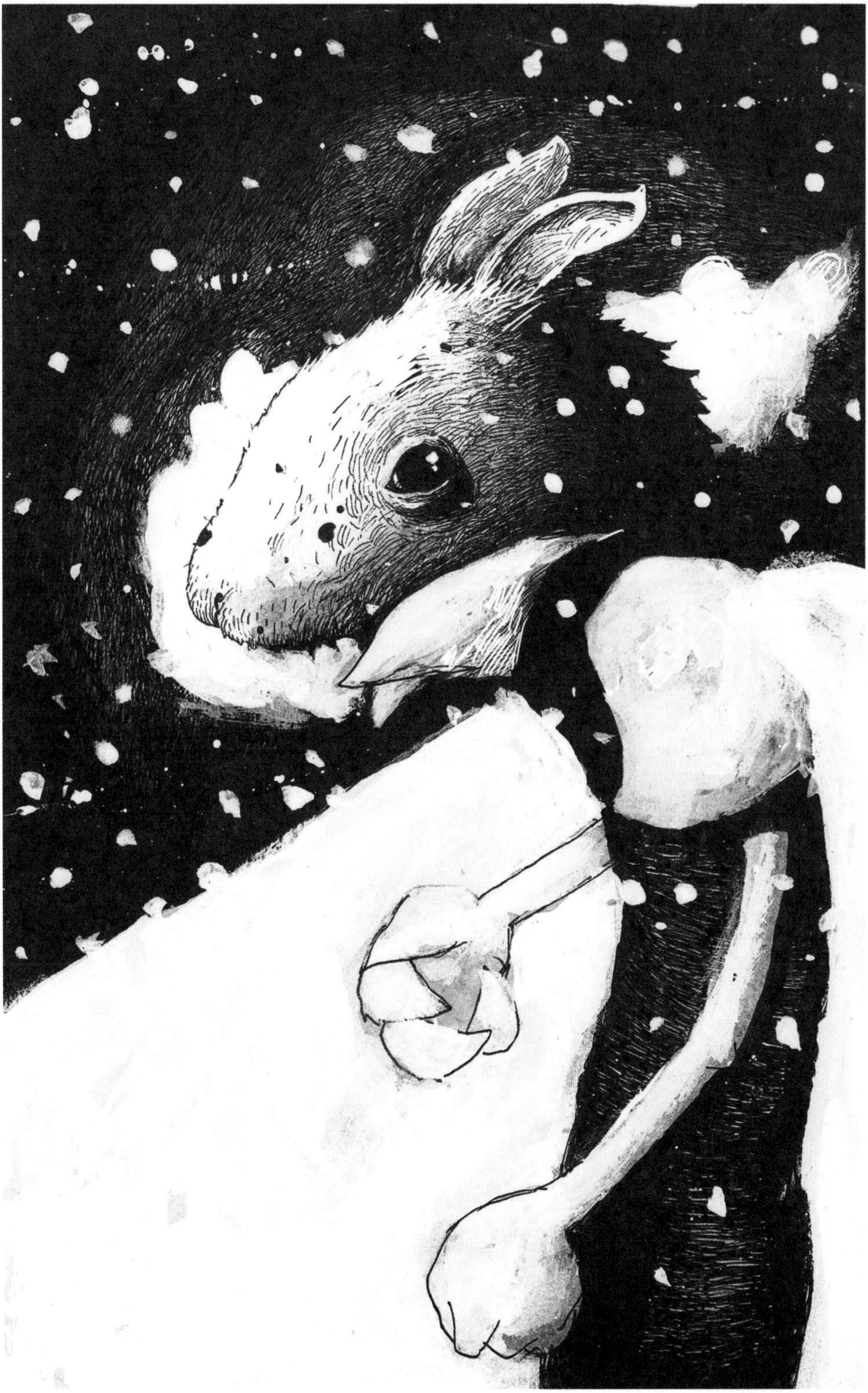

ERIC ORCHARD

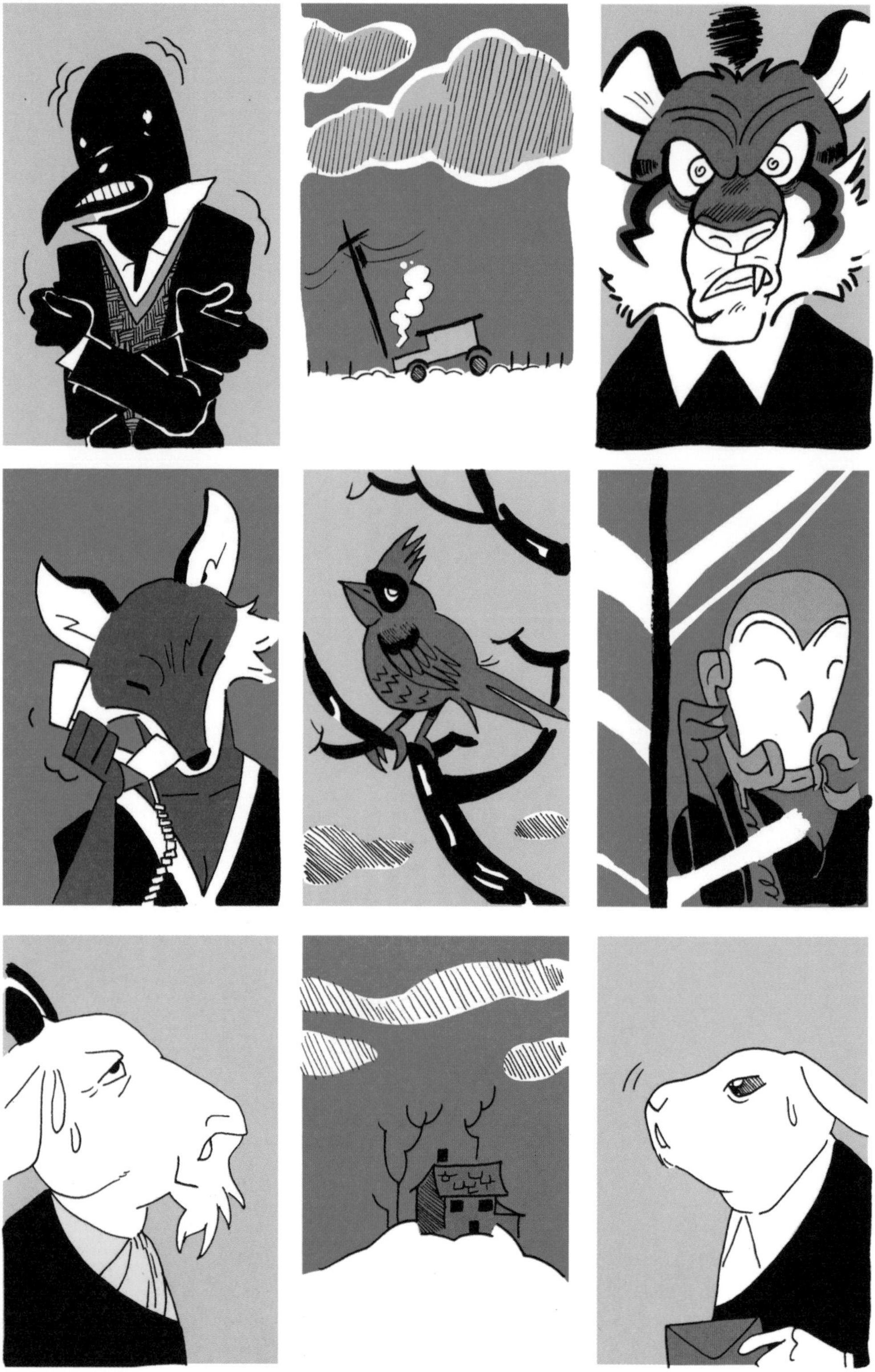

EAMON DOUGHERTY

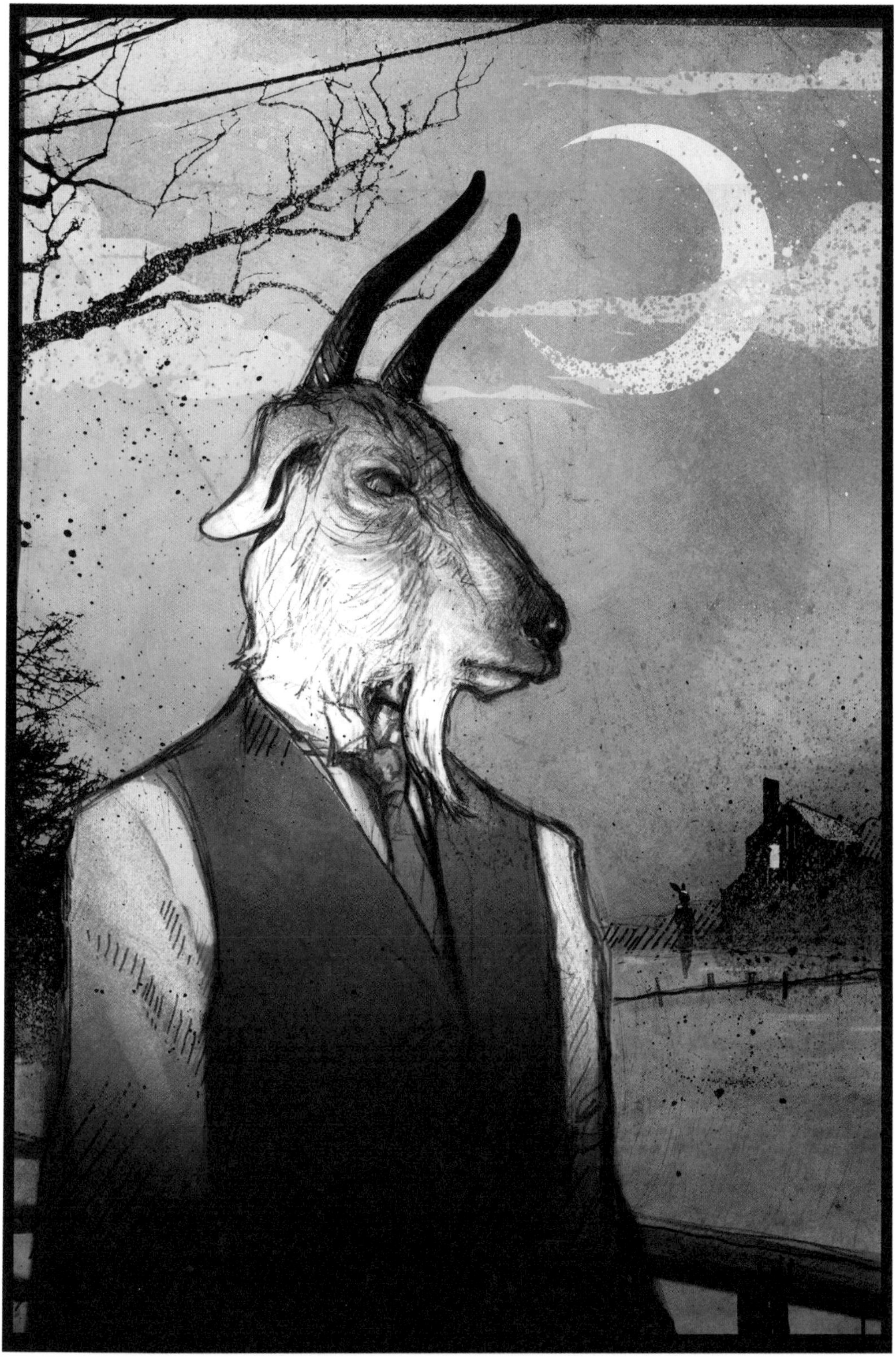

ALEX ECKMAN-LAWN, Illustrator of *Awakening*

ABOUT THE AUTHOR

S.M. Vidaurri was born and raised in northern New Jersey. His previously published works include *Steven Universe: Harmony* and the original graphic novels *Iron: Or the War After* and *Iscariot*. He is currently working on his next project, a graphic novel to be illustrated by Hannah Krieger. His apartment is filled with many animals. He can be found at www.smvidaurri.com.

ACKNOWLEDGMENTS

I had a lot of help finishing *Iron: Or the War After*
and I would like to thank the following:

Without the support and dedication of my Mother I would not have been able to complete this project. I am grateful for the support of my Father, and my Grandparents, who both encouraged and helped me. And I am grateful for my sisters, Tabitha and Chelsea, for their understanding.

A very special thank you to Archaia founder Mark Smylie for taking a chance on *Iron: Or the War After*. And my editor, Rebecca Taylor, who helped me keep my focus. I have to thank Tim Durning for his help with textures and all other aspects technical. Lastly—Kevin, Brian, Alec and Thomas must be mentioned for their unwavering admiration.

Also, for their inspiration: Andrew Wyeth, Erich Maria Remarque, Kenneth Grahame, and E.H. Shepard.

And a special thank you to you, dear reader.